UNDERSTANDING CRIME PREVENTION

THE CASE STUDY APPROACH

EDITED BY
TIM PRENZLER

AUSTRALIANACADEMIC**PRESS**

First published 2017
Australian Academic Press Group Pty. Ltd.
18 Victor Russell Drive
Samford Valley QLD 4520
Australia
www.australianacademicpress.com.au

ISBN: 9781922117939 (paperback)
               9781922117946 (ebook)

Publisher: Stephen May
Copy editing: Rhonda McPherson
Cover design: Luke Harris, Working Type Studio
Typesetting: Australian Academic Press
Printing: Lightning Source

Contents

About the Authors

Mary Baker is a Lecturer in Criminology and Justice at the University of the Sunshine Coast, Australia.

Lyndel Bates is a Senior Lecturer in the School of Criminology and Criminal Justice at Griffith University, Brisbane, Australia.

David Belsham is a Research Officer with the School of Criminology and Criminal Justice at Griffith University, Brisbane, Australia.

Philip Birch is a Senior Lecturer at the Centre for Law & Justice at Charles Sturt University, formerly of Western Sydney University.

Rick Draper is the Chief Executive Officer of Amtac Professional Services, as security consulting firm based in Brisbane, Australia.

Jacqueline Drew is a Senior Lecturer in the School of Criminology and Criminal Justice at Griffith University.

Matt Manning is an Associate Professor in the College of Arts and Sciences, Australian National University, Canberra.

Nadine McKillop is a Lecturer in Criminology and Justice at the University of the Sunshine Coast.

Mateja Mihinjac is a Tutor and PhD student in the School of Criminology and Criminal Justice at Griffith University.

Toby Miles-Johnson is a Lecturer in Criminology in the School of Sociology and Social Policy at the University of Southampton.

Tim Prenzler is a Professor of Criminology and Justice at the University of the Sunshine Coast.

Danielle Reynald is a Senior Lecturer in the School of Criminology and Criminal Justice at Griffith University.

Jessica Ritchie is a PhD student in the School of Law, University of Queensland, Brisbane, Australia.

Rick Sarre is a Professor in the School of Law, University of South Australia, Adelaide.

Eric Wilson is a Tutor in Criminology and Justice at the University of the Sunshine Coast.

Gabriel T. W. Wong is a Research Associate in the Centre for Social Research and Methods at the Australian National University.

Preface

This book is intended to contribute to improved practice in crime prevention, primarily through the lessons from successful projects. It provides an overview of current research in the field, and an exposition of some of the best studies from the past. The target audience includes security practitioners, crime prevention and community safety officers, police, research and policy officers, politicians, and students and academics.

The book represents an outgrowth of the original Australian Academic Press collection, *Professional Practice in Crime Prevention and Security Management*, published in 2014. That book was focused on situational prevention and the work of the security industry. The present book contains a wider range of approaches, including criminal justice, developmental and community strategies. A number of the chapters from the earlier book have been reproduced with updates and additions. Others have been consolidated into a smaller set. As a result, the new book covers a wide spectrum of approaches, designed to address crime problems from multiple angles. Crime is complex, the causes of crime are complex and, consequently, diverse methods are required to make the very large reductions in offending urgently needed around the world.

The first chapter is titled 'Crime Prevention: Setting Standards'. It emphasises the importance of an informed and planned approach to preventive interventions — one that considers justice issues and also evaluation methods that assess as many aspects of project processes and impacts as possible. All this is essential for ensuring the best chances of success, hopefully demonstrating success with robust data but also indicating areas where alternative strategies or refinements might be needed.

Chapter 2 examines the controversial area of 'Policing, Deterrence and Incapacitation'. In its traditional form this approach is often seen as repressive and discriminatory, with little to show, at best, beyond a static crime containment effect. However, there is evidence that police actions — and associated processes of sanctioning offenders — can be enhanced through creative and more scientific methods to make large and sustained reductions in victimisation and improvements in community safety. The issue of dealing with offenders is taken further in Chapter 3, 'Offender Management and Rehabilitation', which examines how programs set by courts and administered by corrective services can generate changes in attitudes and behaviours that help reduce future victimisation and also help offenders find more successful ways of living.

There is also a growing body of evidence, reviewed in Chapter 4 on 'Developmental Interventions', which shows that the expensive and often fraught interventions occurring 'downstream' in criminal justice can be substantially reduced through smarter investments in 'upstream' measures — focused on integrating children and young people into mainstream society through parenting and school support programs. These approaches often overlap with diverse forms of 'Community-based Prevention', discussed in Chapter 5, which aim to mobilise resources against crime at the local level, including support-oriented programs designed to address social deficits as well as approaches concerned more with surveillance and guardianship.

Chapter 6, 'The Evolution of Situational Crime Prevention', enlarges on the lessons from situational prevention and associated opportunity theories, including routine activity theory. The evidence base behind situational prevention is reviewed, including summaries of notable interventions, along with a critique of social issues and potential drawbacks that need to be considered in project design. Chapter 7 on 'Crime Prevention Through Environmental Design' (CPTED) provides an exposition of the role of CPTED — as a variant of situational prevention — in successful crime reduction.

Chapters 8 and 9 then provide a series of more developed case studies — one in the areas of property crime and fraud, and one in the areas of violence and disorder — which demonstrate large-scale successes in crime prevention projects. The accounts incorporate key aspects of project processes — including diagnostics, consultation, planning, and cooperation between stakeholders.

Chapter 10 on 'Principles of Security Management' shows how traditional security management methods can be enhanced by integrating situational techniques within a comprehensive, systematic, multilayered and tailor-made approach to security. Chapter 11, 'Best Practice in Physical Security and People Management', develops this theme, focusing on the principle of defence-in-depth, the role of the security survey in identifying vulnerabilities and closing gaps in protection, and the need to engage all staff in a multilayered approach to security.

Chapter 12, 'The Security Industry and Crime Prevention', — develops the theme of the role of security providers in applying situational and CPTED principles on a daily basis to protect assets, premises and people. The combination of dedicated security staff and situational techniques can be potent. The chapter also considers some of the conduct and competency problems that have arisen in the field. Effective regulatory mechanisms are needed to optimise the crime prevention potential of the industry outlined in the chapter in terms of 'smart regulation'.

Tim Prenzler

Chapter 1

Crime Prevention: Setting Standards

Lyndel Bates, David Belsham, and Toby Miles-Johnson

Crime prevention — as an organised function of government, business or not-for-profit groups — should be based on evidence. Unfortunately, this does not always occur, especially in the 'public policy' domain of government. Instead, the crime prevention policy agenda is often driven by political ideology and anecdotal evidence with insufficient planning and evaluation (Sherman, Farrington, Welsh, & MacKenzie, 2002). Therefore, in many cases, the effectiveness of various crime prevention measures is unknown or unintended consequences are generated, including displacement of crime or deterrence of legitimate activities (Grabosky, 1996). With this in mind, this chapter emphasises the importance of 'standards', focusing on planning, consultation, social and procedural justice, sustainability, and systematic evaluation. The chapter begins with an outline of four types of prevention methods, described by Homel (2015) as 'developmental', 'community', 'criminal justice' and 'situational'.

Types of Crime Prevention

Crime prevention is evolving and is becoming an increasingly sophisticated science, which is no longer considered as solely in the domain of traditional law enforcement bodies. A new level of scrutiny has been applied to the basic constituents of a crime: a location and its agents (both victim and offender). As such, there has been concurrent development of theories and interventions that have required a reimagining of the role of police and the wider community in crime prevention. The field of crime prevention has been divided up in different ways. The following section draws on the four-part structure adopted by Homel (2015), but it must be remembered that these are not mutually exclusive and that prevention programs often involve overlapping categories.

Developmental

Developmental crime prevention occurs when interventions are targeted at individuals who have known risk factors for offending, in order to prevent them committing crimes in the future. Generally this occurs by providing support to individuals, families, schools and communities to target these problems (Homel, 2013, 2015). The basis for these initiatives is the evidence indicating there are long term benefits to interventions that develop children and young people in healthy ways and that subsequently prevent or limit criminal offences, aggression and drug or alcohol abuse (Homel, Freiberg, & Branch, 2015). Successful developmental programs are well resourced, staffed by well-trained professionals and are based in theory (although the specific theory varies). They also tend to work with the individuals in a number of contexts such as the school and at home (Homel, 2013; see also Chapter 4).

Community

Unlike developmental crime prevention, there is limited agreement regarding what constitutes community crime prevention (see Chapter 5). Homel (2015) states that crime can be seen as 'a social problem that requires social ways of thinking and social solutions' (p. 345). When using a community prevention approach, social institutions such as families, churches and youth clubs are used to deliver programs that are designed to reduce crime issues within local communities (Welsh & Hoshi, 2002). This type of program is influenced by theories such as community disorganisation theory, community empowerment theory and community regeneration theory (Welsh & Hoshi, 2002). However, it is difficult to scientifically identify whether or not these types of programs reduce crime or help solve other social problems. This is due in part to the difficulty and expense associated with collecting the appropriate information at a community level, as opposed to an individual level (Homel, 2015).

Criminal Justice

Prevention through the criminal justice system occurs when the police, courts or prisons deter, rehabilitate or otherwise block people from committing crimes (Homel, 2015; see Chapter 2 and Chapter 3). Deterrence occurs when individuals act a certain way because they fear punishment. Deterrence has been shown to be very effective in reducing road offences such as drink driving, as one example (Freeman & Watson, 2009). However, it appears to be less successful as an approach for younger drivers who are greater risk-takers (Allen, Murphy, & Bates, 2015; Bates, Darvell, & Watson, 2015). In contrast, rehabilitation occurs when individuals receive some form of therapy designed to reduce their offending (Homel, 2014). Cognitive–behavioural interventions and restorative justice are examples of rehabilitation programs (Lab, 2010). Finally, one method to prevent people from committing crimes is to incapacitate them. The most common way to do this is to place them in prison, although the electronic monitoring of individuals is another method (Lab, 2010). The evidence regarding preventing crime through the criminal justice system is mixed (Homel, 2015). Therefore, each type of intervention needs to be considered on an individual basis.

Situational

'Situational Crime Prevention' is a framework for understanding the circumstances surrounding offending, and based on this, countermeasures to reduce it. It is one of the most important frameworks for conceptualising and constructing successful crime reduction strategies (see Chapter 6). The framework draws on Rational Choice Theory and Routine Activity Theory (Clarke, 1995). Rational Choice Theory asserts that offenders perform a cost–benefit analysis of their actions, taking into account the ease of committing crime, the rewards for doing so, and the likelihood of being caught. This means observations about the behaviours of the general population can influence crime prevention strategies.

The situational approach has now been adopted throughout the world (Freilich, 2015). It is pragmatic and flexible, and can be easily operationalised via established techniques. For example, Hodgkinson, Curtis, MacAlister, and Farrell (2015) illustrate how it can be applied to student academic dishonesty using Cornish and Clarke's (2003) '25 techniques of situational prevention', including increased surveillance during exams, improving clarity in questions, communicating rules, and promoting and applying plagiarism software technology. The capacity of situational prevention to foster cooperation and target problem situations makes it ideally positioned to address complex international problems as diverse as piracy (Shane, Piza, & Mandala, 2015) and cyber-crime (Hinduja & Kooi, 2013).

Standards

While there are many crime prevention interventions, they are not of equal quality. Strong crime prevention programs are planned systematically, involve appropriate consultation, operate according to the principles of social and procedural justice and are sustainable.

Systematic Planning

Successful crime prevention programs solve problems within local contexts. To do this effectively requires systematic planning. However, even before this planning can occur, a decision needs to be made about what constitutes the crime problem (Sutton, Cherney, & White, 2014). Once this has been clearly conceptualised, there are several models that provide guidance in implementing problem solving approaches. One model — the '5Is model' — suggests five steps: 'intelligence, intervention, implementation, involvement and impact' (Ekblom, 2010). In the intelligence stage, information regarding the crime problem and its effects is obtained and analysed. The second step, intervention, involves deliberating on all mechanisms that could be used to prevent or limit the crime problem. Implementation occurs when the plan is put into action, while involvement refers to relevant organisations and individuals undertaking this action. Finally, impact refers to the evaluation of the crime prevention initiative. (See also the five stages of situational prevention in Chapter 6.)

Consultation

In order for crime prevention programs to work effectively there must be consistency in the goals of the program from all levels of government (Cherney, 2017). This ensures there is ownership of the program from local stakeholders. When programs are implemented from the top-down, there may be a lack of cooperation from those involved in delivering the crime prevention programs (Homel & Masson, 2016). Therefore, consultation becomes a very important process in developing crime prevention programs. Consultation is a conversation that is used to collect opinions and responses to a proposal before any decisions are made. They can occur between the various agencies delivering a program as well as the end users of an intervention.

Social Justice

The aim of social justice is to equitably distribute societal benefits and costs amongst individuals (Capeheart & Milovanovic, 2007). There are numerous examples of where justice systems have not acted in a socially just manner. For instance, many Indigenous peoples were repressed through the idea of *terra nullius*, which meant that their land was forcibly taken from them in a legal but highly unjust manner. They then became trespassers on their ancestral lands. In many places, individuals who are gay, lesbian or transgender are unable to legally marry. A quality crime prevention intervention will seek to ensure that the principles of social justice are present in both the selection of individuals for the program and throughout its delivery in that, for example, poor and dispossessed persons are not overly targeted and subject to discrimination.

Procedural Justice

Procedural justice occurs when individuals assess the way in which interactions with law enforcement occur rather than the outcomes of the interaction. There are four components to procedural justice: 'voice, neutrality, respect and trustworthiness' (in Bates, 2014). The law being applied has to be seen to be legitimate, and the enforcement fair and respectful, for reasonable people to comply. Australian research has shown that a short interpersonal interaction that incorporates these principles between police officers and citizens can influence levels of compliance (Mazerolle, Bennett, Antrobus, & Eggins, 2012). These types of interactions can also positively affect the motivation of police officers (Bates, Antrobus, Bennett, & Martin, 2015).

Sustainability

There is a history of crime prevention programs being launched and then ceasing to operate a few years later. Frequently, this is the result of interventions being introduced using a grant and lacking access to ongoing sources of funding (Sutton, Cherney & White, 2014). For programs to consistently operate, they need to be funded in a different manner. Additionally, crime prevention programs need to be staffed by informed and educated individuals to remain sustainable. While there are written guides regarding crime prevention techniques, the highly differing contexts that the programs operate within mean that some level of skill is required to translate this knowledge into sustainable practices (Ekblom, 2010).

International Guidelines

There are a number of internationally endorsed crime prevention standards that enlarge on the principles set out above. For example, in 2010 the United Nations Office on Drugs and Crime (UNODC) published *The Handbook on the Crime Prevention Guidelines: Making Them Work*. The handbook was created as a tool to support nations in the application of international norms regarding crime prevention strategies. UNODC sought to create a set of guidelines that could be implemented, sustained and entrenched by nations over time, summarised in the following statement (UNODC, 2010, p. 115):

> Approaches to prevention range from tackling the social and economic roots of crime and violence to strengthening the capacities of local communities to modifying environments in order to deter offenders or promote an increased sense of safety. There is no one approach that is optimal, but a careful strategy will balance and utilise a range of approaches which can respond to specific problems of crime and victimization in both the short and longer term. Such a strategy will respond to the needs of all sectors of society, in a way that does not increase the social or economic exclusion of particular groups and will promote respect for the rule of law.

Another example is the 'Beccaria Standards', focused, again, on fairness and effectiveness. This includes a systematic, step-by-step, approach (Marks, Meyer, & Linssen, 2005, p. 4):

1. Description of the problem
2. Analysis of the conditions leading to the emergence of the problem
3. Determination of prevention targets, project targets and targeted groups

4. Determination of the interventions intended to achieve the targets
5. Design and execution of the project
6. Review of the project's implementation and achievement of objectives (evaluation)
7. Conclusion and documentation.

In addition, the guidelines emphasise the importance of overall quality management, in part by ensuring the clear delegation of responsibilities for program development and implementation, and ensuring expert input. Program managers should ensure that:

a) they align the planning, implementation and review of crime prevention projects with the quality criteria outlined in science and literature

b) projects are designed in such a way that they can be evaluated

c) scientific experts, advisors, contracting bodies and sponsors are at hand to provide a technical basis for judging the project's targeting of objectives and quality. (Marks et al., 2005, p. 4)

Evaluation

Systematic evaluation is the final key 'standard' in crime prevention, treated separately here because of its importance. Evaluation is essential for assessing the effectiveness of crime prevention measures and informing the development of future policy and procedures. There are two main types of evaluation: process and outcome. Ideally, an evaluation of a crime prevention project would include both process and outcome measures. A process evaluation assists in identifying whether the crime prevention method has been implemented as planned and develops a greater understanding of the activities used within the method (Morgan & Homel, 2013). As part of this process, evaluators should consider the consultation that has occurred as part of the intervention as well as whether elements of procedural justice are present and social justice issues are addressed. Process evaluations frequently begin by considering the aims of the initiative, staffing numbers and qualifications, financial and broader support available, whether the program was delivered as planned, quality of data and whether any changes were made to the program over time (Lab, 2010). The benefits of undertaking a process evaluation include ensuring it has been implemented correctly and identifying whether or not it is possible to generalise the program to other contexts.

In contrast, an outcome evaluation looks at the overall effectiveness of a program in relation to crime (Morgan & Homel, 2013). Examples would include whether an intervention program delivered in a custodial correctional facility reduces recidivism. However, there are often complex issues in undertaking outcome evaluations. For instance, interventions are frequently not introduced by themselves (Lab, 2010). They are often introduced as a suite of measures. Thus, a new intervention program may be delivered at the same time as penalties for offending are increased. While this may be appropriate, it becomes difficult to identify if any subsequent reduction in recidivist offending is because of the intervention program or the harsher penalties.

Another form of evaluation that can be undertaken for crime prevention initiatives is a financial cost–benefit analysis (Lab, 2010). This type of evaluation identifies if the costs of implementing an intervention are reasonable given the identified benefits. This type of evaluation looks at both process and outcomes. It assesses the costs of putting in place the intervention and then subtracts these costs from the beneficial outcomes.

Methods of Evaluation

Crime prevention interventions can be evaluated through the use of experimental, quasi-experimental or naturalistic designs. A randomised controlled experiment is considered the best evaluation design. In this these types of evaluations, individuals who, for instance, are eligible to complete an intervention are randomly allocated to either the experimental or control group. The experimental group completes the crime prevention intervention. A control group is a group that is identical to the experimental group but does not receive the treatment or intervention that was given to the experimental group. Given that both groups were similar before completing the intervention, any differences between the two after the intervention can be identified as being the result of the intervention.

A quasi-experiment lacks the key element of randomised allocation. One example of a quasi-experiment occurs when information from before the intervention was introduced is compared to information from afterwards (Welsh & Farrington, 2006). This is known as pre and post design. While quasi-experiments do not require the random assignment of participants to different groups, there may be other factors that are not measured within the evaluation that affect the outcomes. For instance, policing strategies may change which affects the levels of crime. There may also be natural fluctuations in crime over time or by season. Finally, differences in how outcomes such as crime are measured over time will also affect the results (White & Coventry, 2000).

While there are many benefits to experimental and quasi-experimental designs, it is important to consider that there are other methods of developing an understanding of crime prevention. Practitioners should continue to undertake evaluations in situations where it is not feasible or desirable to undertake a full experiment. They could use methods such as observations or looking at relationships between factors that they believe influence crime prevention. In that regard, Pawson and Tilley (1997) propose that there are advantages to 'realistic evaluation'. Realistic evaluation is an approach that is theoretically informed and considers what works in what circumstances

(Tilley, 2000). Thus, these types of evaluations are less focused on using the 'best' evaluation method (randomised control trials) and instead on choosing the best available method of assessing if an intervention works based on the problem, the theoretical foundation and the context.

In all types of evaluations, the issue of the length of the follow up period needs careful consideration for two reasons. Firstly, it may take time for the benefits of the intervention to be measurable. Thus, the follow up period should not occur too early. Secondly, there may be benefits within a short time frame but these will disappear over time. Ideally, the follow up of the outcomes of an intervention should occur at several time points such as one month, three months, six months and 18 months. This will enable policy makers to identify how quickly the program has an impact and if this changes over time (Lab, 2010).

Evaluation quality

The quality of all evaluations is not equal. One key tool that is used to assess the quality of evaluation methods is the Maryland Scientific Methods Scale (SMS). This tool is designed for use by scholars, policymakers and practitioners. The scale lists five levels that indicate the rigour of the evaluation method used (see Table 1.1).

Undertaking scientific evaluations is often difficult due to resourcing constraints. In these cases, there are still benefits in undertaking more applied evaluations. This could include targeting evaluation to the areas where there will be the most benefit. One example where this would be beneficial is in situations where the scale of the project makes it difficult to undertake a full scientific evaluation. Additionally, the performance of projects should be monitored on a regular basis to assess both the implementation and the impact. Finally, central agencies can establish mechanisms to support evaluation. Some of these mechanisms can include appointing appropriately skilled individuals to undertake evaluations on behalf of organisations, reviewing and providing suggestions to local partners regarding evaluation design, and assisting in developing the capacity of agencies to undertake evaluations (Morgan & Homel, 2013).

One example of the evaluation of a crime prevention initiative is the Surfers Paradise Safety Action Project (see Chapter 9). This project was designed to reduce violence in and around licenced venues on the Gold Coast, Australia. The evaluation methods included structured observations before and after the implementation of the project as well as examining police and security data. The researchers decided not to use a control area for this evaluation. They argued that the Surfers Paradise area was unique and that it was not possible to match a control area. Additionally, they found it difficult to identify an area that would not be affected by the diffusion effects of the study. The costs of the evaluation would have doubled with the use of

Table 1.1

Maryland Scientific Methods Scale

Level	Definition	Example
Level 1	Correlation between a prevention program and a measure of crime at one point in time	Areas with CCTV have lower crime rates than areas without CCTV
Level 2	Measures of crime before and after the program, with no comparable control condition	Crime decreased after CCTV was installed in an area
Level 3	Measures of crime before and after the program in experimental and comparable control conditions	Crime decreased after CCTV was installed in an experimental area, but there was no decrease in crime in a comparable control area
Level 4	Measures of crime before and after the program in multiple experimental and control units, controlling for other variables that influence crime	Victimisation of premises under CCTV surveillance decreased compared to victimization of control premises, after controlling for features of premises that influenced their victimization
Level 5	Random assignment of program and control conditions to units	Victimsation of premises randomly assigned to have CCTV surveillance decreased compared to victimization of control premises

Source: Adapted from Farrington, 2003, pp. 58–59. (Used with permission.)

a single control area and tripled with the use of two control areas. This was another consideration. The researchers suggested that the internal relationships, particularly between alcohol and violence, identified within the evaluation as well as the variations in time within the community were important for identifying causality. Additionally, the replication of this form of study in other locations and contexts would also contribute to an understanding of the causes of violence. The evaluation indicated that there were reductions in crime and violence within and external to the licensed venues as well as improvements in security practices, entertainment, handling of patrons and transport policies (Homel, Hauritz, Wortley, McIlwain, & Carvolth, 1997).

Conclusion

Planned crime prevention is essential for reducing levels of crime within society. This chapter has outlined the various methods of crime prevention including developmental crime prevention, community prevention, prevention through the criminal justice system and situational crime prevention. While there are many different approaches, the best programs involve systematic planning and consultation prior to their implementation. They also operate according to the principles of social and procedural justice. Finally, the programs are sustainable. The chapter concluded with a discussion of how to measure, or evaluate, if a crime prevention program is successful. The randomised controlled experiment is considered the best way of conducting an evaluation. However, this is not always possible. In these situations, it is possible to use a range of alternative evaluation methods to assess the value of a crime prevention initiative.

References

Allen, S., Murphy, K., & Bates, L. (2015). What drives compliance? The effect of deterrence and shame emotions on young drivers' compliance with road laws, *Policing and Society*. doi: 10.1080/10439463.2015.1115502

Bates, L. (2014). *Procedural justice and road policing: Is it important?* Australasian Road Safety Research, Policing and Education Conference, 12–14 November, Melbourne, Australia.

Bates, L., Antrobus, E., Bennett, S., & Martin, P. (2015). Comparing police and public perceptions of a routine traffic encounter. *Police Quarterly, 18*(4), 442–468.

Bates, L., Darvell, M., & Watson, B. (2015), Young and unaffected by road policing strategies: Using deterrence theory to explain provisional drivers' (non)compliance, *Australian and New Zealand Journal of Criminology*. doi: 10.11770004865815589824

Capeheart, L., & Milovanovic, D. (2007). *Critical issues in crime and society: social justice – theories, issues and movements*. New Brunswick, Canada: Rutgers University Press.

Cherney, A. (2017). Designing and implementing programmes to tackle radicalization and violent extremism: lessons from criminology, *Dynamics of Asymmetric Conflict*, doi: 10.1080/17467586.2016.1267865

Clarke, R. (1995). Situational crime prevention. *Crime and Justice, 19*(19), 91–150.

Cornish, D., & Clarke, R. (2003). Opportunities, precipitators and criminal decisions: A Reply to Wortley's critique of situational crime prevention. *Crime Prevention Studies, 16*, 41–96.

Ekblom, P. (2010). *Crime prevention, security and community safety using the 5Is framework*. Basingstoke, England: Palgrave Macmillan

Farrington, D. (2003). Methodological quality standards for evaluation research. *The Annals of the American Academy of Political and Social Science. 587*(1), 49–68.

Freeman, J., & Watson, B. (2009). Drink driving deterrents and self-reported offending behaviours among a sample of Queensland motorists. *Journal of Safety Research, 40*(2), 113–120.

Freilich, J. (2015). Beccaria and situational crime prevention. *Criminal Justice Review, 40*(2), 131–150.

Grabosky, P. (1996). Unintended consequences of crime prevention. *Crime Prevention Studies, 5*, 25–56.

Hinduja, S., & Kooi, B. (2013). Curtailing cyber and information security vulnerabilities through situational crime prevention. *Security Journal, 26*(4), 383–402.

Hodgkinson, T., Curtis, H., MacAlister, D., & Farrell, G. (2015). Student academic dishonesty: The Potential for situational prevention. *Journal of Criminal Justice Education, 27*(1), 1–18.

Homel, R. (2013). Developmental crime prevention. In N. Tilley (Ed.), *Handbook of crime prevention and community safety* (pp. 71–106). London, England: Willan.

Homel, R. (2015). Crime prevention. In H. Hayes & T. Prenzler (Eds.), *Introduction to crime and criminology* (pp. 341–352). Melbourne, Australia: Pearson.

Homel, R., & Masson, N. (2016). Partnerships for human security in fragile contexts: Where community safety and security sector reform intersect. *Australian Journal of International Affairs.* Advanced online publication. doi:10.1080/10357718.2015.1126803

Homel, R., Freiberg, K., & Branch, S. (2015). CREATE-ing capacity to take developmental crime prevention to scale: A community-based approach within a national framework. *Australian & New Zealand Journal of Criminology*, 48(3), 367–385.

Homel, R., Hauritz, M., Wortley, R., McIlwain, G., & Carvolth, R. (1997). Preventing alcohol-related crime through community action: The Surfers Paradise Safety Action Project. *Crime Prevention Studies, 17*, 35–90.

Lab, S. (2010). *Crime prevention: Approaches, practices and evaluations.* New Providence, NJ: Lexis Nexis.

Marks, E., Meyer, A. & Linssen, R. (2005) *Beccaria-Standards for ensuring quality in crime prevention projects.* Hanover, Germany: Council for Crime Prevention of Lower Saxony.

Mazerolle, L., Bennett, S., Antrobus, E. & Eggins, E. (2012). Procedural justice, routine encounters and citizen perceptions of police: Main findings from the Queensland Community Engagement Trial (QCET), *Journal of Experimental Criminology, 8*, 343–367.

Morgan, A., & Homel, P. (2013). Evaluating crime prevention: Lessons from large-scale community crime prevention programs. *Trends and Issues in Crime and Criminal Justice, 458*, 1–6.

Pawson, R., & Tilley, N. (1997). *Realistic evaluation.* London, England: SAGE.

Shane, J., Piza, E. & Mandala, M. (2015). Situational crime prevention and worldwide piracy: A Cross-continent analysis. *Crime Science, 4*(1), 1–13.

Sherman, L., Farrington, D., Welsh, B., & Mackenzie, D. (2002). Preventing crime. In L. Sherman, D. Farrington, B. Welsh, & D. MacKenzie (Eds.), *Evidence-based crime prevention* (pp. 1–12). London, England: Routledge.

Sutton, A., Cherney, A., & White, R. (2014). *Crime prevention: Principles, perspectives and practices.* Melbourne, Australia: Cambridge University Press

Tilley, N. (2000). *Realistic evaluation: An overview.* Presented at the Founding Conference of the Danish Evaluation Society. September 2000. Retrieved from www.danskevalueringsselskab.dk/pdf/Nick%20Tilley.pdf.

United Nations Office on Drugs and Crime (UNODC). (2010). *The handbook on the crime prevention guidelines: Making them work.* New York, NY: Author.

Welsh, B., & Farrington, D. (2006). Evidence-based crime prevention. In B. Welsh, & D. Farrington (Eds.), *Preventing crime: What works for children, offenders, victims and places* (pp. 1–17). London, England: Springer.

Welsh, B., & Hoshi, A. (2002). Communities and crime prevention. In L. Sherman, D. Farrington, B. Welsh, & D. MacKenzie (Eds.), *Evidence-based crime prevention* (pp. 165-197). London, England: Routledge.

White, R., & Coventry, G. (2000). *Evaluating community safety — A guide.* Melbourne, Australia: Department of Justice Victoria.

Chapter 2

Policing, Deterrence and Incapacitation

Jacqueline M. Drew

This chapter examines incapacitation and deterrence in the context of policing. Laws provide the sanctions for criminal acts while the role of police is one of detection and apprehension of offenders. This chapter addresses the role of police as the first step in the chain of events that need to occur prior to incapacitation. Specific organisational police strategies employed by police agencies in their efforts to deter crime are examined. These policies are critically assessed by examining empirical research and contemporary theorising to determine their relative contribution to deterrence, specifically their effectiveness on crime prevention and control outcomes. The policing strategies discussed in this chapter include crackdowns, hot spots policing strategies and pulling levels policing and the impact of police-community relations in crime prevention and control efforts. Mounting empirical support demonstrates that police strategies and tactics can be significantly undermined if such operational strategies erode police–community relations. As such, the role of procedural justice principles and police legitimacy in the implementation of police approaches is addressed.

Incapacitation and Deterrence Effects

In theory, the criminal justice system apprehends, prosecutes and punishes those individuals who break the law. The police, courts and correctional systems work together to impact on criminal behaviour and crime. Police are responsible for apprehending the offender and bringing them before the courts. The role of incapacitation and punishment of offenders is the mandate of the courts and correctional system.

Incapacitation and deterrence are the two key pillars of the criminal justice system, focused on crime prevention and crime control (Nagin, 2013a). Rather than rehabilitation, the emphasis lies with punishment of offenders, the perceived likelihood and use of sanctions to deter and curtail criminal behaviour (Nagin, 2013a, 2013b; Vito & Maahs, 2015). Based on the seminal work of Bentham and Beccaria, the elements that make punishment effective include *certainty* of punishment, *swift* reaction to crime and sufficient *severity* that ensures the punishment outweighs any potential rewards that are perceived by the offender for engaging in the crime (for more detailed discussion see: Apel & Nagin, 2011; Nagin, 2003a). Punishment of offenders can take many forms, including such options as imprisonment, home detention, monitoring of offenders through the use of such devices as security bracelets or vehicle interlocks, community service orders, monetary fines and penalties, disqualification of professional accreditation and restitution orders.

Punishment through *incapacitation* that involves incarceration of offenders, ensures that potential offenders have no capacity to commit further crime, at least for the period of imprisonment (Nagin, 2013a). The judicial system will institute responses to crime such as mandatory minimum sentencing and "three strikes" policies for targeted crimes (Paternoster, 2010). Incapacitation can be categorised as 'collective incapacitation' or 'selective incapacitation'. In the case of collective incapacitation, this involves a change to sentencing, for example introducing or increasing mandatory minimum sentences (Paternoster, 2010; Vito & Maahs, 2015). This type of approach is able to affect a large number of offenders (Vito & Maahs, 2015). Alternatively, a more tailored approach to incapacitation may be undertaken, known as selective incapacitation. This involves targeting individual, specific, chronic offenders who are determined to pose an elevated risk of reoffending and giving them longer prison sentences (Vito & Maahs, 2015).

Deterrence involves the threat of punishment that discourages criminal behaviour, that is crime prevention (general deterrence) and the impact of punishment on future re-offending (specific deterrence; Braga & Weisburd, 2014). As discussed by Nagin (2013a, 2013b) empirical support for *certainty* of punishment, relative to *severity* of punishment, has been found to have more impactful deterrent effects.

The Role of Police

Deterrence theorists have sought to empirically test the proposition that formal punishment is associated with real and significant reductions in criminal behaviour. Given the focus of this chapter on the role of police, it is important to consider how deterrence has been adapted and can be understood in this context. In order for offenders to be convicted and subsequently punished, the police must first apprehend the offender (Nagin, 2013a). Police may also influence crime outcomes without apprehension, by influencing the behaviour of potential offenders through their presence and actions (Nagin, 2013a).

Arrests and Re-offending

If apprehension results in subsequent imprisonment, police enhance crime prevention through their contribution to incapacitation of offenders and potentially, may also impact on future criminal behaviour. In respect to police impact on future criminal behaviour, we must understand the relationship between arrest and re-offending. Some of the most interesting research in this area has focused on domestic violence.

In the United States in the 1970s, police sought to address domestic violence where possible, through such strategies as referral to social service agencies rather than arrest (Maxwell, Garner, & Fagan, 2001). During the 1980s this approach was questioned and police moved from therapeutic models to more punitive, arrest-based, responses (Maxwell et al., 2001). Empirical evidence to support either approach had largely not been undertaken. This gap in knowledge was addressed, beginning with the Minneapolis Domestic Violence Experiment (MDVE). Broadly, this research found that arrests were associated with around a 50% decrease in re-offending across the 6 month follow-up period. The findings saw many police agencies adopt pro-arrest policies (Maxwell et al., 2001). However, subsequent replication studies demonstrated that the relationship was not quite so definitive.

These inconsistencies reflect the likely complexities of the relationship between arrest and re-offending. Maxwell and colleagues' (2001) sophisticated re-analysis of six replications revealed that arrest of offenders did impact on re-offending however the size of the deterrent effect was modest in comparison to the relationship between arrest and other measures such as prior criminal record and age. Further, the majority of offenders did not re-offend even if they were not arrested. As such, it was concluded that mandatory arrest for all offenders is likely to be unwarranted and identifying and responding to chronic or high-risk offenders is a better use of police resources and more prudent implementation of arrest policy.

Durlauf and Nagin (2011) have asserted that crime prevention can be improved by 'shifting resources from imprisonment to policing' (p. 9-10). The approach of targeting or focusing police resources on high risk crimes, places and in the case discussed here, high risk offenders, is emerging as a strong theme of contemporary police approaches. This approach is further discussed later in the chapter relevant to operational police practices of hot spots policing and pulling levers policing.

The Impact of Police Presence

The intensity and perception of police presence is related to crime outcomes (Nagin, 2013). When there is a perception that risk of apprehension is high, crime will be prevented. Nagin (2013) concludes that more rigorous research is needed that examines how the perceived risk of apprehension, reducing the perceived attractiveness of criminal opportunities, can be influenced by both police presence but also importantly, by different types of police tactics. Researchers have examined how crime can be prevented and influenced through changes in police numbers and resources. Specifically, this involves studying the relationship between numbers of police and crime rates.

Researchers have also examined how police can better influence crime prevention outcomes through the use of different types of police strategies and tactics (Nagin, 2013).

Police Numbers

Prior to discussing police numbers, it is important to highlight the distinction between absolute and marginal deterrence, a distinction that has been at times neglected in the police literature (Vito & Maahs, 2015). 'Absolute deterrence' refers to the impact of having a formal system in place that seeks to influence and prevent the likelihood that potential offenders will engage in criminal behaviours (Vito & Maahs, 2015). The complete absence of laws, police and correctional facilities undoubtedly would influence crime rates (Lee, Eck, & Corsaro, 2016; Vito & Maahs, 2015). Related to police, studies of this nature include research that has examined instances of police strikes where police officer numbers have been significantly and dramatic decreased for a period of time (Sherman, 1997).

A recent study of this was provided by Shi (2009). In Cincinnati, heavy rioting and significant media attention resulted from an incident where an unarmed African American suspect was shot by a white police officer. It was reported that officers responded by decreasing their use of arrest for misdemeanour crimes. Shi (2009) found that during this period there was significant decline in officer productivity and a substantial increase in crime rates (38% increase for violent crime and 22% increase for property crime).

Of perhaps more interest and importance, given that the abolishment or general absence of police responses is unusual, is the concept of marginal deterrence. The majority of studies examine marginal deterrence, seeking to understand how incremental changes in criminal sanctions impact on crime (Tonry, 2008). Marginal deterrence can be studied as small changes to current police numbers within an established and functioning police agency (Lee et al., 2016; Weisburd & Eck, 2004).

Summaries of relevant police numbers research have been provided by Lee et al. (2016) and Marvell and Moody (1996). It was concluded by Sherman and Eck (2002) that the evidence related to increasing police numbers will impact on crime is at best, weak. Lee et al. (2016) found that the relationship between police numbers and crime is small, negative and nonsignificant.

Marvell and Moody (1996) did provide some insight into the potential impact of deployment patterns. This review found a differential impact of increases in police numbers dependent on deployment location, with greater reductions in crime being realised in more densely populated areas (i.e., large cities) rather than simply adding officers to all locations (Sherman, 1997). Bradford (2011) working from Marvel and Moody's (1996) analysis of the literature reviewed 13 more recent studies of police numbers. Despite noted methodological issues with the research reviewed, Bradford (2011) found that there is a significant and negative relationship between numbers of police and some forms of recorded crime, specifically property crime rather than violent crime. Lee et al. (2016) asserted, based on a systematic review of 62 studies of police size and crime, that 'changing police strategy is likely to have a greater impact on crime than adding more police' (p.431).

Police Strategies and Tactics

Reflecting on the experiences of the United States during the 1990s, there were relatively large increases in police numbers and a wave of new and more innovative police strategies being trialled and implemented across many police agencies. It has been estimated that there was an approximate 14% increase in officers per capita at this time (Paternoster, 2010). Given the preceding discussion that heavily questioned the efficacy of generic increases in police resources impacting on crime outcomes, it is unlikely that the dramatic decreases in crime that were experienced in the United States during the 1990s simply resulted from more police (Paternoster, 2010). Of interest is what police did during this time in terms of the development of more effective policing strategies and tactics. As such, a combination of more police, but importantly what police 'did' with their existing and now increased human resources, is perhaps of more significance.

Research examining the effectiveness of operational police practices, dominated by 'reactive policing', that was undertaken across the 1970s and 1980s became a catalyst for the development of new and more innovative police approaches (Drew & Prenzler, 2015). The mainstays of police work – rapid response policing and random patrolling – as they were being implemented in their traditional form, were found to be largely ineffective in crime prevention and control (Weisburd & Eck, 2004). The value of policing as an effective approach to crime prevention came under increasing scrutiny (Nagin, 2013b). Traditional police strategies seek to maximise detection and arrest outcomes. As described by Nagin (2013b) police act as 'apprehension agents'. Evidence to support the deterrent effect of police as apprehension agents is limited (Nagin, 2013b). The Kansas City Preventative Patrol Experiment is undoubtedly the landmark study that initiated a new wave of thinking about how to maximise the effectiveness of the police function.

Police Patrols and Hot Spots Policing

Beginning in 1972, the Kansas City Preventative Patrol study tested the effects of certainty of punishment by undertaking a study of police patrol resources. Patrol resources were experimentally manipulated in order to empirically test the impact of preventative patrol on crime outcomes and community perceptions of crime (Kelling, Pate, Dieckman, & Brown, 1974). The findings were surprising. The study found that increasing or decreasing preventative patrols had no effect on crime, fear of crime, community attitudes towards police, response time or traffic accidents (Kelling et al., 1974). Although the Kansas City study has been heavily criticised for its methodological weaknesses and research design, its contribution and role in sparking renewed interest in not only how to improve patrol strategies but the need to empirically test long held and unquestioned assumptions about the effectiveness of police practices is undeniable (Drew & Prenzler, 2015).

The significant questions that were raised by the Kansas City Preventative Patrol Experiment subsequently resulted in a better appreciation and understanding of how focused and targeted police strategies could be more effective. In the case of patrolling, the seminal work undertaken in the Minneapolis Hot Spots Study was essential to the progression in thinking of patrol practices. The Minneapolis study manipulated patrol frequency within 110 small geographic areas (55 control areas and 55 experimental areas) that had the highest concentration of crime (Sherman & Weisburd, 1995). Experimental areas compared to control areas experienced two to three times more patrols, with patrols specifically increased during the hours when there was increased criminal activity (11 pm and 3am). Doubling patrols significantly decreased calls for service (decrease between 6 and 13 per cent) and reductions specifically were identified for soft crimes, for example vandalism and disorderly behaviour (Sherman & Weisburd, 1995). This study became the impetus for the further development and widespread use of what has become known as hot spots policing.

Hot spots policing can be described within the context of intensive law enforcement approaches that are designed to have a deterrent effect. As discussed, it seeks to identify particular geographic locations, specific crimes and/or target high-risk offenders, focusing police resources (often patrol resources), increasing the certainty of arrest and punishment on these areas of concentration (Braga & Apel, 2016; Braga, Papachristos, & Hureau, 2012). Using Nagin's (2013b) role description as discussed earlier, police are apprehension agents.

However, hot spots policing also necessitates what Nagin (2013b) refers to as a 'sentinel role'. This is an important distinction, as it reflects the broadening of policing during the 1990s to more fully embrace strategies beyond detection and arrest, and to explicitly adopt a crime prevention focus. When enacting the sentinel role, police seek to prevent crime by influencing the perception of offenders that areas that have been identified and are the target of hot spots policing due to their disproportionate high crime rates are now too risky for offenders to engage in criminal behaviour. Further, police who simultaneously adopt a broader problem solving approach (developed within a problem oriented policing framework) will influence offender behaviour by altering the criminal opportunity structures of the hot spots thereby making the location a less desirable and a more difficult location to commit crime (Braga & Apel, 2016). Braga and colleagues (2012) undertook a systematic review of 19 studies of hot spots policing based on 25 interventions. They found that in 20 out of 25 interventions, hot spots policing produced significant and important crime reduction effects.

It is important to acknowledge, that while hot spots policing was gaining momentum as a strategy that embraced both intensive law enforcement and sought to achieve crime prevention outcomes, other intensive law enforcement strategies were being trialled and implemented. Approaches such as 'police crackdowns' and 'zero tolerance policing' also attracted significant attention during this time (Paternoster, 2010).

Police Crackdowns and Zero Tolerance Policing

Case Example: New York Police Department

Perhaps the best known example of these approaches is the alleged 'zero tolerance' policing approach undertaken by the New York Police Department (NYPD) in the 1990s. Zero tolerance policing in New York involved a focus on certain, swift and severe enforcement of minor offences including pubic drunkenness, loitering, littering and many public order offences (Paternoster, 2010). The premise was based in 'broken windows' theory, that a determined focus on minor violations would send a strong deterrent message that would in turn impact on more serious crime (Wilson & Kelling, 1982). During this time, NYPD also instituted a new management system known as 'COMPSTAT' that focused on rigorous performance evaluation and more targeted, analytical and accountable allocation and use of police resources (Paternoster, 2010). It was reported that New York was able to halt a spiralling crime wave, felonies dropped by 44.3%, murders decreased by 60.2% and there was a 48.4% drop in robbery (Greene, 1999). Many would argue that evidence to support what some had referred to as the 'New York miracle' has no substantive basis and the fall in crime was already occurring prior to the policy changes and strategy implementation (Tonry, 2008). Regardless, the zero tolerance policy adopted by NYPD provides an interesting example of intensive enforcement that strongly influenced police practices at this time.

It must be noted that zero tolerance policing has not been subsequently adopted with the same vigour that we have seen with hot spots policing. This in part can be explained due to its unintended consequences. Specifically, zero tolerance policing can have a negative impact on police–community relations. While many police departments were actively focusing on building and enhancing community relations through community policing initiatives, zero tolerance policing has been described as 'hyperaggressive' and characterised as aggressive enforcement (Greene, 1999). This resulted in increases in allegations of misconduct and excessive force used by police (Greene, 1999). The detrimental impact on police effectiveness that results from strategies that undermine good community relations, perceptions of procedural justice and police legitimacy are discussed later in this chapter.

Pulling Levers Policing

Most recently, focused deterrence policing approaches have been proposed as a promising way forward. Their benefit seemingly derives from a better understanding under what conditions deterrence is most effective, including in what contexts, with what type of offences, types of offenders and types of victims (Vito & Maachs, 2015). 'Focused deterrence' is a more specific approach that sits within the generic framework of problem oriented policing (POP). Also, similar to hot spots policing, this approach follows a contemporary understanding of crime concentration. Only a small percentage of people are responsible for a large percentage of crime (Weisburd & Eck, 2004). Hence, police resources need not be evenly distributed throughout our communities but effective deployment involves identification and targeting of likely offenders and high crime locations (Braga et al., 2012).

Consistent with the core tenets of deterrence theory, this approach focuses on the identification of high-risk offenders for identified, specific crimes. Strategies are applied to influence the perception of likely offenders that the benefits of engaging in the criminal behaviour does not outweigh the costs and further, that apprehension is likely (US Department of Justice Violence Reduction Network, 2015). The targeted offenders are informed via explicit and direct messages designed to deter future criminal behaviour that the consequences of not disengaging will result in punishment and sanctions (US Department of Justice Violence Reduction Network, 2015). Importantly, these strategies involve multiple stakeholders, expanding beyond police. Strategies involve police, mobilise communities and include social service actions (Braga & Weisburd, 2014). If offenders do not positively respond to the messages provided, the 'levers' (enforcement actions) are 'pulled' (actioned by police; US Department of Justice Violence Reduction Network, 2015). As such, strategies used by police within a focused deterrence framework are often referred to as 'pulling levers' policing (Kennedy, 2008).

Pulling levers policing builds on traditional deterrence strategies founded on the core idea of increasing the risk for offenders committing crime, by identifying creative ways to use both traditional and nontraditional law enforcement methods to de-incentivise criminal behaviour (Braga & Weisburd, 2012b). Responses that are developed are customised to the specific circumstances of the target problem/s and are developed in light of local conditions and within available operational capacities (Braga & Weisburd, 2014). The core elements of pulling levers policing are identified in Table 2.1.

The focused deterrence approach adopted by police was originally developed in Boston in the 1990s, and was known as Operation Ceasefire.

Table 2.1

Core elements of Pulling Levers Policing Strategies

Element	Description
Problem selection	Selection of a particular, specific crime problem
Partnership formation	Convene interagency working group, including law enforcement, social services and community-based practitioners
Research and analysis	Identify key offenders, groups and behavioural patterns
Response development	Frame a response to offenders and groups of offenders, utilising varied menu of sanctions ('pulling levers') to stop identified criminal behaviour/s
Focus resources	Focus social services and community resources on target offenders and groups, matching law enforcement efforts

Source: Adapted from Braga & Weisburd, 2012b, p. 5.

Operation Ceasefire focused on combatting serious gang violence (Braga & Weisburd, 2012b; Kennedy, Piehl, & Braga, 1996). While some questioned the true effectiveness of the approach, many have heralded this strategy as an unprecedented success (Braga & Weisburd, 2012b).

Pulling Levers – Case Example: Operation Ceasefire, Boston Gun Project

The operation utilised two strategies focused on preventing inter-gang gun violence (Braga, Kennedy, Waring, & Piehl, 2001; Braga & Weisburd, 2014). It was identified that the offenders were a small population of chronic offenders (between 1100 to 1300) that were involved in approximately 61 informal, loosely grouped, predominantly neighbourhood groups. This small group, representing less than one per cent of the all youth aged between 14 and 26, perpetrated more than 60% of youth homicides in Boston.

One strategy involved targeting the suppliers of weapons to the youth gangs and the second strategy involved gathering together the youth gang members in order to directly communicate with them. On multiple occasions the youth gang members at these group meetings (known as forums or call-ins) were informed by police that serious violence would be met with strong and multifaceted enforcement. This also included prosecution of nonrelated, nonviolent, crimes, such as drug dealing. Police disrupted low-level street crime such as public drinking and trespassing, served outstanding warrants and strictly enforced probation and parole conditions. In addition to police action, probation and parole officers, gang outreach workers and eventually church and other community groups became involved in the strategy.

The strategy sought to impact on violent crime by increasing severity and certainty of punishment under specific and targeted circumstances. It was important that the intervention was focused, in particular the messages being given to the identified group of offenders. The messages were direct and targeted, ensuring that it was clearly communicated what kind of behaviours were being targeted and what responses should be expected. Those who are the focus of the intervention need to be made beware of changes to punishment and the direct relationship between behaviour and responses. When sanction risk and certainty are recognised by the target group, deterrent outcomes are enhanced (Durlauf & Nagin, 2011).

Beyond Operation Ceasefire

Subsequently, these methods and approach was adopted elsewhere, spawning many policing initiatives based within the deterrence-based framework (Brunson, 2015). These have included programs and evaluations in Los Angeles (Tita et al., 2004), Chicago (Papachristos, Meares, & Fagan, 2007) and Indianapolis (McGarrell, Chermak, Wilson, & Carsaro, 2006). Evaluations, similar to Operation Ceasefire, demonstrated important crime reduction outcomes. Based on a narrative review of the effectiveness of the identified programs and a meta-analysis of the main effects on reported crime, nine of the ten evaluations of pulling levers policing reported a significant impact on crime (Braga & Weisburd, 2012b). While Braga and Weisburd (2012b) cautioned that there was a lack of rigorous evaluation designs such as randomised experiments, the crime reductions effects were noted as strong, large and significant.

The Impact of Focused Deterrence on Police–Community Relations

Many herald the success of more focused policing methods, however it must be acknowledged that some have raised concerns about the impact of targeted strategies on police–community relations. This issue was highlighted earlier in the chapter related to intensive law enforcement enacted through zero tolerance policing.

A focused approach in its implementation necessitates a focus on places where crime clusters (Brunson, 2015). High crime areas are often those that have disproportionate numbers of people that are socially and economically disadvantaged and minority members of our community (Brunson, 2015). It is these types of communities that often experience greatest levels of mistrust and suspicion of police, feeling that they are unfairly targeted and over-policed (Braga & Apel, 2016). As such, a focus on high crime areas, while effective from a crime prevention and crime control perspective, can pose significant challenges to police–community relations.

An important body of work has emerged that examines how police–community relations can underpin the success of a diversity of police strategies and tactics being pursued by police agencies. Community policing began in the 1980s with an emphasis on community involvement in setting police priorities, collaborative problem-solving by police with the community and an emphasis on local, community-level solutions to community crime problems (Skogan, 2006).

Undoubtedly, police effectiveness is enhanced by the voluntary cooperation of members of the community who support police in their duties (Mazerolle, Bennett, Davis, Sergeant, & Manning, 2013). Recently, significant work has been conducted in relation to the concepts of 'procedural justice' and 'police legitimacy'. Cooperation with police is heavily influenced by the perceived legitimacy of police authority held by community members (Tyler, 2001). Police legitimacy results largely from the fair and just application of authority, known as procedural fairness (Mazerolle et al., 2013). Perceptions of legitimacy lead to increased compliance. Based on a systematic review of relevant police legitimacy literature, it was found that legitimacy is associated with increased willingness of the public to cooperate and comply with police directives, reductions in revictimisation and importantly, reducing reoffending when used in the direct contact with offenders (Mazerolle et al., 2013).

Pulling Levers and Police Legitimacy – Case Example: Project Safe Neighborhoods in Chicago

As part of the Project Safe Neighborhoods initiative sponsored by the US Department of Justice, a focused deterrence strategy was implemented in Chicago targeting gun and gang-involved offenders on parole (Papachristos et al., 2007). The strategy involved increases in federal prosecutions for convicted offenders that carried or used guns, increased mandatory sentencing, law enforcement strategies aimed at increasing gun seizures and offender notification forums. A 37% drop in quarterly homicide rates across treatment districts was reported.

The specific relevance of this case study, to the current discussion relates the study findings in respect to offender notification forums. Those offenders returning to high-risk neighbourhoods were required to attend offender notification forums. The forums notified offenders of federal firearm laws and mandatory minimum sentences for re-offending, social services were offered and they were spoken to by other ex-offenders who had been successful in not re-offending. Rather than threatening offenders, forums were explicitly designed on procedural justice principles seeking to change offender behaviour though persuasive communication strategies. Architects of focused deterrence strategies assert that offenders should be treated in a procedurally fair manner, with interactions characterised by respect (Braga & Weisburd, 2012a; Kennedy, 2008). The findings of the Chicago strategy found that the observed decrease in homicides was attributable specifically to offender notification forums.

Conclusions

Police are important to crime prevention and crime control. Police enact the necessary first step in the chain of events that lead to incapacitation. Laws provide the sanctions for criminal acts while the role of police is one of detection and apprehension of offenders (Paternoster, 2010). The role of police is particularly important in achieving crime prevention and control outcomes through deterrence, with the conclusion that certainty of punishment is a more effective deterrent compared to severity of punishment (Nagin, 2013a, 2013b). As reviewed in this chapter, the influence of police is likely to result from a combination of police numbers and their strategic deployment to where their presence and associated specific police strategies and tactics are going to have most impact (Nagin, 2013a, 2013b).

Based on the critical analysis undertaken in this chapter of relevant empirical studies and theorising, it is concluded that hot spots policing and focused deterrence strategies, specifically pulling levers policing are key operational strategies for police (Braga et al., 2012; Braga & Weisburd, 2012b). Further, a growing body of empirical support clearly demonstrates the impact that community and offender perceptions have on police legitimacy, with police actions supported and reinforced when community–police relations are positive and respectful (Mazerolle et al., 2013).

References

Braga, A., & Weisburd, D. (2014). Focused deterrence and the prevention of violent gun injuries: Practice, theoretical principles and scientific evidence. *The Annual Review of Public Health, 36,* 55–68.

Brunson, R.K. (2015). Focused deterrence and improved police–community relations: Unpacking the proverbial 'black box'. *Criminology and Public Policy, 14*(3), 507–514.

Drew, J., & Prenzler, T. (2015). *Contemporary police practice.* Melbourne, Australia: Oxford University Press.

Durlauf, S., & Nagin, D. (2011). Imprisonment and crime: Can both be reduced? *Criminology and Public Policy, 10*(1), 13–54.

Greene, J. (1999). Zero tolerance: A Case study of police policies and practices in New York City. *Crime & Delinquency, 45*(2), 171–187.

Kelling, G., Pate, T., Dieckman, D., & Brown, C. (1974). *The Kansas City preventative patrol experiment: A Summary report.* Washington, DC: Police Foundation.

Kennedy, D. (2008). *Deterrence and crime prevention: Reconsidering the prospect of sanction.* London, England: Routledge Press.

Kennedy, D.M., Piehl, A.M. & Braga, A.A. (1996). Youth violence in Boston: Gun markets, serious youth offenders, and a use-reduction strategy. *Law and Contemporary Problems, 59*, 147–196.

Lee, Y., Eck, J. & Corsaro, N. (2016). Conclusions from the history of research into the effects of police force size on crime — 1968 through 2013. *Journal of Experimental Criminology, 12*, 431–451.

Marvell, T., & Moody, C. (1996). Specification problems, police levels, and crime rates. *Criminology, 34*(4), 609–646.

Mazerolle, L., Bennett, S., Davis, J., Sergeant, E., & Manning, M. (2013). *Legitimacy in policing: A systematic review.* Oslo, Norway: The Campbell Collaboration.

Maxwell, C., Garner, J., & Fagan, J. (2001). *The Effects of arrest on intimate partner violence: New evidence from the spouse assault replication program.* Washington, DC: US Department of Justice.

McGarrell, E., Chermak, S., Wilson, J. & Carsaro, N. (2006). Reducing homicide through a 'lever-pulling' strategy. *Justice Quarterly, 23*, 214–229.

Nagin, D. (2013a). Criminal deterrence research at the outset of the twenty-first century. In M. Tonry (Ed.), *Crime and justice: A review of research.* Vol. 23 (pp. 1–42). Chicago, IL: University of Chicago Press.

Nagin, D. (2013b). Deterrence: A review of the evidence by a criminologist for economists. *Annual Review of Economics, 5*, 83–105.

Papachristos, A., Meares, T. & Fagan, J. (2007). Attention felons: Evaluating Project Safe Neighborhoods in Chicago. *Journal of Empirical Legal Studies, 4*, 223–272.

Paternoster, R. (2010). How much do we really know about criminal deterrence. *The Journal of Criminal Law and Criminology, 100*(3), 765–823.

Sherman, L. (1997). Policing for crime prevention. L.W. Sherman, D. Gottfredson, J. Eck, P. Reuter, & S. Bushway (Eds.), *Preventing crime: What works, what doesn't, what's promising.* Washington, DC: US Department of Justice.

Sherman, L., & Eck, J. (2002). Policing for prevention. In L.W. Sherman & D. Farrington & B. Welsh (Eds.), *Evidence based crime prevention* (pp. 295–329). New York, NY: Routledge.

Sherman, L., & Weisburd, D. (1995). General deterrent effects of police patrol on crime 'hot spots': A Randomised, controlled trial. *Justice Quarterly, 12*(4), 625–648.

Shi, L. (2009). The limits of oversight in policing: Evidence from the 2001 Cincinnati riot. *Journal of Public Economics, 93,* 99–113.

Skogan, W. (2006). The Promise of community policing. In D.Weisburd & A. Braga (Eds.), *Police innovation: Contrasting perspectives* (pp. 27–43). Cambridge, England: Cambridge University Press.

Tita, G., Riley, K., Ridgeway, G., Grammich, C., Abrahamse, A., & Greenwood, P. (2004). *Reducing gun violence: Results from an intervention in East Los Angeles.* Santa Monica: RAND.

Tonry, M. (2008). Learning from the limitations of deterrence research. *Crime and Justice, 37*(1), 279–311.

Tyler, T. (2001). Public trust and confidence in legal authorities: What do majority and minority group members want from legal authorities. *Behavioral Sciences and the Law, 19,* 215–-235.

US Department of Justice Violence Reduction Network. (2015). *Ceasefire: The effects of "pulling levers" focused deterrence strategies on crime.* Retrieved from https://www.vrnetwork.org/Clearinghouse/Resource/108

Vito, G., & Maahs, J. (2015). *Criminology: Theory, research and practice.* Burlington, MA: Jones & Bartlett Learning.

Weisburd, D., & Eck, J. (2004). What can the police do to reduce crime, disorder, and fear? *The Annals of the American Academy of Political and Social Science, 593*(1), 42–65.

Wilson, J., & Kelling, G. (1982). Broken windows: The police and neighbourhood safety. *The Atlantic Monthly,* March, 29–38.

Chapter 3

Offender Management and Rehabilitation

Mary Baker and Nadine McKillop

Desistance from offending is the system-wide aim of corrective services. Offenders are a heterogeneous group — they (and their offences) come in all shapes and sizes. Assessment, management and treatment of offenders must therefore attend to this diversity. Over the past two decades significant efforts have been made to design and deliver programs tailored to these unique risks and needs. In this chapter we introduce best practice frameworks (risk-need-responsivity [RNR] model, good lives model (GLM), and therapeutic jurisprudence) under-pinning current offender management and rehabilitation practices. We then review some promising approaches implemented at different stages of the correctional process (probation through to reintegration) and identify areas for continued development.

Offender Management

Over the past two decades, imprisonment rates have risen globally (see Figure 3.1); the highest rates being in the United Sates (707 per 100,000). This calls attention to the need for effective offender management practices and accountability, within and outside prison, to improve community safety (Day, Casey, Ward, Howells, & Vess, 2010). This includes the management of custodial offenders awaiting trial (i.e., remand), convicted and awaiting sentencing (i.e., reception), or sentenced, and those on community-based orders. Although governed by statutes, frameworks for managing offenders vary across jurisdictions.

The primary aims of offender management are to (1) identify offenders' risks and needs; (2) to protect society by monitoring offenders in accord with identified risk; and (3) to ensure access to, and help motivate engagement in, appropriate treatment programs (Golias, 2004). Corrective services and community corrections staff are provided with training in risk assessment, compliance and management. Tasked primarily with law enforcement, their role is often complicated by the rehabilitative ideals of corrective practice (Allard, Wortley, & Stewart, 2003). It is also shaped by the current political culture, a corrective services officer's personality, the

Figure 3.1

Global prison population 1992–2012.

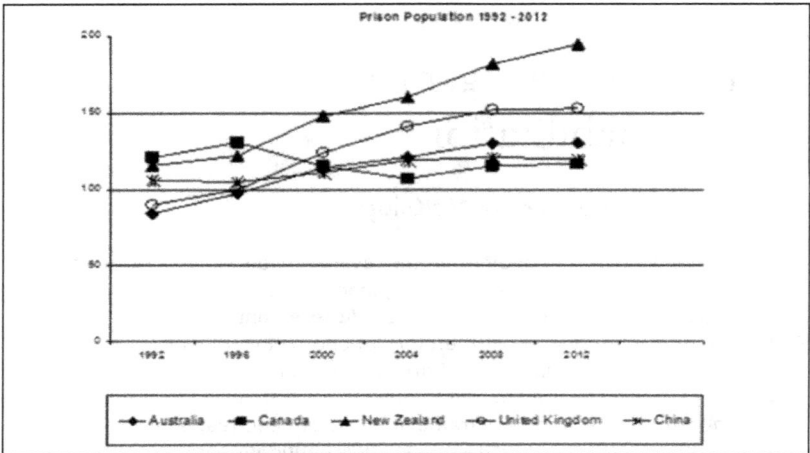

Source: Institute for Criminal Policy Research, 2014.

type of offender being supervised and institutional aims (Schaefer, Cullen, & Eck, 2016).

To improve coherence, consistency and continuity in service provision for offenders throughout their sentence, the integrated offender management model was introduced in Australia and New Zealand in 1998 (Mellor, 2002). Its purpose is to bring together the multitude of professionals working with offenders to address the factors associated with their offending and streamline custodial and community-based services (White & Graham, 2010), as depicted in Figure 3.2. One key component of offender management is rehabilitation.

Figure 3.2

Integrated offender management model.

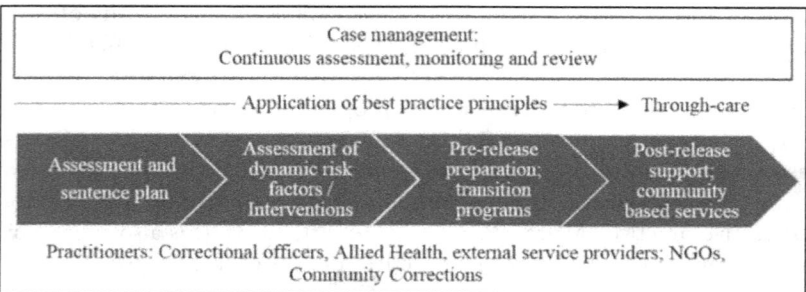

Source: Originally published in White & Graham, 2010. (Used with permission.)

Offender Rehabilitation

Generally, rehabilitation refers to therapeutic interventions that help individuals recover both physically and psychologically from illness, injury or addiction; and programs aimed at prosocial behavioural change (White & Graham, 2010). In the context of corrections, this latter behavioural change approach to rehabilitation is a key part of offender management both in prison and in the community, through probation and parole.

Offender rehabilitation itself has borne considerable influence, criticism, rejection and resurgence. Notably, Martinson's (1974) 'nothing works' proclamation brought about cynicism concerning the effectiveness of rehabilitative practices, resulting in widespread abandonment of programs. This shift away from rehabilitative to more retributive ideals persisted despite Martinson (1979) later revising his position (see Cullen & Gendreau, 2000). Since this time, there have been profound developments and shifts in perspective, and renewed enthusiasm for rehabilitation.

Since the late 1980s, more nuanced questions concerning 'what works, for whom, and in what circumstances?' have been raised. The development and application of best practice principles ensued (Andrews & Bonta, 2010), and concerted efforts have been made to attend to differences in risk, age, gender, culture and intellectual capacities that comprise offender populations. An expanding empirical-base (see Andrews & Bonta, 2010) demonstrates generally positive rehabilitative outcomes; more so, at least, than standard criminal justice methods focused on punishment and deterrence alone (Chen & Shapiro, 2007). It is these best practice frameworks to which we now turn.

Best Practice Frameworks

Three main theoretical frameworks underpin current offender management and rehabilitation practices:

- the Risk-Need-Responsivity (RNR) model
- the Good Lives Model (GLM)
- Therapeutic Jurisprudence.

The RNR model was developed in Canada by Andrews, Bonta and Hoge (1990) to guide the design and implementation of effective correctional programs. Since this time it has been used with increasing success globally and is arguably the dominant model of effective correctional practice. Essentially, it guides service providers on *who* to treat ('risk' principle), *what* to treat ('need' principle) and *how* to deliver treatment ('responsivity', 'integrity' and 'flexibility' principles) (Bonta & Andrews, 2007), as summarised in Figure 3.3.

Figure 3.3

Risk-Need-Responsivity model.

THEORETICAL PRINCIPLES	PRACTICE PRINCIPLES
RISK	• Intervention matched to offender's assessed level of risk • Higher the risk, more intensive the intervention
NEED	• Interventions targeted to address dynamic factors (e.g. criminogenic needs) likely to increase reoffending
RESPONSIVITY	• Programs adapted to match learning style, in ways that motivate participation; culturally appropriate
INTEGRITY	• Evidence-based; underpinned by theory • Program integrity maintained throughout
FLEXIBILITY	• Adapted to suit individual needs and local capacity

Source: Andrews & Bonta, 2010.

The GLM (Ward & Stewart, 2003) was subsequently developed to address some perceived limitations of the RNR model. Ward and Stewart (2003) argued that although it is necessary to focus on risk-reduction, this one-dimensional focus was not sufficient. Advocating a strength-based approach (i.e., focusing on offenders' personal strengths and skills that complement interventions), the GLM extends the focus beyond risk-management strategies to include plans aligned with life enrichment that forge new ways to live, attain goals (termed 'primary goods') and interact with others in socially (and legally) acceptable ways (Ward & Stewart, 2003). Table 3.1 lists 'primary goods' that are the essential ingredients for change.

In effect, developing and implementing meaningful life plans and the strategies to achieve them promotes psychological wellbeing and, in turn, reduces the risk of further offending (Ward & Stewart, 2003). Despite some contentious debates in the field (e.g., Ward, Yates, & Willis, 2012), the GLM continues to receive international attention and is being incorporated into case management and offender (especially sex offender) programs worldwide (McGrath, Cumming, Burchard, Zeoli, & Ellerby, 2010).

Although offender rehabilitation is often viewed within the realm of corrective services, the courts also play a significant role in diverting offenders, before sentencing, for the purposes of offender management and rehabilitation. 'Therapeutic jurisprudence' (Wexler & Winick, 1996) is a legal theory premised on the benefits of a rehabilitative, rather than punitive, approach to offender management. It considers how an offender's encounter with the

Table 3.1

Definitions of 'Primary Goods'

Primary Good	Definition
1. Life	Healthy living and functioning
2. Knowledge	Learning and knowing; feeling well informed
3. Excellence in play	Striving for mastery and excellence in hobbies and leisure activities
4. Excellence in work	Striving for mastery and excellence in work
5. Excellence in agency	Seeking autonomy and self-directedness
6. Inner peace	Peace of mind; absence of emotional turmoil or distress
7. Relatedness	Relationships and friendships; close mutual connections and bonds
8. Community	Sense of belonging to a wider group and sharing common values
9. Spirituality	Finding a sense of purpose and meaning in life
10. Happiness	Desire to experience happiness and pleasure in the 'here and now'
11. Creativity	Desire to be innovative and try new things; expressing oneself through alternative forms

Source: Ward & Stewart, 2003.

law, legal institutions and practices can affect their wellbeing (Winick, 2003). Judges and lawyers contribute to achieving justice principles by suggesting treatment options that address the causes of offending rather than criminality per se (White & Perrone, 2015). It provides a holistic approach to offender rehabilitation by considering 'internal responsivity factors', such as emotional and psychological needs, and 'external responsivity factors', such as the use of therapeutic agents, the treatment setting and the social needs of the offender (Birgden, 2004, p. 283).

Promising Approaches

There are now many promising programs underpinned by these frameworks.[1] Some are still in their infancy, not all have been subject to scientifically robust evaluations, but nevertheless they show promise in reducing reoffending, improving community safety and producing more meaningful lives for offenders. At the very least, they provide direction for future program development and research. The remainder of this chapter showcases a small selection of these.

---

1 See www.crimesolutions.gov/Programs.aspx for a comprehensive overview.

Managing Probationers

Probation is not always taken seriously and some recalcitrant offenders violate their orders knowing there will be no immediate consequences and likely delays to prosecution. To address this problem, the Hawaii Opportunity Probation with Enforcement (HOPE) program was introduced as a result of a Judge's frustration with conventional probation. Operating since 2004, the HOPE program is a court-based probation-violation deterrence program for illegal drug users and other high-risk offenders (National Institute of Justice, 2012). It is aimed at reducing reoffending by imposing 'nonsevere graduated sanctions' on probation violators (Duriez, Cullen, & Manchak, 2014, p. 57). During 'warning hearings', probationers are advised of the expectations and conditions of probation (i.e., intense monitoring and random drug testing), and the immediate, proportionate consequences (e.g., short stays in prison) for violations, including repeat violators serving their entire original prison sentence (National Institute of Justice, 2012). Consistent with classical criminology, HOPE advocates that effective punishment should be certain and swift. Its appeal is that probationers are held accountable for their decision-making around compliance through 'tough love' (Duriez et al., 2014, p. 61). In theory then, the program will have a deterrent effect through the acute threat of punishment, while offering probationers opportunities for change.

An initial evaluation, comparing 493 male and female high-risk probationers, found improvements across a range of indicators after one-year for those randomly assigned to HOPE compared to those receiving regular probation services, as follows (Hawken & Kleiman, 2009, p. 64):

- 55% reduction in new arrest rates (47% of the non-HOPE group were rearrested compared to 21% of the HOPE group)
- 72% reduction in drug use (46% of the non-HOPE group tested posted to a urine test compared to 13% of the HOPE group)
- 61% reduction in non-compliance (23% of the non-HOPE group missed probation supervision appointments compared to 9% of the HOPE group)
- 53% reduction in probation revocation (15% of non-HOPE group had their probation revoked compared to 7% of the HOPE group).

The findings from a longer-term follow-up study were limited to re-arrest statistics, expressed in summary form in the following terms (Hawken et al., 2016, pp. 12–13).

> At 10-year follow-up the original HOPE pilot group had significantly less criminal involvement as measured by the number of charges for new crimes ($p = 0.00$). The probationers who were referred to HOPE in the original pilot had an average of 0.19 new charges by 10-year follow-up,

compared with an average of 0.78 for those who were in the group that receives routine supervision ... For subjects assigned to HOPE, the return-to-prison rate was 13 per cent compared with 27 per cent for subjects assigned to control.

Evaluations of other 'HOPE-style' programs in the United States have shown mixed results, with some showing similar positive outcomes to the Hawaiian program (Hawken, 2016).

Male Offenders: Domestic Violence Programs

Since the 1980s, a range of domestic violence (DV) programs has been developed in response to the problems of male-perpetrated intimate-partner violence. The literature places the Duluth model and cognitive–behaviour therapy (CBT) at the forefront of approaches, although 'narrative therapy' and 'restorative justice' principles are increasingly being used (Australia's National Research Organisation for Women's Safety Limited [ANROWS], 2015). The Duluth model posits that the cause of violence is not in offenders' mental or behavioural health but rather in their perceptions of entitlement to dominate and control their partners (ANROWS, 2015). CBT challenges offenders' irrational beliefs about violent behaviour, teaching them to construct and rehearse alternative behaviours (White & Graham, 2010). Narrative therapy seeks to have offenders tell their stories about why they offend and explore possibilities for change. Restorative justice adopts this narrative approach and attempts to heal the harms caused by domestic violence through victim and offender dialogue (White & Graham, 2010).

Evaluations of domestic violence programs underpinned by these models have shown some success. Babcock, Green, and Robie's (2004) meta-analysis, which included both quasi-experimental (with nonequivalent control groups, $n = 17$) and randomised experimental ($n = 5$) designs, examined effects for treatment type, study design and report type (police and victim data). Overall, they found little difference in effect size between Duluth-type or CBT interventions. Program completers in the quasi-experimental designs showed a 15% reduction in reoffending compared to 5% for those in the more rigorous randomised experiments, suggesting little impact on repeat offending. Nonetheless, Babcock and colleagues (2004) emphasised that this equates to approximately 42,000 US women per year protected from DV because of perpetrators' involvement in treatment rather than simply being dealt with by sanctioning. Other meta-analytic studies have found similar results (e.g., Miller, Drake, & Nafziger, 2013). However, these programs tend to focus on norms and attitudes of masculinity without concern for the structural gender inequalities that enable domestic violence (Salter, 2016). They fail to consider problems such as economic inequality and poverty that marginalise women and increase their risk of victimisation. That is, victims' needs are largely ignored in domestic violence offender treatment programs.

Some Australian domestic violence programs that address victims' needs include security-oriented services, such as safe houses for emergency accommodation; safe phones that prevent harassment, tracking and stalking by offenders; a cross-border domestic violence intelligence desk that shares information on victim and offender movement across specific state and territory borders; and Community Engagement Police Officers for increased protection of Indigenous women in communities (Giles & Turnbull, 2015). As such, a combination of treatment programs, services and legal sanctions that address offender and victim needs may offer the most effective response.

Youth Offenders: Multisystemic Approaches

It is widely recognised that interventions for youth must attend to maturational (e.g., cognitive, emotional, social) factors that separate youth from adult offenders. They are generally more impulsive, lack emotional maturity and are highly influenced by their peers compared to adults (Richards, 2011). To maximise responsivity, a holistic approach is required that addresses the factors that directly impact youth within their natural social ecosystem (e.g., family, school, neighbourhood). This is the key focus of multisystemic therapy (MST) programs.

Developed in the United States during the 1980s (Henggeler et al., 1986), MST adopted a 'social-ecological' approach (Bronfenbrenner, 1979) to address the then-perceived limitations of individual treatment of youth, which disregarded the natural social ecosystems within which they live. Originally designed as a short-term (3–5 months; 60 hours) community-based approach, MST targets individual (e.g., antisocial attitudes) and family vulnerabilities through CBT, social learning principles and family-based therapies (Henggeler et al., 1986). Working closely with the youth and their family face-to-face at least twice a week, MST therapists are available 24 hours a day, seven days a week to help develop strategies, provide aid and monitor progress. Parents are regarded as conduits of change in this process and are educated in effective parenting practices to support change in their child. Collaborative partnerships with community-based organisations contribute to positive sustainable outcomes by promoting opportunities to practice new skills in familiar environments (Henggeler et al., 1986).

Several multisite outcome evaluations of MST have been conducted including randomised control trials. These evaluations have consistently demonstrated significant short-term and long-term reductions in reoffending among MST participants compared to control groups (see Swenson & Duncan, 2016a, 2016b) including high-risk and violent youth (Letourneau et al., 2009). These effects extend to siblings of treated youth (Wagner,

Borduin, Sawyer, & Dopp, 2014). The most recent and longest follow-up of MST was conducted by Sawyer and Borduin (2011) using a sample of youth court-referred to the Missouri Delinquency Project (MDP) between 1983 and 1986. The MDP was developed in 1983 to deliver MST treatment services targeting serious and chronic (i.e., arrested at least twice) youth offenders aged 12 to 17 years old. The findings demonstrated sustained effects over a 22-year period with 34.8% of the MST group rearrested for an indictable offence compared to 54.8% of the individual therapy (IT) group. Those who received IT were 4.1 times more likely to be arrested for a violent offence and almost two times more likely to be rearrested for a nonviolent offence than MST participants (Sawyer & Borduin, 2011). Now widely adopted in the United States, Canada, the United Kingdom, Australia and New Zealand, MST is fast becoming the predominant intervention model for offending youth.

Female Offenders: Gender-responsive Programs

Females constitute 2% to 9% of the global prison population (Walmsley, 2015). Consequently, criminological theory has been largely based on the contributors to, and patterns of, male offending. Such explanations and associated interventions might have little relevance to female offending and its prevention. For example, the aetiology of female offending is interfaced with their experiences of physical, emotional and sexual victimisation, usually at the hands of family members and partners. As such, many females enter correctional systems with mental health issues, drug dependency and post-traumatic stress disorder (PTSD; Covington & Bloom, 2007). These females tend to be disadvantaged in terms of access to resources and basic needs such as education, employment, housing and quality healthcare services (Stathopoulos & Quadara, 2014). These multilevel structural disadvantages shape their patterns of criminal behaviour in different ways to males. More recent recognition of these differences has led to the development of gender-responsive approaches.

One promising program evident across the US prison system is therapeutic communities (TC; Eliason, 2006). TCs are designed for nonviolent and first-time offenders. Participation is voluntary. Participants share a positive family environment and are accommodated in a residential dormitory style treatment facility within the prison grounds. Programs generally require stays between 90 days and 24 months. Staff work with community-based health-care providers to run programs including parenting, substance dependency and job skills training. Regular random drug testing occurs as part of all TCs. Innovative techniques, including 'psychodrama' (feelings articulated through movement rather than words), are used to strengthen participants' capacity for effective decision-making and enhance coping skills (Covington & Bloom, 2007).

Females are most susceptible to relapse or reoffending in the immediate post-release period (Heilbrun et al., 2008). So many TCs include community aftercare services to assist females with this transition. Delaware's CREST program is one TC that provides secondary transitional treatment between prison and the community for female offenders with drug abuse issues. This six-month program combines a clinical drug treatment program with life skills and job training. Six-month and 18-month follow-up evaluations of CREST found that participating females were initially less likely to relapse than the control group (39% vs. 50% respectively). However, at 18-months there was no effect on reoffending. Although participants were able to create and maintain support networks in a structured setting, they had difficulty fostering similar support networks post-release to support their desistance from crime (Farrell, 2000). This may be linked to program length.

One consistent finding in TC evaluations is that success (e.g., reduced reoffending) is linked with the length of time female offenders spend in treatment. For example, the Forever Free substance abuse treatment program in California has demonstrated an 86% success rate on parole (after 12 months) when in-prison treatment was completed, combined with at least five months of residential aftercare, compared to 27% for the control group (Hall, Prendergast, Wellisch, Patten, & Cao, 2004).

Indigenous Offenders: Culturally Inclusive Programs

Indigenous Australians constitute 3% of the population yet represent 28% of the prison population, and they are also at higher risk of reoffending than non-Indigenous Australians (Australian Bureau of Statistics [ABS], 2011). Until recently, rehabilitation programs largely ignored cultural factors despite calls for more contextualised approaches to assessment and intervention that consider where the offender grew up, literacy levels, interdependence, spirituality and 'readiness' to participate (Hovane, Dalton, & Smith, 2014). Indigenous involvement, including Elder consultation, is now highly recommended as part of program design, delivery and evaluation (Day, 2003).

Western countries with Indigenous populations (e.g., Canada, New Zealand, Australia) have begun implementing some culturally inclusive rehabilitation programs. In Australia, Queensland's Ending Family Violence program is a combination of cognitive–behavioural and 'narrative' approaches (Toby, 2001). The narrative approach allows offenders to talk about the factors influencing DV in their communities and the cultural importance of taking responsibility for their actions. The program consists of ten 2-hour modules usually delivered twice a week, in either custody or the community. The program targets dynamic risk factors, including links between alcohol and violence, but also offenders' self-esteem. For Indigenous offenders, raising self-esteem has been linked to empowering individuals and changing their thinking patterns (Toby, 2001). Changes in Indigenous offenders' sense of wrongdoing and responsibility are tested through language usage, imitation and performance (Gergen, 1990). Pre- and post-program evaluations gather qualitative data to inform future interventions. However, no outcome evaluations currently exist.

Similarly, limited evaluations exist in relation to Indigenous Sex Offender programs. This is due to the ethical implications concerning denying treatment to control groups and small sample sizes (MacGregor, 2008). In New Zealand the Kia Marama treatment program operates as a group-based CBT program for child-sex offenders. It has a strong cultural emphasis, focusing on learning styles, but does not separate Indigenous from non-Indigenous offenders. The Te Piriti special treatment program uses these same treatment methods but combines them with 'tikanaga' (a way of living correctly, guided by the past) Maori practices. Evaluations of both programs have found significant reductions in sexual reoffending compared to control groups, but the culturally-attuned Te Piriti program demonstrates superiority ($n = 81$, 13.6% recidivism vs. $n = 68$, 4.4% recidivism respectively; NZ Department of Corrections, 2009).

Reintegration Programs

At least 95% of prisoners will be released back into the community (Hughes & Wilson, 2002), but many will relapse and return to prison (Durose, Cooper, & Snyder, 2014). Given that the aim of offender management and rehabilitation is desistance from offending, through-care is integral to managing risk at this stage in the offender's sentence (Cullen & Gendreau, 2000). Better outcomes have been found when after-care services have adequate release planning that engage significant (formal and informal) community-based partners in this process. Surveillance and monitoring alone have little impact (Schaefer et al., 2016).

One promising — yet controversial program — developed to assist reintegration of convicted child-sex offenders is Circles of Support and Accountability (COSA). COSA was established in Canada in 1994 in response to concerns about reoffending among adult child-sex offenders released from prison (Wilson & McWhinnie, 2013). Underpinned by 'restorative justice' principles, its purpose is to help offenders gain accommodation, employment and financial assistance, and engage with formal and social support networks.

A resource-intensive program, COSA is supported by a group (i.e., 'circle') of volunteers who work together to assist and support the offender (see Figure 3.4). Essentially, each circle comprises the offender (the core member) and 4 to 6 community volunteers (the 'inner circle' of support) who regularly meet with the core member. Volunteers receive formal training and have access to an advisory committee comprising psychologists, justice,

Figure 3.4

Circles of support and accountability.

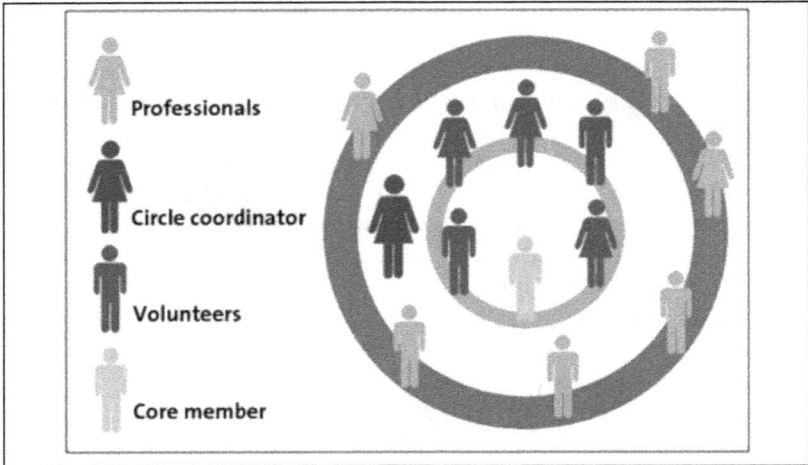

Source: Wilson & McWhinnie 2013. (Used with permission.)

social service and law enforcement professionals who represent the 'outer circle' and provide ongoing support and guidance (Wilson & McWhinnie, 2013). At least one community volunteer (the 'primary' volunteer) meets with the core member every day in the initial post-release period (e.g., first 60–90 days). The duration of each circle varies, but generally lasts at least 12 months. COSA has been adopted in the United States (Minnesota), the United Kingdom and recently in Australia.

COSA's pilot evaluation found significant overall reductions in reoffending by COSA participants compared to a matched comparison group (Wilson, Picheca, & Prinzo, 2007, p. 332) including:

- 35% reduction in overall recidivism (charges of a new offence including sexual and violent offences; 43.4% non-COSA group vs. 28.3% COSA group)
- 70% reduction in charges for sexual offences (16.7% non-COSA group vs. 5% COSA group)
- 27% reduction in charges for violent (including sexual) offences (35% non-COSA group vs. 15% COSA group).

These findings were replicated in a separate Canadian sample (e.g., Wilson, Cortoni, & McWhinnie, 2009). Success of the program has been attributed to its alignment with RNR and GLM principles — working in concert to provide risk management strategies (e.g., accountability, compliance and supervision) with the attainment of meaningful life plans. This fosters well-being and personal efficacy, and lessens feelings of social isolation and disconnection (Duwe, 2012; Wilson et al., 2009). Initiating the circle prior to release appears to improve outcomes overall, emphasising the importance of pre-planning and continuity of care when transitioning from custody (Duwe, 2012). Other UK-based studies demonstrate within-treatment gains (e.g., Bates, Saunders, & Wilson, 2007). Results from initial outcome evaluations of the Minnesota COSA, which began operating in 2008, are also promising (Duwe, 2012). Given that COSA is a relatively recent program, evaluation studies have been constrained by small samples (e.g., $n = 40$) and brief follow-up periods. Further evaluations will provide more clarity regarding their long-term effectiveness.

Conclusion

Generally, a holistic collaborative approach to offender management that observes statutory requirements, focuses on offender health and wellbeing, and provides tailored interventions offers the best chance for promoting desistance from offending (Raynor & Vanstone, 1994). Although rehabilitation is an integral component of offender management, not all programs are effective for all offenders. Programs that adhere to RNR principles and are strengths-based (e.g., GLM) seem to enhance motivation, engagement and outcomes. Synthesised and coordinated aftercare services improve reintegration success rates. The approaches discussed in this chapter are certainly underpinned by these characteristics, although many (e.g., women's programs, Indigenous programs) remain underevaluated. Continued development of an evidence-base demonstrating key components for effective offender management and rehabilitation, for different subgroups of offenders, remains the task at hand.

References

Allard, T., Wortley, R., & Stewart, A. (2003). Role conflict in community corrections, *Psychology, Crime & Law, 9*(3), 279–289.

Andrews, D., & Bonta, J. (2010). *The Psychology of criminal conduct*. Newark, NJ: LexisNexis.

Andrews, D., Bonta, J., & Hoge, R. (1990). Classification for effective rehabilitation: Rediscovering psychology. *Criminal Justice and Behaviour, 17*, 19–52.

Australian Bureau of Statistics (ABS). (2011). *Aboriginal and Torres Strait Islander offenders*. Retrieved from http://www.abs.gov.au

Australia's National Research Organisation for Women's Safety Limited (ANROWS). (2015). *Landscapes: State of knowledge paper, Part One*. Retrieved from http://anrows.org.au/publications/landscapes

Babcock, J., Green, C., & Robie, C. (2004). Does batterers' treatment work? A Meta-analytic review of domestic violence treatment. *Clinical Psychology Review, 23*, 1023–1053.

Bates, A., Saunders, R., & Wilson, C. (2007). Doing something about it: A follow-up study of sex offenders participating in Thames Valley circles of support and accountability, *British Journal of Community Justice, 5*(1), 19–42.

Birgden, A. (2004). Therapeutic jurisprudence and sex offenders: A psycho-legal approach to protection. *Sexual Abuse: A Journal of Research and Treatment, 16*(4), 351–364.

Bronfenbrenner, U. (1979). *The ecology of human development: Experiments by nature and design.* Cambridge, MA: Harvard University Press.

Chen, M., & Shapiro, J. (2007). Do harsher prison conditions reduce recidivism? A discontinuity-based approach. *American Law and Economics Review, 9*, 1–29.

Covington, S., & Bloom, B. (2007). Gender-responsive treatment and services in correctional settings, *Women & Therapy 29*(3-4), 9–33.

Cullen, F., & Gendreau, P. (2000). Assessing correctional rehabilitation: Policy, practice, and prospects. In J. Horney (Ed.), *Criminal Justice 2000, Volume 3* (pp. 109–175). Washington, DC: US Department of Justice.

Day, A. (2003). Reducing the risk of re-offending in Australian Indigenous offenders: What works for whom? *Journal of Offender Rehabilitation, 37*(2), 1–15.

Day, A., Casey, S., Ward. T., Howells, K., Vess, J. (2010). *Transitions to better lives: Offender readiness and rehabilitation.* Cullompton, England: Willan.

Durose, M., Cooper, A., & Snyder, H. (2014). *Recidivism of prisoners released in 30 states: Patterns from 2005–2010.* US Department of Justice. Retrieved from https://www.bjs.gov/content/pub/pdf/rprts05p0510.pdf

Duriez, S., Cullen, F., & Manchak, S. (2014). Is Project HOPE creating a false sense of hope? A Case study in correctional popularity. *Federal Probation, 78*(2), p. 57.

Duwe, G. (2012). Can Circles of Support and Accountability (COSA) work in the United States? Preliminary results from a randomised experiment in Minnesota. *Sexual Abuse: A Journal of Research and Treatment, 25*(2), 143–165.

Eliason, M. (2006). Are therapeutic communities therapeutic for women? *Journal of Substance Abuse Treatment, Prevention, and Policy, 1*(3), 1–7.

Farrell, A. (2000). Women, crime and drugs, *Women & Criminal Justice, 11*(1), 21–48.

Gergen, K. (1990). Therapeutic professions and the diffusion of deficit. *Journal of Mind and Behaviour, 11*, 353–368.

Giles, A., & Turnbull, M. (2015, September 24). Australia: Praise for $100 million commitment on domestic violence. *MENA Report, 1.*

Golias, P. (2004). *Offender management framework: Prisons and community correctional services.* Melbourne, Australia: Corrections Victoria.

Hall, E., Prendergast, M., Wellisch, J., Patten, M., & Cao, Y. (2004). Treating drug-abusing women prisoners: An outcomes evaluation of the Forever Free program. *The Prison Journal, 84,* 81–105.

Hawken, A. (2016). All implementation is local. *Criminology & Public Policy, 15*(4), 1229–1239.

Hawken, A., & Kleiman, M. (2009). *Managing drug involved probationers with swift and certain sanctions: Evaluating Hawaii's HOPE.* Washington DC: US Department of Justice.

Hawken, A, Kulick, J., Smith, K., Yiwen Zhang, J., Jarman, S., Yu, T., Carson, C., & Vial, V. (2016). *HOPE II: A follow-up to Hawai'i's HOPE Evaluation.* Washington, DC: National Institute of Justice.

Heilbrun, K., DeMattco, D., Fretz, R., Erickson, J., Yasuhara, K., & Anumba, N. (2008). How 'specific' are gender-specific rehabilitation needs? *Criminal Justice and Behaviour, 35,* 1382–1397.

Henggeler, S., Rodick, J., Borduin, C., Hanson, C., Watson, S., & Urey, J. (1986). Multisystemic treatment of juvenile offenders: Effects on adolescent behaviour and family interaction. *Developmental Psychology, 22,* 132–141.

Hovane, V., Dalton (Jones), T., & Smith, P. (2014). Aboriginal offender rehabilitation programs. In P. Dudgeon, H. Milroy & R. Walker (Eds.), *Working together: Aboriginal and Torres Strait Islander Mental Health and Wellbeing Principles and Practice.* (pp. 509–522). Canberra, Australia: Department of Prime Minister and Cabinet.

Hughes, T., & Wilson, D. (2002). *Reentry trends in the United States.* Washington, DC: US Department of Justice, Bureau of Justice Assistance.

Institute for Criminal Policy Research. (2014). *World prison brief.* University of London. Retrieved from http://www.prisonstudies.org/world-prison-brief

Letourneau, E., Henggeler, S., Borduin, C., Schewe, P., McCart, M., Chapman, J., & Saldana, L. (2009). Multisystemic Therapy for juvenile sexual offenders: 1-Year results from a randomized effectiveness trial. *Journal of Family Psychology, 23*(1), 89-102.

MacGregor, S. (2008). *Sex offender treatment programs: Effectiveness of prison and community based programs in Australia and New Zealand.* Sydney: Indigenous Justice Clearinghouse.

Martinson, R. (1974). What works? Questions and answers about prison reform. *The Public Interest, 35*(Spring), 22–54.

Martinson, R. (1979). New findings, new views: A note of caution regarding sentencing reform. *Hofstra Law Review, 7,* 243–258.

McGrath, R., Cumming, G., Burchard, B., Zeoli, S., & Ellerby, L. (2010). *Current practices and emerging trends in sexual abuser management: The Safer Society 2009 North American survey.* Brandon, VT: Safer Society Press.

Mellor, T. (2002). *Integrated offender management changing the way we work with offenders in New Zealand.* Paper presented at the Probation and Community Corrections: Making the Community Safer Conference. Perth, Australia, 23–24 September.

Miller, M., Drake, E., & Nafziger, M. (2013). *What works to reduce recidivism by domestic violence offenders?* Olympia: Washington State Institute for Public Policy.

National Institute of Justice. (2012). *'Swift and certain' sanctions in probation are highly effective: Evaluation of the HOPE program.* Office of Justice Programs. Retrieved from http://www.nij.gov/topics/corrections/community/drug-offenders/pages/hawaii-hope.aspx

New Zealand Department of Corrections. (2009). *Maori focus units and Maori therapeutic programs: Evaluation report.* Wellington: Department of Corrections.

Raynor, P., & Vanstone, M. (1994). Probation practice, effectiveness and the non-treatment paradigm. *British Journal of Social Work, 24*(4), 387–404.

Richards, K. (2011). Trends in juvenile detention in Australia. *Trends & Issues in Crime and Criminal Justice, 416,* 1–6.

Salter, M. (2016). 'Real men don't hit women': Constructing masculinity in the prevention of violence against women. *Australian & New Zealand Journal of Criminology 49*(4), 463–479.

Sawyer, A.M. & Borduin, C.M. (2011). Effects of multisystemic therapy through midlife: A 21.9-year follow-up to a randomized clinical trial with serious and violent juvenile offenders. *Journal of Consulting and Clinical Psychology, 79*(5), 643–652.

Schaefer, L., Cullen, F., & Eck, J. (2016). *Environmental corrections: A new paradigm for supervising offenders in the community.* Thousand Oaks, CA: SAGE.

Stathopoulos, M., & Quadara, A. (2014). *Women as offenders. Women as victims: The role of corrections in supporting women with histories of sexual abuse.* Sydney, Australia: NSW Corrective Services.

Swenson, M. & Duncan, M. (2016a). *Multisystemic therapy: An overview.* Retrieved from http://mstservices.com/files/overview_a.pdf

Swenson, M. & Duncan, M. (2016b). *Multisystemic therapy: Clinical outcomes and cost savings.* Retrieved from http://mstservices.com/files/outcomes_1a.pdf

Toby, B. (2001). *Best practice in program delivery for Aboriginal and Torres Strait Islander offenders.* Paper presented at the Best Practice Interventions in Corrections for Indigenous People Conference, Sydney, Australia, 8–9 October 2001.

Wagner, D., Borduin, C., Sawyer, A., & Dopp, A. (2014). Long-term prevention of criminality in siblings of serious and violent juvenile offenders: A 25-year follow-up to a randomized clinical trial of multisystemic therapy. *Journal of Consulting and Clinical Psychology, 82*(3), 492–499.

Walmsley, R. (2015). *World female imprisonment list.* Institute for Criminal Policy Research. Retrieved from http://www.prisonstudies.org/sites/default/files/resources/downloads/world_female_imprisonment_list_third_edition_0.pdf

Ward, T., & Stewart, C. (2003). The treatment of sex offenders: Risk management and good lives. *Professional Psychology: Research and Practice, 34,* 353–360.

Ward, T., Yates, P., & Willis, G. (2012). The good lives model and the risk need responsivity model: A critical response to Andrews, Bonta, and Wormith (2011). *Criminal Justice and Behaviour, 39,* 94–110.

Wexler, D., & Winick, B. (1996). *Law in a therapeutic key: Developments in therapeutic jurisprudence.* Durham, NC: Carolina Academic Press.

White, R., & Graham, H. (2010). *Working with offenders: A guide to concepts and practices.* New York, NY: Willan.

White, R., & Perrone, S. (2015). *Crime, criminality and criminal justice.* Melbourne, Australia: Oxford University Press.

Wilson, R., Picheca, J., & Prinzo, M. (2007). Evaluating the effectiveness of professionally facilitated volunteerism in the community-based management of high-risk sexual offenders: Part Two — a comparison of recidivism rates. *The Howard Journal, 46*(4), 327–337.

Wilson, R., Cortoni, F., & McWhinnie, A. (2009). Circles of Support and Accountability: A Canadian national replication of outcome findings. *Sexual Abuse: A Journal of Research and Treatment, 21,* 412–430.

Wilson, R., & McWhinnie, A. (2013). Putting the 'community' back in community risk management of persons who have sexually abused. *International Journal of Behavioral Consultation and Therapy, 8* (3-4), 72–79.

Winick, B. (2003). Therapeutic jurisprudence and problem solving courts. *Fordham Urban Law Review, 30,* 1055–1090.

Chapter 4

Developmental Interventions

Gabriel T.W. Wong and Matthew Manning

This chapter introduces the developmental and life-course (DLC) paradigm and provides examples showing how DLC intervention can be effective in producing short- and long-term positive impacts on individual development and wellbeing. We begin by briefly introducing the DLC approach. In Section 2, principles of DLC intervention are discussed including risk and protective factors, developmental pathways and the core concepts of DLC. We then consider the origins and types of DLC intervention and their common forms and aims (Section 3). Section 4 reviews the effectiveness of DLC intervention programs and provides a case study of the Seattle Social Development Project. Finally, we provide some closing remarks regarding the development of sustainable DLC policy.

Background

Children who are developmentally vulnerable, display early signs of antisocial behaviour, who are unprepared or perform poorly at school or who live in a disadvantaged environment are at a greater risk of developing social, health and psychological problems later in life. Such 'situations' have the potential to amplify over time and may result in undesirable trajectories that steer an individual down a path that hinders their potential to succeed or affect their quality of life and that of their future children. Undesirable trajectories could lead to poor educational outcomes (e.g., school drop-out), reduced economic success (e.g., welfare dependence), increased deviance and contact with the criminal justice system, family dysfunction and chronic health disease (Manning, Homel, & Smith, 2010; Manning, Smith, & Homel, 2013).

The overall aims and objectives of DLC interventions are planning and employing efforts to reduce undesirable trajectories, while preserving or increasing positive pathways for individuals, particularly those who are disadvantaged or vulnerable due to circumstances often beyond their control. Such prevention involves targeting risk and protective factors in order to alter potential negative trajectories with an emphasis on: (a) investing in institutions (e.g., schools or other learning environments such as playgroups); (b) communities and social policies that manipulate multiple risk and protective factors at different levels of the social ecology; and (c) crucial transition points (e.g., the commencement of school).

DLC perspectives highlight the wide range of factors (e.g., individual, cultural, social, environmental and economic) that contribute to within-individual variations in offending throughout life. In particular, these factors or life events can impose 'risk' or 'protection' to an individual by making them more vulnerable or assisting them to overcome adversity. The influences of different factors are assumed to interact with the individual's age/stage of life. A comprehensive understanding of this dynamic process, acknowledging that deviance and delinquencies represents a multicomponent problem influenced by multiple causal factors, can therefore allow the identification of: (a) factors for moderation; and (b) points of transition (i.e., turning points) (Manning, 2008).

Risk and Protective Factors

Risk and protective factors underpin the DLC perspective. Risk factors are measurable characteristics that precede an outcome and are used to divide the population of interest into a range of groups (e.g., high and low risk). They can be classified as fixed (e.g., race and gender) or variable (e.g., parental child rearing practices). Protective factors are variables that reduce the probability of negative outcomes - for example, the presence of a stable emotional bond to a caregiver. It is important to understand that what may be a risk factor in one situation may be a protective factor in another. Risk and protective factors, in some situations, function simultaneously. For example, the divorce of a child's parents might have a negative impact on the child and may constitute a risk factor. Conversely, a volatile family environment coupled with marital conflict and perhaps even domestic violence is likely to have a negative impact on the child's social and emotional wellbeing — so divorce may actually act as a protective device from the child being subjected to further stress. Das (2010) found this to be the case in minority ethnic families whose culture is highly resistant to divorce.

Developmental Pathways

With respect to developmental pathways to adolescent and adult antisocial behaviour, Vitaro, Barker, Brendgen and Tremblay (2011), propose that young people are susceptible to two categories of pathways — behavioural and socio-environmental. The behavioural pathway recognises that early disruptiveness in childhood predicts antisocial behaviour during adolescence, which, in turn, predicts adult criminal involvement (Farrington, 1995). Critical points of intervention, therefore, focus on modelling early signs of behavioural problems in transitions such as from kindergarten/childcare to formal schooling. Socio-environmental pathways include:

- the parental supervision pathway (including positive parenting practices)— lack of parental supervision can be linked to adolescent antisocial behaviour and can be used to predict later criminal behavior (Larzelere & Patterson, 1990)
- peer-related pathway— an association with antisocial deviant peers can nurture an antisocial lifestyle and contact with the criminal justice system (Elliott & Menard, 1996);
- school-related pathway— school engagement (including being prepared for various transitions such as from preschool to primary school) is positively correlated with perseverance, school adjustment, and school completion. Being prepared to learn, having positive social experiences in school, and ultimately being successful at school will minimise the chances of adolescent and adult antisocial behaviour and engagement in criminal activity (Reynolds, Ou & Topitzes, 2004).

Table 4.1 lists some risk and protective factors across five settings/systems. The list is by no means exhaustive, but it aims to provide the reader with a general sense of what may be explanatory factors of offending and delinquency.

Points of Transition and When To Implement DLC Strategies

Loeber and Le Blanc (1990) suggest that DLC intervention can be particularly effective in periods of greatest behavioral transformation (e.g., in early childhood and juvenile years). Transition points can either serve to initiate or reinforce vulnerability (Manning, Homel, & Smith, 2011) or, if protective steps are taken, reduce vulnerability. In reality, almost all nonbiological transitions require an individual to identify with new social institutions, many of these requiring an individual to cope with a new set of developmental tasks and challenges (Laub & Sampson, 2005). For example, some children are vulnerable when moving from home to a formal school setting. The transition into this new setting can be stressful, frightening and overwhelming if strategies are not in place to protect the child and equip them with the necessary skills and resources to cope. These strategies are often needed before the transition (e.g., preparing to learn in the kindergarten years) or at the time of the transition (e.g., strategies aimed at reducing stress and uncertainty— this could be as simple as having an older 'buddy' to assist the child in negotiating a new and unfamiliar environment).

Starting DLC interventions early in life is important. At this stage in the life-course, individuals can minimise the effect of adverse life circumstances, disadvantage, and vulnerability, and shape opportunities for developing new pathways that ultimately promote improved quality of life (Meisels & Shonkoff, 2000). This is not to say that there is no hope for those who are not cared for early in life. Humans, on the whole, are resilient and, as such, it is

Table 4.1

Risk and Protective Factors Associated with Antisocial and Criminal Behaviour

System	Risk Factors	Protective Factors
Child	Poor problem-solving; Beliefs about aggression; Attributions; Poor social skills; Low self-esteem; Lack of empathy; Alienation; Hyperactivity/ disruptive behaviour; Impulsivity; Prematurity; Low birth weight; Disability; Prenatal brain damage; Birth injury; Low intelligence; Difficult temperament; Chronic illness; Insecure attachment	Social competence; Social skills; Above average intelligence; Attachment to family; Empathy; Problem-solving skills; Optimism; School achievement; Easy temperament; Internal locus of control; Moral beliefs; Values; Self-relative cognitions; Good coping style
Family	*Parental characteristics*: Psychiatric disorder (especially depression); Substance abuse; Criminality; Teenage mothers; Single parents; Antisocial models*Family environment*: Family violence and disharmony; Marital discord; Disorganised negative interaction/social isolation; Long-term parental unemploy-ment; Large family size; Father absence *Parenting style*: Poor supervision and monitoring of the child; Discipline style (harsh or inconsistent); Rejection of the child; Abuse; Lack of warmth and affec-tion; Low involvement in child's activities; Neglect	Supportive caring parents; Family harmony; More than two years between siblings; Responsibility for chores or required helpfulness; Secure and stable family; Supportive relationship with other adult; Small family size; Strong family norms and morality
School context	School failure; Normative beliefs about aggression; Deviant peer group; Bullying; Peer rejection; Poor attachment to school; Inadequate behaviour management	Positive school climate; Pro-social peer group; Responsibility and required helpfulness; Sense of belonging/bonding; Opportunities for some success at school and recognition of achievement
Community and cultural factors	Socio–economic disadvantage; Population density and housing conditions; Urban area; Neighbourhood violence and crime; Cultural norms concerning violence as acceptable response to frustration; Media portrayal of violence; Lack of support services	Access to support services; Community networking; Attachment to the community; Participation in church or other community group; Community/cultural norms against violence; A strong cultural identity and ethnic pride
Stressful life events and transitions	Divorce and family break-up; War or natural disasters; Death of a family member	Meeting significant person; Moving to a new area; Opportunities at critical turning points or major life transitions

Source: Adapted from National Crime Prevention, 1999.

never too late to learn or change, but the process becomes increasingly complex and expensive (Manning, 2004, in press).

Core Concepts of DLC and Crime

DLC approaches identify and offer explanations for many important aspects of crime, including: 'prevalence'; 'age of onset'; 'duration of offending career'; 'escalation' and 'de-escalation'— in terms of frequency and seriousness of criminal involvement; and, finally, 'desistance' from crime. Regarding the commonly used terminology, Loeber and Le Blanc (1990) summarise and propose the generic concepts of offending, define temporal boundaries and present dynamic concepts (i.e., *activation, aggravation* and *desistance*), which are employed extensively in the DLC literature (see Table 4.2).

The generic concepts, which apply to offending as a whole and synthesise all the offenses committed by an individual, include: (1) *participation* — current or cumulative (formerly called prevalence of offending); (2) *Lambda* — annual and cumulative frequency of offending or the number of crimes committed by an individual within a given time period (formally incidence); (3) *Crime mix*, which refers to the combination of crimes committed by an individual; (4) *Seriousness*, which classifies the number of individuals for each different level of seriousness involved; (5) *Variety*, which centres on the number of types/categories of offenses accumulated.

Boundary concepts represent the temporal boundaries of offending and include: (1) *Age at onset* (i.e., age at the time of the first offense); (2) *Age at termination* (i.e., age at the time of the last offense); (3) *Duration of offending* (i.e., the interval between the first and the last crime; (4) *Transfer/crime*

Table 4.2

Summary of Core Concepts of DLC Perspectives

Generic Concepts	Boundary Concepts	Dynamic Concepts
Participation	Age at onset	Activation:
Lambda	Age at termination	Acceleration
Crime mix	Duration	Diversification
Seriousness	Transfer/crime switching	Stabilisation
Variety		Aggravation:
		Developmental sequence
		Escalation
		Desistance:
		Deceleration
		De-escalation

SpecialisationSource: Adapted from Loeber & Le Blanc, 1990.

switching (i.e., transfer from one type of criminal activity to another, or the transfer of offending from juvenile delinquency to adult offending.

Based on findings from empirical studies, which investigate the relationship between generic concepts of offending and temporal boundaries, DLC theorists conceptualise dynamic processes and construct models of offending. There are three basic processes (*activation, aggravation and desistance*). *Activation* refers to the way the development of criminal activities is motivated and the way its continuity, frequency, and diversity is secured. Activation incorporates three sub-processes: (1) acceleration — increased frequency of offending over time; (2) stabilisation— increased continuity over time; and (3) diversification — the propensity for individuals to become involved in more diverse criminal activities. For a*ggravation*, a developmental sequence of diverse forms of delinquent activities may be identified. This process reflects how a problem may be escalated or increased in seriousness over time. It should be noted that individuals can progress or regress within this developmental sequence. Regarding the final process, *desistance,* a trajectory may reflect a drop in the frequency of offending (deceleration), a reduction in its variety (specialisation), and a reduction in its seriousness (de-escalation).

The Origins of DLC Criminology

Tracing the origins of the DLC criminology approach is difficult. Some texts begin with Wolfgang's 1972 Philadelphia birth cohort study (Wolfgang, Figlio, & Sellin, 1987). This study analysed antisocial/delinquent development up to age 17 in a sample of 10,000 boys born in Philadelphia in 1945.

Other scholars point to the work of Blumstein (1986) in a National Academy of Sciences report of the panel research on criminal careers. This panel attempted to assess the extent to which future criminal development could be predicted and outline the possible contribution of such predictions to policies of general and selective incapacitation.

A number of notable longitudinal studies predate Wolfgang and colleagues (1987) and Blumstein (1986). For example, Sheldon and Elanor Glueck (1950) studied the delinquent development, up to age 32, of 500 adolescent boys remanded to Massachusetts reform schools. The Gluecks performed a number of longitudinal studies, including a study of 1,000 juvenile delinquents referred to Judge Baker Foundation Behaviour Clinic and a 15-year follow up of 510 reformatory inmates.

Other criminological classics, conducted by the University of Chicago's Sociology Department, include the *The Jack Roller* (Shaw, 1930) and *The Professional Thief by a Professional Thief* (Sutherland, 1956), both of which were interest in the processes and dynamics of within-individual change in criminal behavior — similar to that of Quetelet (1833).

Types of DLC Interventions

DLC interventions can be divided into four categories:

1. preschool
2. primary school
3. family
4. community/centre-based.

Table 4.3 provides examples of the focus of activities that fall under each category. Depending on the contextual and cultural variations and other diverse needs faced by parents and families, special programs may also be delivered. For example, the targetting of specific groups or subpopulations in the community with different cultural backgrounds (e.g., non-English speaking, Aboriginal and Torres Strait Islander).

Table 4.3

Categories of DLC

Category/Activities	Focus
1.Intellectual and developmental enrichment; conduct disorder/behaviour management; family functioning in the preschool years	Target risk factors that lead to poor school attachment and individual academic achievement, school failure, lack of parental involvement in child's activities and learning, poor parenting skills, child abuse an neglect and unhealthy levels of self-esteem etc.
2. Child protection education, educational welfare services and learning/teaching support for parents and families in school-based settings	Target risk factors that lead to parental and peer conflict, child abuse and neglect, poor school attachment, poor social skills, depression, aggressive behaviour, and bullying etc.
3. Parental skills training, parent helpline, childhood health services and education, home-visiting and relationship building	Target risk factors that lead to poor and inconsistent or harsh parenting, family discord, social isolation and health problems etc.
4. Familial-centred assistance provided by volunteers from the community, community centre, or community advisory groups	Target risk factors that lead to social isolation (due to culture, background and poor English proficiency), disconnection with school, lack of employment or unemployment (economic disadvantage) etc.

Source: Adapted from National Crime Prevention, 1999.

Influential DLC Interventions

The Perry Preschool Project is, arguably, the most famous of all modern DLC interventions. Implemented in the years 1962 to 1967, the project aimed to enhance intellectual development and subsequent school achievement in disadvantaged three-year-old and four-year-old children. The goal was to promote effective decision-making, self-discipline, collaboration, self-expression, reasoning, and understanding and acceptance of people's differences. Children were followed-up annually from age 3 through 11 and then at ages, 14,15, 19, 27 and 40 (Schweinhart et al., 2005).

Another prominent DLC intervention is the Montreal Prevention Project. Beginning in 1984, the project aimed to reduce juvenile delinquency by identifying the most disruptive boys (classified in terms of how disruptive, hyperactive and aggressive they were) and providing social skills development and self-control strategies. The project followed boys to age 12 in order to assess school achievement, antisocial and self-reported delinquent behaviour (Tremblay, Pagani-Kurtz, Masse, Vitaro, & Pihl, 1995).

Implemented in 1981, the Seattle Social Development Project (Hawkins, Kosterman, Catalano, Hill, & Abbott, 2008) was a multi-year, school-based intervention that used risk-reduction and skill-development to moderate later offending. The underlying belief was that offending would be discouraged in children who established strong bonds with their families, schools and communities. Children were followed up to age 21 to assess outcomes such as risky sexual behaviour, school success, use of illegal drugs, and contact with the criminal justice system.

In Australia, the Pathways to Prevention Project, which began in 2001, is aimed at primarily preventing antisocial behaviour in young people from disadvantaged and marginalised backgrounds (Homel et al., 2006). The intervention targeted four-year-old to six-year-old children in the Brisbane suburb of Inala with a focus on the transition from before-formal schooling (e.g., preschool) to primary school. Two main services were offered: (1) a preschool intervention program (PIP) — aimed to enhance children's communication and social skills; and (2) family independence program (FIP) — to assist caregivers and families to create a stimulating home environment that is harmonious and conducive to child development (Homel et al., 2006). Outcomes of the intervention show that it is effective in improving the level of children's communication skill and reducing their level of difficult behaviour, over and above the effect of the regular preschool curriculum. The strongest effects of the program involvement were found in the FIP+PIP group, which gained significantly lower problem behaviour scores than PIP, FIP and no program groups alone.

Does DLC Work?

A number of meta-analyses (Farrington & Welsh, 2003; MacLeod & Nelson, 2000; Manning et al., 2010) and economic analyses (Manning, Homel, & Smith, 2006; Manning et al., 2013; Washington State Institute for Public Policy, 2012) have been conducted. These studies highlight the efficacy of the DLC approach on a range of outcomes, such as offending, cognitive development, educational attainment, social–emotional development, social participation, and health and familial wellbeing. Manning and colleagues (2010), for example, found evidence that the impact of carefully designed and well-conducted DLC programs on quality of life of participants can be substantial. The authors found that the mean effect size[1] across all programs and outcomes (see Figure 4.1) was 0.313, equivalent to a 62% higher mean score for an intervention group than for a control group. The largest effect was for educational success (effect size 0.528) followed by deviance (0.481), social participation (0.371), cognitive devel-

Figure 4.1

The impact of DLC interventions on outcomes in adolescence.

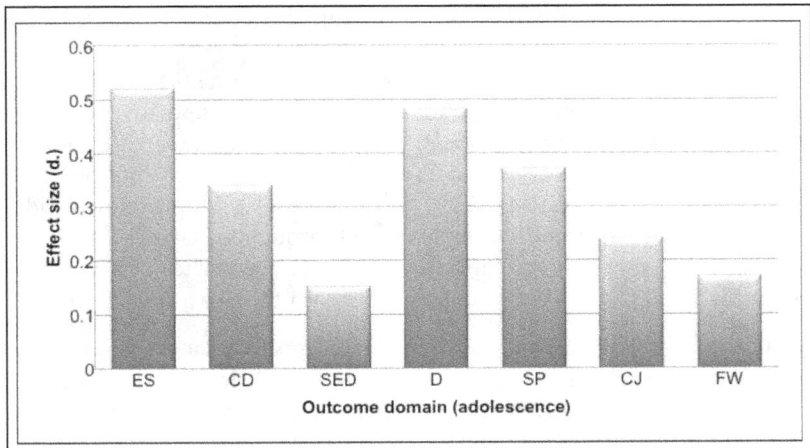

Note: ES = educational success, CD = cognitive development, SED = social–emotional development, D = deviance, SP = social participation, CJ = involvement in crime, FW = family wellbeing.

Source: Manning, Homel, & Smith, 2010.

---

1 Based on Cohen's (1992) proposition that effect sizes of 0.20 are small, 0.50 are medium, and 0.80 are large, one can compare effect sizes to established benchmarks. However, it must be noted that Cohen's descriptions of effect sizes may be misleading in some instances. Effect sizes in the human services and crime prevention literatures, for example, are often in the 0.20–0.30 range, yet these effects correspond to substantial and often cost-effective benefits in the population.

opment (0.339), involvement in crime (0.243), family wellbeing (0.178), and social–emotional development (0.157).

In addition, programs that lasted longer than three years were associated with larger sample means than programs that were longer than one year but shorter than three years. More intense programs (those with more than 500 sessions per participant) also had larger means than less intense programs. There was a marginally significant trend for programs with a follow-through component into the early primary school years (e.g., Preschool to Grade 3) to have more positive effects than programs without a follow-through.

The Seattle Social Development Project

The Seattle Social Development Program (SSDP) is a multicomponent intervention for teachers, students and parents during elementary school (Grades 1 to 6), through random assignment, targeting children and family from schools in high crime urban areas. The theoretical model (a social development model) that underpins the SSDP hypothesise that high levels of social bonding (attachment and commitment) to family and school (prosocial groups and activates) set children on a positive developmental trajectory (Catalano & Hawkins, 1996). The goal was to promote positive functioning and prevent mental health problems, crime and substance use in adolescence and adulthood.

Beginning in 1981, SSDP provided training to (a) *teachers*— in proactive classroom management, interactive teaching and cooperative learning; (b) *parents*— in child behaviour management, academic support, and skills to reduce risks for drug use; and (c) *children*— to shape interpersonal problem solving and refusal skills. There were two intervention conditions— the 'full' intervention, implemented throughout Grades 1 through 6 and the 'late' intervention, implemented for two years when children were in Grades 5 and 6. The main differences between the two groups were:

- for the full-intervention group, Grade 1 teachers were taught to use a cognitive- and social skills-training curriculum in their classes and parents (of children in Grades 1 through 3) were provided (voluntarily) a 7-session curriculum in child behaviour management skills and a 4-session curriculum in skills for supporting children's academic development
- for parents of children in the full- and late-intervention groups (during Grades 5 and 6), a 5-session curriculum was provided which aimed to strengthen parental skills to reduce risks of drug use and other problem behaviours.

The sample consisted of 592 consenting students (full intervention = 143, late intervention group = 243 and control condition = 206). Students in the sample were from eight schools in high crime areas within the Seattle public school system. Two schools were administratively assigned to receive intervention, two were assigned as control classrooms and the remaining six were randomly assigned to intervention or control conditions. In the fifth grade, all students in the 18 Seattle elementary schools were included in the study.

SSDP was funded by the National Institute on Drug Abuse (Prevention Research Branch), the Office of Juvenile Justice and Delinquency Prevention, the Robert Wood Johnson Foundation, and the Burlington Northern Foundation. The project was managed by the Social Development Research Group (SDRG) and implemented by public and private elementary schools.

Outcomes and Long-term Impacts of the SSDP

Previous evaluation and follow-up studies of the SSDP intervention found significant effects in childhood and adolescence across various health- and nonhealth-related outcomes from Grade 2 through to age 27. Examples of outcomes include:

- Grade 2: less aggressiveness and externalising antisocial behaviour among boys, less self-destructiveness among girls (Hawkins, Von Cleve, & Catalano, 1991)
- Grade 5: less initiation of alcohol use, reduced delinquency, better family management and communication, greater attachment to family, higher school attachment and commitment (Hawkins et al., 1992)
- Grade 6: less initiation of cigarette use, more classroom and team learning opportunities, more classroom participation, more bonding and commitment to school, improved social skills, better school commitment, improved achievement test scores, and less antisocial peers among low income boys (O'Donnell, Hawkins, Catalano, Abbot, & Day, 1995)
- Age 16 to 18: higher school bonding among full-intervention participants, less likely to report lifetime violence, less heavy alcohol use in the past year, fewer lifetime multiple sex partners, improved school attachment school achievement and reduced school misbehaviour among full-intervention participants (Hawkins, Catalano, Kosterman, Abbot, & Hill, 1999)
- Age 21: fewer sexual partners and pregnancies and births to female full-intervention participants (Hawkins, Kosterman, Catalano, Hill & Abbott, 2005), reductions in the prevalence of sexually transmitted disease among African American full-intervention participants (Lonczak, Abbott, Hawkins, Kosterman, & Catalano, 2002), better functioning in school (e.g., more engaged in classes and activities and with other students) and work (e.g., more longevity at their present job on average), better regulation of emotions, fewer symptoms of social phobia, fewer suicidal thoughts, less involvement in crime and drug dealing, fewer reports of possessing an official lifetime court record, lower arrest rate

among male full-intervention participants and higher arrest rate among female participants (Hawkins et al., 2005; Lonczak et al., 2002)

- Age 24: constructive engagement in school and/or work among full treatment group males, less likely to meet sufficient criteria for a Generalised Anxiety Disorder diagnosis among low-income participants, higher responsibility on the job among Caucasians (Hawkins et al., 2008)
- Age 27: more likely to be at or above the median in socioeconomic status (education or household income), fewer symptoms of mental health disorders, lower prevalence of having been diagnosed with a sexually transmitted disease, higher involvement in community groups among low-income participants; higher household income and fewer past-year sex partners (Hawkins et al., 2008).

An independent cost–benefit analysis of SSDP was undertaken by the Washington State Institute for Public Policy (2012). It estimated that the net benefits associated with SSDP in US dollars are $12,148 producing a benefit to cost ratio of $4.27. That is, for every dollar spent on the program, $4.27 is returned in benefits. Benefits from SSDP are derived from reductions in crime ($1,244), labour market earnings associated with high school graduation ($17,678), less grade repetition from kindergarten to Grade 12 ($220), reduced public assistance ($3), reduced health care associated with educational attainment ($139), costs of higher education (-$1,570) and adjustment for the deadweight cost of the program (-$1,854). Table 4.4 provides a disaggregation of the cost–benefit analysis.

Closing Remarks

The benefits derived from DLC interventions are numerous and span both the health and nonhealth dimensions. In short, the benefits from a DLC paradigm, which should be considered a form of social justice, can readily be quantified. However, we must be cognisant of the fact that not all programs will produce positive net benefits. Although there are clear benefits with regards to health and educational components (in the short and long term), the argument regarding the criminal justice benefits needs further research. This is the case with the economic returns from investment in DLC in the long-term. In saying this, however, longitudinal research gives us confidence that when programs are well designed, properly funded, carefully implemented and thoroughly evaluated the risks associated with funding, moreover, continually funding DLC interventions are minimised.

Manning (in press) proposes that we are not there yet with regards to the efficient and effective management and implementation of DLC interventions. Manning (in press) argues that to become efficient and more effective in the long term (i.e., to develop sustainability and longevity of a DLC inter-

Table 4.4

Cost–Benefit Analysis of SSDP

Benefits	
Taxpayer	$5,096
Participants	$8,468
Others*	$3,701
Indirect**	-$1,406
Total Benefits	**$15,860**
Net program cost	$3,712
Net Benefits	$12,148
Benefit to cost ratio	4.27

Note:

* Others include benefits resulting from reductions in crime victimisation, the economic benefits from a more educated workforce, and the benefits from employer-paid health insurance.

** Indirect benefits includes estimates of the net changes in the value of a statistical life and net changes in the deadweight costs of taxation.

Source: Adapted from Washington State Institute for Public Policy, 2012.

vention) policymakers must reduce system silos, which hinder individual service providers working collaboratively to deal with the complex problems (and the complex set of solutions) that are associated with the most marginalised in our community. To achieve this, policymakers should aim to:

- increase the efficacy of individual child-serving organisations
- enhance the capacity of people at every level of an organisation
- facilitate openness and commitment to change and organisational reform where needed
- motivate clear-headed reflection on the appropriateness of current practice, and reduce the use of ineffective and inefficient strategies
- translate knowledge about the causes of poor developmental outcomes into well-implemented evidence-based DLC programs.

References

Blumstein, A. (1986). *Criminal careers and 'career criminals'*. Washington, DC: National Academy Press.

Catalano, R., & Hawkins, J. (1996). The social development model: A theory of antisocial behavior. In J. Hawkins (Ed.), *Delinquency and crime: Current theories* (pp. 149–197). New York, NY: Cambridge University Press.

Cohen, J. (1992). Quantitative methods in psychology: A power primer. *Psychological Bulletin, 112*(1), 155–159.

Das, C. (2010). Resilience, risk and protective factors for British-Indian children of divorce. *Journal of Social Science, 25*(1–3), 97–108.

Farrington, D., & Welsh, B. (2003). Family-based prevention of offending: A meta-analysis. *The Australian and New Zealand Journal of Criminology, 36*(2), 127–151.

Glueck, S., & Glueck, E. (1950). Unravelling juvenile delinquency. *Juvenile Court Judges Journal, 2*(1), 32–34.

Hawkins, D., Catalano, R., Kosterman, R., Abbot, R., & Hill, K. (1999). Preventing adolescent health-risk behaviours by strengthening protection during childhood. *Archives of Pediatrics and Adolescent Medicine, 153*(3), 226–234.

Hawkins, D., Catalano, R., Morrison, D., O'Donnell, J., Abbott, R., & Day, L. (1992). The Seattle Social Development Project: Effects of the first four years on protective factors and problem behaviours. In J. McCord & R. Tremblay (Eds.), *Preventing antisocial behaviour: Interventions from birth through adolescence* (pp. 139–161). New York, NY: The Guilford Press.

Hawkins, D., Kosterman, R., Catalano, R., Hill, K., & Abbott, R. (2005). Promoting positive adult functioning through social development intervention in childhood: Long-term effects from the Seattle Social Development Project. *Archives of Pediatrics & Adolescent Medicine, 159*(1), 25–31.

Hawkins, D., Kosterman, R., Catalano, R., Hill, K., & Abbott, R. (2008). Effects of social development intervention in childhood 15 years later. *Archives of Pediatrics & Adolescent Medicine, 162*(12), 1133–1141.

Hawkins, D., Von Cleve, E., & Catalano, R. (1991). Reducing early childhood aggression: Results of a primary prevention program. *Journal of the American Academy of Child and Adolescent Psychiatry, 30*(2), 208–217.

Laub, J., & Sampson, R. (2005). A General age-graded theory of crime: Lessons learned and the future of life-course criminology. In D. Farrington (Ed.), *Advances in criminological theory, Volume 14: Advances in Criminological Theory* (pp. 165–181). New Brunswick, NJ: Transaction Publishers.

Loeber, R., & Le Blanc, M. (1990). Toward a developmental criminology. *Crime and Justice, 12*, 375–473.

Lonczak, H., Abbott, R., Hawkins, D., Kosterman, R., & Catalano, R. (2002). Effects of the Seattle Social Development Project on sexual behavior, pregnancy, birth, and sexually transmitted disease outcomes by age 21 years. *Archives of Pediatrics & Adolescent Medicine, 156*(5), 438–447.

MacLeod, J., & Nelson, G. (2000). Programs for the promotion of family wellness and the prevention of child maltreatment: A meta-analytic review. *Child Abuse and Neglect, 24*(9), 1127–1149.

Manning, M. (2004). *Measuring the costs of community-based developmental prevention programs in Australia* (Master's dissertation, Griffith University, Brisbane, Australia).

Manning, M. (2008). *Economic evaluation of the effects of early childhood intervention programs on adolescent outcomes.* (Doctoral thesis, Griffith University, Brisbane, Australia).

Manning, M. (in press). Addressing developmental challenges to improve the wellbeing of children. In S. Garvis & D. Pendergast (Eds.), *Health & wellbeing in childhood* (2 ed.). Melbourne, Australia: Cambridge University Press.

Manning, M., Homel, R., & Smith, C. (2006). Economic evaluation of a community-based early intervention program implemented in a disadvantaged urban area of Queensland. *Economic Analysis and Policy, 36*(1 & 2), 99–120.

Manning, M., Homel, R., & Smith, C. (2010). A Meta-analysis of the effects of early developmental prevention programs in at-risk populations on nonhealth outcomes in adolescence. *Children and Youth Services Review, 32*(4), 506–519.

Manning, M., Homel, R., & Smith, C. (2011). An economic method for formulating better policies for positive child development. *Australian Review of Public Affairs, 10*(1), 61–77.

Manning, M., Smith, C., & Homel, R. (2013). Valuing developmental crime prevention. *Criminology and Public Policy, 12*(3), 305–332.

Meisels, S., & Shonkoff, J. (2000). Early childhood intervention: A continuing evolution. In S. Meisels & J. Shonkoff (Eds.), *Handbook of Early Childhood Intervention* (pp. 3–31). New York: Cambridge University Press.

National Crime Prevention. (1999). *Pathways to prevention: Developmental and early intervention approaches to crime in Australia.* Canberra: Author.

O'Donnell, J., Hawkins, D., Catalano, R., Abbot, R., & Day, L. (1995). Preventing school failure, drug use, and delinquency among low-income children: Long-term intervention in elementary schools. *American Journal of Orthopsychiatry, 65*(1), 87–100.

Quetelet, A. (1833). *Recherches sur le penchant au crime aux différens âges.* Bruxelles: Hayez.

Schweinhart, L., Montie, J., Xiang, Z., Barnett, W., Belfield, C., & Nores, M. (2005). *Lifetime effects: The HighScope Perry Preschool study through age 40.* Ypsilanti, MI: High/Scope Press.

Shaw, C. (1930). *The Jack roller.* Chicago, IL: University of Chicago Press.

Sutherland, E. (1956). *The professional thief by a professional thief.* London, England: University of Chicago Press.

Tremblay, R., Pagani-Kurtz, L., Masse, L., Vitaro, F., & Pihl, R. (1995). A bimodal preventive intervention for disruptive kindergarten boys: Its impact through mid-adolescence. *Journal of Consulting and Clinical Psychology, 63*(4), 560–568.

Washington State Institute for Public Policy. (2012). *Seattle Social Development Project*. Retrieved from http://www.wsipp.wa.gov/BenefitCost/Program/70.

Wolfgang, M., Figlio, R., & Sellin, T. (1987). *Delinquency in a birth cohort*. Chicago, IL: University of Chicago Press.

Chapter 5

Community-based Prevention

Philip Birch and Tim Prenzler

Community-based prevention is focused on locations where potential offenders, potential victims and associated third parties share their lives in close proximity. The approach is primarily concerned with building positive interactions against crime. The chapter identifies the theories of crime behind this approach, emphasising the role of poverty, inequality and the breakdown of community support mechanisms. A variety of strategies are then briefly described, before moving on to more detailed accounts of programs that illustrate the diversity of methods within this framework. The chapter concludes by discussing major issues around community-based prevention, in particular those of community economics and evidence of success.

Parameters

Community-based crime prevention is difficult to define. A 'community' can be merely a 'setting' for prevention initiatives, although the concept of 'community-based' prevention tends to be more about the 'direct involvement' of community members (Gill, 2013, p. 14). Differences can also occur around what constitutes a 'community' and what is a genuine community-based strategy (Gill, 2013). One fairly narrow approach would see community-based prevention occurring within small neighbourhood settings where residents tend to know or recognise each other. Examples include a village or small town or perhaps a suburb or part of a suburb where there tends to be a sense of common identity. Smaller community areas can also be defined in terms of local government areas, postcodes or areas served by a police station. Broader approaches will include larger zones such as districts or even regions, business areas or industrial areas, as well as non-geographically-based 'communities' of people with common interests. Nowadays, communities can be online and include members across the globe.

Community-based approaches tend to focus on supportive practices. Programs along these lines attempt to develop pro-social values and behaviours, and build resilience, through improved relationships. Welfare services delivered to offenders and victims by professionals in a community setting could be considered community-based prevention, although the service can operate independently of other community members. At the other end of the spectrum are surveillance-based approaches in which citizens observe and report suspicious activity, and may even act to intervene in crime events.

Community-based approaches often overlap with other types of prevention. For example, early-childhood interventions (see Chapter 4) can be organised and delivered through local institutions and involve local participants. Numerous successful prevention programs categorised as 'situational' or 'CPTED' have been implemented in villages and residential estates, business districts and industrial estates (see Chapter 6 to Chapter 9). The effectiveness of these interventions has been attributed in part to limited access to these sites, common interests, and high levels of participation and communication. Offender management programs (see Chapter 3) can also involve community-based orders in which offenders have to work with local groups, such as charities, and mix with ordinary citizens. The 'community policing' movement (see Chapter 2) sought to optimise police work through formalised cooperation between officers and their local constituencies. This can involve communication from citizens to police about crime issues through forums, committees and surveys. It can also include the direct involvement of citizens in prevention by means such as reporting crime, enhancing their own security in response to police requests or volunteering to assist police in outreach work.

The question of where to draw the line around what is and is not a 'community-based' strategy is probably not one that is easily answered to the point of consensus. It is likely that the term will persist nonetheless and it remains common in criminology as a nebulous but convenient shorthand, along with terms such as 'street crime' and 'white collar crime'.

Diagnostics and Design

Community-based crime prevention as a philosophy and organised program of practical activity grows out of the sociological tradition of criminology that developed in the 1800s. However, the practice of community-based prevention goes back much further and can be seen wherever individuals and groups attempt to improve local interpersonal interactions for purposes that include crime reduction. Community-based approaches can therefore be ad hoc and partly intuitive or theorised and programmatic. In either case there is a recognition that family dysfunction and personality deficits, often seen as fundamental to the development of criminal behaviour, can be mitigated or exacerbated through broader community influences. This is the idea that 'it takes a village to raise a child'.

One of the earliest crime theories to focus on community was the Chicago School, which analysed crime and social conditions in American cities in the 1920s and 1930s, and showed that crime was concentrated in impoverished inner-city neighbourhoods (Shaw & McKay, 1942).

Importantly, crime was one element of a concentrated social malaise. High-crime communities, which can be suburban and rural as well, are often characterised by high rates of poverty and unemployment, congestion and urban blight, mental illness and suicide, single parent households and absent fathers, poor physical health and reduced longevity. The Chicago School researchers noted that these high-crime inner city areas tended to be transitional zones for immigrants. New groups failed to put down roots and moved to the suburbs as soon as they could. Groups came and went but the problems remained in the same locations. The inability of host communities to provide adequate employment and activities often led to the development of youth gangs in slum areas, and adult organised crime gangs, such as the mafia, sometimes exercised control. Australian cities have also suffered from this problem in inner city zones as well as in welfare suburbs built by governments on the outskirts of cities (Vinson & Rawsthorne, 2015).

The association between concentrated social problems and a breakdown in 'normal' community ties was summed up in the concept of 'anomie'. The term simply refers to the loss of community cohesion, common values and purpose (Durkheim, 1933). Immigration, and lack of cultural and economic fit, is a common cause, but immigrant groups often move out of anomic zones and build new lives elsewhere. In other cases, anomie becomes deeply embedded amongst one group and is intergenerational. This situation is often evident in Indigenous communities devastated by colonialism, and unable to regroup and rebuild in the contemporary post-colonial period (Jang, 2015). In other cases, changes in an economy, such as a shift in manufacturing to other locations, can destroy communities and leave behind an environment of enduring poverty, crime and inertia.

A number of other theoretical perspectives feed into the case for community-based prevention. These are generally described as theories of 'social disorganisation' or 'conflict' theories. Conflict criminology and associated economic strain theories focus on crime as a symptom of social and economic deprivation and exclusion caused by class exploitation and competition, with crime concentrated amongst low wage communities and 'surplus' populations (Merton, 1938). Poverty can drive offending based on economic need. Exploitation, economic exclusion and perceived inequality can also breed resentment and provoke forms of rebellion that include crime and violence. As one example, Wilkinson and Pickett (2010) have shown that rates of violence are generally higher in less equal societies.

Social disorganisation theories have been advanced in the last few decades by concepts such as 'collective efficacy'. Survey research by Sampson, Raudenbush and Earls (1997) showed that respondents in neighbourhoods with strong shared norms and values, and a willingness of members to intervene in crime problems, had reduced experiences and perceptions of violent crime. More generally, residential mobility and low home ownership rates are commonly associated with higher crime rates (Hayes & Prenzler, 2015, p. 92). Wilson and Kelling's (1982) 'broken windows' theory argued that failure to fix signs of disorder, including lower level street crimes, contributed to a culture in which people withdrew behind closed doors, and the lack of guardianship encouraged criminal behaviour. 'Social control' or 'social bonding' theories also highlighted how crime was influenced by deficits in 'attachment, commitment, involvement and belief' in families and communities (Hirschi, 1969). Even labelling theory (Becker, 1963) has relevance in that stigma and the development of a criminal identity can occur within neighbourhood domains. Theories of 'differential association' (Sutherland & Cressy, 1978) and 'drift' (Matza, 1964) also described how normal social learning processes leading to participation in criminal subgroups occurred in community settings.

Drawing on these strands of theory, community-oriented prevention programs usually have a strong social justice and welfare flavour in attempting to redress social deficits (Hauritz, Mackay, Hayes, & Prenzler, 1996). In many or most cases, crime is one target along with overlapping and mutually reinforcing problems of mental illness, suicide, poor health, isolation, boredom, drug abuse, unemployment and poverty. While economically deprived communities tend to be the area of focus, more prosperous, 'normal' and even wealthy suburbs can suffer from a range of crime-related problems that can become targets of locally based prevention initiatives.

Types

As noted earlier, community-based prevention programs operate across a spectrum from 'softer' forms of support or welfare to 'harder' forms of surveillance and control. Examples of supportive programs include employment schemes, where unemployed people at-risk of crime are connected to local employers; accommodation services, which help prevent sleeping out, begging and petty crime; and 'drop in' centres that provide counselling as well as referrals to services such as training, employment and accommodation. There are also a number of school-based programs, covering before-and-after care and vacation care, that provide a safe environment for students outside school hours, helping them to avoid becoming victims as well as perpetrators of crime. School truancy schemes involve volunteers that assist students with transport to school.[1]

One type of intermediate intervention involves 'restorative justice', such as 'community conferences' which are fairly common in the youth justice field. As well as victims and offenders and a mediator, they often include support

---

1 For example see:
  www.dpmc.gov.au/indigenous-affairs/education/remote-school-attendance-strategy

persons and local police. The input of elders and other community members can be particularly important in Indigenous communities. Conferences are very beneficial in reconciling the main parties, but there is limited evidence about their effectiveness in preventing re-offending (Strang, Sherman, Mayo-Wilson, Woods, & Ariel, 2013). Another intermediate type of measure is 'safety houses'[2] that provide an accessible refuge to potential victims of crime, mainly children, who might be targeted in public places.

Surveillance-oriented programs attempt to mobilise citizens to protect themselves and, to some extent, serve as the 'eyes and ears' of authorities such as police and security services. Surveillance schemes are aimed at enhancing specific deterrence and incapacitation by increasing the chances of offenders being arrested; although efforts to inform potential offenders of the scheme can have general deterrence as an aim. Prominent examples include Neighbourhood Watch, Business Watch and School Watch. 'Eyes on the Street' is an initiative in Perth, in Western Australia, that involves the managers and staff of local businesses receiving training in recording and reporting suspicious activity (Prenzler & Sarre, 2016). An 'Eyes on the Street' team follows up on reports, usually through police action. The program is meant to have high visibility, through displays of the logo for example, in order to encourage participation, deter offenders and support feelings of safety. There is some evidence that these programs can contribute to improved arrest and conviction rates, but there is limited evidence of a primary prevention effect (Prenzler & Sarre, 2016). One exception is the famous 'cocoon watch' project in the United Kingdom (see Chapter 8).

Community-based Crime Prevention Case Studies

The following six case studies highlight diverse prevention programs operating in the community space. Where possible, evaluation data have been included in the descriptions.

- 'Community Night Patrols' have been implemented in numerous Indigenous communities in Australia since the 1980s. In the Northern Territory in 2011 there were 80 patrols operating with financial support from the federal government (Beacroft, Richards, Andrevski, & Rosevear, 2011). The initiative involves volunteers and/or paid community members patrolling the streets of a community, usually at night and in a vehicle, offering support to those at-risk of offending and/or victimisation. The patrols often target intoxicated persons, and they operate in part as a diversion from arrest and incarceration by taking potential

---

2 www.australianpolice.com.au/the-safety-house-program/

arrestees home or to a 'sobering-up shelter'. More broadly, the patrol groups can serve as an alternative means of justice and peacekeeping in mediating disputes, providing security at events and advising courts (Blagg & Valuri, 2004). These patrols have become embedded in many communities and despite the absence of strict scientific evaluations there are numerous reports of reduced crime and improved feelings of safety (Beacroft et al., 2011).

- Business Improvement Districts (BIDs) involve local business communities combining resources to improve the amenity and security of an area to attract more customers. BIDs can take different forms but usually they involve spending funds from the group as well as a government partner to renovate locations, put in seating and plants, repair vandalised property, remove graffiti, and activate private security patrols. Cook and MacDonald (2011) reported there were approximately 1,000 BIDs in the United States in 2010. Evaluations showed some successes in crime reduction without displacement, including burglary and motor vehicle theft. One review reported that 'most neighbourhoods with established BID security programs have experienced double-digit reductions in crime rates (sometimes up to 60%)' (Vindevogel, 2005, p. 237). Another assessment, with an economic focus, claimed BIDs could provide substantial public benefits, including significantly reducing the costs of criminal justice processing of offenders (Cook & MacDonald, 2011). Police involvement is usually an important part of the mix. A BID was established in Canberra in 2007 in an effort to enliven the central business district (In the City Canberra, 2015). The security aspect was extended in 2010 with a police 'BizSafe' program, essentially an education program about countering crime risks. There do not appear to be any proper impact reports involving crime. However, Canberra has consistently scored in the highest category of liveable cities, including on the criterion of safety (Sibthorpe, 2016).

- 'Circles of Support and Accountability', described in Chapter 3, is a charity-based rehabilitation program for sexual offenders focused on 'reintegration ... into a local community' (Circles UK, 2016, p. 4). 'Social isolation and emotional loneliness' are seen as major risk factors for reoffending and are addressed through the enlistment of volunteers from the community (p. 4). The offender, or 'core member', and a small group of trained volunteers commit to regular meetings and ad hoc communication. The focus is on supporting the emotional and practical needs of the offender but also on communicating and reinforcing community expectations about self-control and responsibility. The circles are supervised by a coordinator and they work with an outer circle of professionals, including probation officers. In 2016 there were 16 circles operating in England and Wales (Circles UK, 2016, p. 2). There are also programs in Canada and the United States. At least two evaluations have indicated success (see Chapter 3; Wilson, Cortoni, & McWhinnie, 2009; Wilson, Picheca & Prinzo, 2007).

- 'U-Turn', established in Tasmania in 2003, was a diversionary rehabilitation program for young people involved in vehicle-related crimes, such as motor vehicle theft. Run by Mission Australia, it gave participants the opportunity to develop employment-related skills in the motor vehicle industry. Participants spent 10 weeks in a workshop environment learning from local experts about vehicle maintenance. The wider needs of the young people were addressed through a case management process. The award winning program claimed many successes in reducing recidivism amongst participants and significantly improving their lives (e.g., Kellow, Julian, & Alessandrini, 2005). However, it came to an end in 2015 when the state government broke an election promise and withdrew funding (Lohberger, 2015).

- Police Citizen Youth Clubs (PCYCs) are an Australian charity established in 1937 by a New South Wales Police Commissioner.[3] The management and operation of clubs involve significant input from local police along with other community members. New South Wales has 60 clubs with 85,000 members. Activities are designed around the needs of local young people and include sporting, adventure, fitness and leadership programs. The activities are designed to build resilience and address risk-factors for delinquency, including boredom and inappropriate role models. Early intervention and primary prevention are major aims: 'PCYC aims to get to the kids before the kids get to the Police Station'.[4] There are also programs aimed at young people who have had contact with the criminal justice system, and these are generally located in high-crime economically deprived locations.

- Communities That Care (CTC) provides 'an evidence-based, community-change process for reducing youth problem behaviours, including harmful substance use, low academic achievement, early school leaving, sexual risk-taking, and violence'[5]. Concerned citizens in a locality can request assistance from CTC, which provides training and facilitation. Examples of activities include drug and alcohol education, restricting

---

3 www.pcycnsw.org.au/mission-history/

4 www.pcyc.org.au/Youth-Programs/Crime-Prevention.aspx

5 www.communitiesthatcare.net/about/

access to alcohol and tobacco, parenting skills development, family therapy, antibullying training, mental health awareness and training, and mentoring (e.g., 'Big Brothers/Big Sisters' which connects young people to suitable older persons; Communities That Care, 2012). However, rather than prescribing any specific actions against crime, CTC uses a version of the action research paradigm to diagnose problems and develop tailor-made solutions. An evaluation by Hawkins, Oesterle, Brown, Abbott, and Catalano (2014) included a control group and used 'abstinence' from a range of harmful behaviours up to Grade 12 as the main outcome criterion. Behaviours included smoking and alcohol consumption as well as more clearly crime-related behaviours. The study found significant differences between the intervention and control groups for 'delinquency' – 41.7% abstinence vs 33% – and use of 'gateway drugs' – 29.4% vs 21.0% (p. 126). CTC has been adopted in several locations in Australia.[9]

Isssues

Community-based crime prevention schemes can be very appealing. They are usually based on social justice principles and attempt to build and sustain 'natural' crime prevention through collective means. Nonetheless, there are a number of problematic aspects. One issue involves representing the interests and needs of diverse groups and individuals. Communities can be intolerant of nonconformists, and they can be managed in authoritarian ways. Community-based crime prevention schemes, such as police-citizen consultative committees or security patrols, can be dominated by members with simplistic and repressive ideas about crime control; and interventions, whether deliberate or not, can lead to exclusion and stigmatisation (Laycock & Tilley, 1995).

A common weakness of community-based programs is that they are run by nongovernment organisations (NGOs), usually 'charities', but are largely dependent on periodic competitive grants from governments (Hauritz et al., 1996). This means there is considerable uncertainty about the longevity of their work, and funds can be reduced or cut off with a change of government or fiscal crisis. The fate of the U-turn program in Tasmania, described above, is one example. In addition, community engagement and involvement are fundamental to this approach, but programs can be difficult to establish in the areas where there is most need (Hope, 1995). Community members may be suspicious of professionals from outside, and poor social skills and low social capital can mitigate against project participation.

One fundamental problem is that programs usually cannot address core deficits at the economic base of a community. In many cases it is low incomes, unemployment and underemployment that lie behind or aggravate social problems. Programs may appear to be addressing crime causation at its heart in dysfunctional communities, but in fact the real economic drivers remain unchanged. In many Indigenous communities, for example, this means not only large numbers of unoccupied young people but adult males with little standing or purpose in the community (Johnston, 1991). Community-based prevention involves a 'micro-level' approach to crime, but in many cases it is 'macro-level' change that is also needed (Bohm & Vogel, 2015).

Finally, as indicated throughout this chapter, a major weakness across community-based programs is the absence of rigorous evaluation, or often the lack of any evaluation. The issue is particularly important given that programs are often funded from tax money or donations by well-meaning citizens. The large 'what works' study of crime prevention in the mid-1990s (see Chapter 1) found that community-oriented approaches were common but concluded that 'there are no community based programs of "proven effectiveness"' (Sherman, 1997, p. 32; see also Welsh & Hoshi, 2002).

Since the 'what works' study, the main program to emerge with scientific credentials is Communities that Care. As outlined earlier in this chapter, a study by Hawkins et al. (2014) found significant differences in outcomes between program participants and a control group. In addition, a US study by Prinz, Sanders, Shapiro, Whitaker, and Lutzker (2009) engaged a control group and identified improved outcomes in child abuse prevention from a Positive Parenting Program (Triple P). The program was a good example of an overlap between early intervention and community-based approaches in that delivery occurred at the county level through a diverse range of local stake-holders. The program targets both child deprivation and child maltreatment. The study concluded that, 'in a community with 100,000 children under 8 years of age, these effects [from Triple P] would translate into 688 fewer cases of CM (child maltreatment), 240 fewer out-of-home placements, and 60 fewer children with injuries requiring hospitalization or emergency room treatment' (Prinz, et al. 2009, p. 9). There is also emerging evidence supporting the Circles of Support and Accountability program (see also Chapter 3).

Conclusion

Community-based crime prevention programs operate in many locations. The central idea of mobilising communities and improving collective measures against crime are sound in theory as one important measure in a battery of measures addressing the complex causes of crime (Sherman, 1997). Unfortunately, however, this approach remains much more in the category of 'promising' than 'proven'. There are many examples of programs that appear to have positive effects in addressing the needs of offenders and changing their lives in ways that include reduced offending. However, adequate scientific evidence of specific program effectiveness is generally lacking. And the small number of programs with stronger evidence of 'success' has been limited in the overall scale of their impacts. It may be the case that inadequate resourcing is a key factor. Certainly it seems to be the case that there are no easy solutions to the problems of concentrated disadvantage, fractured communities and crime. Anomie is easy to diagnose but extremely difficult to fix. The issue highlights the need for improved practice, including at the macro-level where full employment and equal opportunity strategies need to be optimised.

References

Beacroft, L., Richards, K. Andrevski, H., & Rosevear, L. (2011). *Community night patrols in the Northern Territory: Toward an improved performance and reporting framework*. Canberra: Australian Institute of Criminology.

Becker, H. (1963). *Outsiders*. New York, NY: Free Press.

Blagg H., & Valuri. G. (2004). Aboriginal community patrols in Australia: Self-policing, self-determination and security. *Policing & Society, 14*(4), 313–328.

Bohm, R., & Vogel, B. (2015). *A primer on crime and delinquency theory*. Durham, NC: Carolina Academic Press

Circles UK. (2016). *Annual review 2015–2016*. Reading, England: Author.

Communities That Care. (2012). *Guide to Australian prevention strategies*. Parkville, Australia: Author.

Cook, P., & MacDonald, J. (2011). Public safety through private action: An Economic assessment of BIDS. *The Economic Journal, 121*(May), 445–462.

Durkheim, E. (1933). *The division of labor in society*. Translated by George Simpson New York, NY: Free Press.

Gill, C. (2013). Community based crime prevention: What have we learned from systematic reviews? Paper presented at the *Stockholm Criminology Symposium*, June 2013, Stockholm, Sweden. Retrieved from http://www.criminologysymposium.com/download/18.6b82726313f7b2 34a582e7/1372334622925/TUE01+Gill+Charlotte.pdf

Hauritz, M., Mackay, P., Hayes, H., & Prenzler, T. (1996). *Final report of the Youth and Community Combined Action Report*. Brisbane: Queensland Department of Family and Community Services.

Hawkins, D., Oesterle, S., Brown, E., Abbott, R., & Catalano, R. (2014). Youth problem behaviors 8 years after implementing the Communities That Care prevention system: A community-randomized trial. *JAMA Pediatrics, 168*(2): 122–129.

Hayes, H., & Prenzler, T. (2015). Victim and offender characteristics. In H. Hayes & T. Prenzler (Eds.), *An introduction to crime and criminology* (pp. 81–97). Sydney: Pearson.

Hirschi, T. (1969). *Causes of delinquency.* Berkeley, CA: University of California Press.

Hope, T. (1995). Community crime prevention. In M. Tonry and D. Farrington (Eds.), *Building a safer society: Strategic approaches to crime prevention* (pp. 21–90). Chicago, IL: University of Chicago Press

In the City Canberra. (2015). Business Improvement Districts 101. Retrieved from http://www.inthecitycanberra.com.au/business-improvement-districts-101/

Jang, H. (2015). *Social identities of young Indigenous people in contemporary Australia.* New York, NY: Springer.

Johnston, E. (1991). *National Report: Royal Commission into Aboriginal Deaths in Custody, Volume 3.* Canberra: Australian Government Publishing Service.

Kellow, A., Julian, R., & Alessandrini, M. (2005). *Young Recidivist Car Theft Offender Program (U-Turn), Local evaluation – Tasmania, Final report.* Hobart, Australia: University of Tasmania.

Laycock, G., & Tilley, N. (1995). *Policing and Neighbourhood Watch: Strategic issues.* London, England: Home Office.

Lohberger, L. (2015, 28 March). Emotions high as U-Turn hits wall. *Mercury*, p. 4.

Matza, D. (1964). *Delinquency and drift.* New York, NY: Wiley.

Merton, R. (1938). Social structure and anomie. *American Sociological Review*, *3*(5), 672–682.

Prenzler, T., & Sarre, R. (2016). Public-private crime prevention partnerships. In T. Prenzler (Ed.), *Policing and security in practice: Challenges and achievements* (pp. 149–167). Houndmills, England: Palgrave-Macmillan.

Prinz, R., Sanders, M., Shapiro, C., Whitaker, D., & Lutzker, J. (2009). Population-based prevention of child maltreatment: The US Triple P system population trial. *Prevention Science, 10*, 1–12.

Sampson, R., Raudenbush, S., & Earls, F. (1997). Neighborhoods and violent crime: A multilevel study of collective efficacy. *Science, 277*(5328), 918–924.

Shaw, C., & McKay, H. (1942). *Juvenile delinquency and urban areas.* Chicago, IL: University of Chicago Press.

Sherman, L. (1997). Communities and crime prevention. In L. Sherman, D. Gottfredson, D. MacKenzie, J. Eck, P. Reuter & S. Bushway (Eds.), *Preventing crime: What works, what doesn't, what's promising: A report to the United States Congress* (pp. 1–53). Washington, DC: National Institute of Justice

Sibthorpe, C. (2016). Canberra home to the highest quality of living worldwide, according to Numbeo data. *The Canberra Times*. http://www.canberratimes.com.au/act-news/canberra-life/canberra-home-to-the-highest-quality-of-living-worldwide-website-numbeo-reports-20160721-gqb9gn.html

Strang, H., Sherman, L., Mayo-Wilson, E., Woods, D., & Ariel, B. (2013). *Restorative justice conferencing (RJC) using face-to-face meetings of offenders and victims: Effects on offender recidivism and victim satisfaction. A systematic review.* Oslo, Norway: The Campbell Collaboration.

Sutherland, E., & Cressy, D. (1978). *Criminology.* Philadelphia, PA: Lippincott.

Vindevogel, F. (2005). Private security and urban crime migration: A bid for BIDs. *Criminal Justice, 5*(3), 233–255.

Vinson, T., & Rawsthorne, M. (2015). *Dropping off the edge: Persistent communal disadvantage in Australia.* Melbourne: Jesuit Social Services.

Welsh, B., & Hoshi, A. (2002). Communities and crime prevention. In L. Sherman, D. Farrington, B. Welsh & D. Mackenzie (Eds.), *Evidence-based crime prevention* (pp. 165–197). London, England: Routledge.

Wilkinson, R., & Pickett, K. (2010) *The spirit level: Why equality is better for everyone.* London, England: Penguin.

Wilson, J., & Kelling, G. (1982). Broken windows. *Atlantic monthly, 249*(3), 29–38.

Wilson, R., Cortoni, F., & McWhinnie, A. (2009). Circles of Support and Accountability: A Canadian national replication of outcome findings. *Sexual Abuse: A Journal of Research and Treatment, 21,* 412–430.

Wilson, R., Picheca, J., & Prinzo, M. (2007). Evaluating the effectiveness of professionally facilitated volunteerism in the community-based management of high-risk sexual offenders: Part two – a comparison of recidivism rates. *The Howard Journal, 46*(4), 327–337.

Chapter 6

The Evolution of
Situational Crime Prevention

Tim Prenzler and Eric Wilson

S ituational crime prevention has been the most important theoretical framework for understanding and designing crime prevention strategies that work. This chapter examines the development of the theory, from its roots in rational choice theory, and the overall contribution of the theory to understanding success in applied crime prevention. The associated theory of routine activity is also examined, with some brief attention to problem oriented policing, CPTED, crime mapping, and product design against crime. The chapter concludes by analysing a number of criticisms of situational prevention. Issues of displacement, inconvenience and inequality need to be taken into account when planning and evaluating crime prevention projects. However, these potential problems should not be seen as inevitable and should not inhibit project managers and security managers from making the most of situational prevention techniques.

Opportunity Theories

Situational crime prevention is founded on the 'rational choice' theory of crime. A key source is Cornish & Clarke's (1986) edited book *The Reasoning Criminal: Rational Choice Perspectives on Offending*. Rational Choice theory sits with a group of opportunity-based approaches to crime. These include 'environmental criminology' (concerned with the physical environment of crime), 'routine activity theory' and 'deterrence theory'. This perspective has considerable longevity, including references to crime opportunities in the pioneering work of Edwin Sutherland (1947). However, the idea was crystallised by research in the 1970s and 1980s in the Home Office Research Unit in the United Kingdom, which increasingly focused its efforts on finding solutions to the problem of rising crime (Clarke, 1997). One instructive example concerned the large reductions in suicides in England and Wales from the mid-1960s to the mid-1970s. These were associated with the introduction of nontoxic domestic gas, and, importantly, the loss of this mechanism for suicide did not translate directly into the adoption of other, less convenient, means (Clarke, 2012, p. 4.). Another study found that a very large reduction in motorcycle theft in Germany — from 153,153 in 1980 to 54,208 in 1986 —

was associated with the introduction of compulsory helmet laws. It appeared that motorcycle theft was largely spontaneous and opportunistic, and not having a helmet made thieves conspicuous (Clarke, 2012, p. 4).

The focus on opportunity in these and other studies was summed up in *The Reasoning Criminal*, as follows (Cornish & Clarke, 1986, pp. 1–2):

> The synthesis that we had suggested — a rational choice perspective on criminal behaviour — was intended to locate criminological findings within a framework particularly suitable for thinking about policy-relevant research. Its starting point was an assumption that offenders seek to benefit themselves by their criminal behaviour; that this involves the making of decisions and choices, however rudimentary on occasion these processes might be; and that these processes exhibit a measure of rationality, albeit constrained by limits of time and ability and the availability of relevant information. It was recognised that this conception of crime seemed to fit some forms of offending better than others. However, even in the case of offenses that seemed to be pathologically motivated or impulsively executed, it was felt that rational components were also often present and that the identification and description of these might have lessons for crime-control policy.

Studies of offender decision-making were a major source of support for this approach. For example, interviews with persons who engaged in burglary to feed a drug habit showed they weighed different environmental cues about access and escape routes — deciding what might be worth stealing inside premises, and the likelihood of different types of guardians being present (Macintyre, 2001). The role of rational decision-making in crime was also supported by studies of the types of locations of crimes, the targets of crime, and times of the day or the week when offences occurred — all indicating that offenders avoided detection and sought to minimise effort and maximise rewards (Clarke, 1997; Cornish & Clarke, 1986). Further support was provided by studies which observed how ordinary people often succumbed in situations where they were tempted to cheat or commit a crime and thought they would not be observed or identified (Gabor, 1994).

Some elements of rationale choice theory can be seen in the 'classical' school of criminological thought developed in Enlightenment Europe in the 17th and 18th centuries (Curran & Renzetti, 2001; see Chapter 1). This approach set itself against the brutal punishments of the time, arguing they were not only inhumane but ineffective. Instead, reformers believed that the right combination of 'severity, certainty and swiftness' of punishment would deter would-be criminals, most of whom engaged in a cost-benefit analysis of the risks and potential rewards entailed in criminal conduct. The problem with this approach was that it put too much faith in the criminal justice system to ensure 'certainty and swiftness'.

Rational choice differs from classical theory when identifying the more complex conditions under which offenders will decide to act. This includes a focus on perceptions of the probability of apprehension. A key element here is observability. For example, Clarke (1997, p. 6) refers to studies in the 1920s showing children were more likely to be dishonest when they were subject to less supervision, and that property crime rates were higher during winter when there was more cover provided by longer hours of darkness. Traffic law enforcement provides a good example of the idea of modifying an environment to change human perceptions and the opportunity structure for crime (Bates, Soole, & Watson, 2012). Random speed testing, and random drug and alcohol testing, are designed to make drivers feel that non-compliance could be detected at any time. However, rational choice theorists are also interested in the ways in which environmental changes can simply make it more difficult or impossible to break the law. Examples from traffic law enforcement include speed bumps, bollards and barriers that force drivers to slow down or to stop them from entering prohibited areas. Ignition immobilisers or vehicle confiscation can also be applied to repeat offenders who are unresponsive to increases in the likelihood of detection and punishment.

Rational choice theory was developed at a time when criminology was dominated by sociological theories of crime focused on inequality and poverty (Curran & Renzetti, 2001). Equality of opportunity and the redistribution of wealth were seen as the solutions to the crime problem. However, crime rates escalated despite postwar prosperity and the rise of the welfare state. Anticrime programs focused on reducing poverty and improving social capital were poorly managed and largely ineffective. Crime also continued to rise despite the preferences of many governments to employ more police and increase penalties. Imprisonment and offender rehabilitation programs also appeared to be ineffective, prompting the promulgation of a 'nothing works' thesis in criminal justice (Martinson, 1974; see also Chapter 3).

The intersection of rising crime rates and failed crime policies also provided the setting for the development of 'routine activity theory'. Cohen and Felson's (1979) groundbreaking article, 'Social Change and Crime Rate Trends: A Routine Activity Approach', published in *The American Sociological Review*, correlated increasing crime rates with increasing freedom and the availability of consumer goods. The researchers highlighted the proliferation of opportunities for crime, famously asserting that (1979, p. 589):

> Structural changes in routine activity patterns can influence crime rates by affecting the convergence in space and time of the three minimal elements of direct-contact predatory violations:
>
> 1. motivated offenders
> 2. suitable targets
> 3. the absence of capable guardians against a violation.

The long postwar economic boom generated enormous increases in the number of lightweight, high-value, easily transportable goods that could be stolen. There was much more cash in circulation and more valuables in the possession of more people. The rapid growth in motor vehicle ownership created a new opportunity for thieves and a means of accessing desired targets and escaping crime scenes. In addition, more people worked away from home during the day, including increasing numbers of women, while workplaces were abandoned at night in the commute back to the suburbs. People also went out more and travelled more, exposing themselves to robbery and assault. There were more people living alone who were more vulnerable to burglary, robbery and assaults. This separation of guardians from targets was a key factor in the escalating crime problem. In many countries, crimes reported to police increased three- and four-fold between the 1960s and 1990s (van Dijk, 2008, 2012). In Australia, between 1973 and 1974, and 1995 and 1996, the total volume of crime reported to police increased by 121% as a rate per 100,000 population, while violent crime increased by 373% (Makkai & Prenzler, 2015).

Rational choice and routine activity theories challenged the police monopoly on crime control. Analysis of crime opportunities highlighted the extremely limited capacity of police to provide a preventive presence or an effective interdiction through a rapid response to crimes in progress. For example, Felson (1998) estimated the extent of police coverage of premises in Los Angeles County if patrol officers were deployed on a per capacity basis. He concluded that this would give each location fifteen seconds of protection in 24 hours. Doubling the number of police would therefore provide 30 seconds of protection: 'like putting two drops in a bucket instead of one' (p. 9).

Opportunity theories also showed how many businesses and organisations exposed themselves to crime. Walker, for example, described how retail stores 'almost invite shoplifting' with wide access, minimal staffing and open display of products (1994, p. 17). Felson described how many modern schools 'produce' crime by poor building design (e.g., creating hiding places for offenders), poor student-teacher ratios and poor supervision (1994, p. 97). Manufacturers produced goods with little regard for their security, making crime prevention the responsibility of consumers who lacked the means to protect their purchases.

Analysis of the factors that make a 'suitable target' assisted in understanding crime rates in greater depth than was permissible through the reporting of aggregate data. Crime rates across nations and jurisdictions are inflated by multiple offences committed against the same victims, including organisations as victims. This phenomenon of repeat victimisation informed the concept of 'risky facilities'. Researchers such as Eck, Clarke, and Guerette (2007) focused on the concept of 'place management' as a major explanation for this phenomenon. Place managers can be responsible, often unconsciously, for management practices that are 'crime enablers':

> The concentration of crime at a few facilities can seldom be dismissed as a random fluke or 'just a lot of targets' or active offenders... Comparing the way similar facilities with different crime levels are managed can test crime enabling. If compared to low crime facilities, the high crime locations have fewer rules, lax enforcement, easy access, poor security, and other features that help offenders detect targets, commit crimes, and get away... If the high crime facilities have many targets or more highly desirable targets (either hot products or repeat victims) compared to low crime facilities, but managers do little to enhance target protection, this also suggests place management is at the heart of the problem. (2007, p. 240)

Research identified many dramatic cases of repeat victimisation. Eck et al. (2007) cited examples such as motel crimes in Chula Vista, California, where 19% of local motels were responsible for 51% of calls to police; and shoplifting in Danvers, Connecticut, where 20% of stores were responsible for 85% of incidents. A UK study in Merseyside found that 43 schools were subject to eight or more burglaries in one year, and 57 retail/manufacturing facilities were subject to four or more burglaries (Bowers, Hirschfield, & Johnson, 1998). Repeat victimisation occurs in part because a successful crime will motivate offenders to return to the same location; often with a short time frame, such as a month (Bowers et al., 1998).

Clarke also analysed features of consumer products that made them attractive targets for thieves. He coined the term 'CRAVED' to describe products that are 'concealable, removable, available, valuable, enjoyable and disposable' (Clarke, 1999, p. vi). Some items are high value but easily concealed after being stolen. Examples include small items such as smartphones, tablets and wallets. Due to their high demand they are easily disposed of for cash on the black market.

A useful way of picturing crime opportunities, building on the work of routine opportunity theory (discussed earlier), is with the 'crime triangle', developed by Clarke & Eck (2003; see Figure 6.1). The inner triangle summarises the three primary ingredients for crime: (a) an offender, (b) a target, and (c) a place where the crime occurs. The outer triangle shows primary human agents who can facilitate or inhibit crime by their actions. A 'manager' has responsibility for conduct in a specific location, 'such as a bus conductor or teacher at a school' (p. 27). A 'handler' is someone who has a relationship with a potential offender and can exercise some control or influence over their behaviour. Handlers include teachers, parents and friends. 'Capable guardians' are 'usually people protecting their own belongings' or those of other people (p. 26).

Figure 6.1

The Crime Triangle

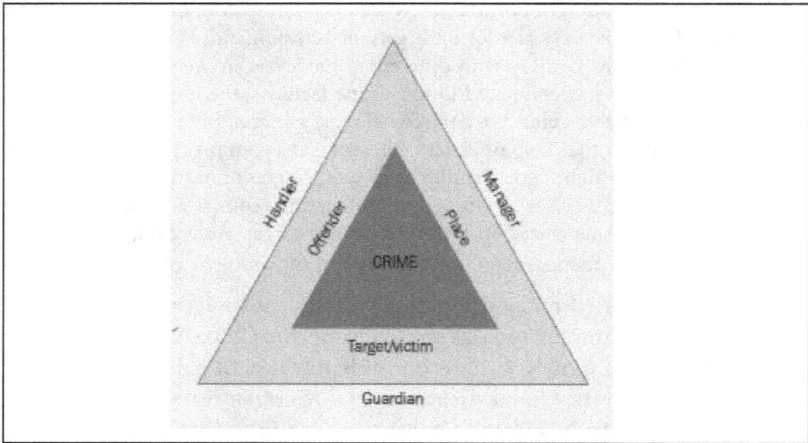

Source: Clarke & Eck, 2003, p. 27. (Used with permission.)

Situational Crime Prevention

Opportunity theories focused on the role of situational factors in crime causation and led to the development of the idea of situational interventions to prevent crime. The key text here is Clarke's edited book *Situational Crime Prevention: Successful Case Studies* first published in 1992. Clarke's introduction is arguably the most important manifesto in the science of crime prevention. Following the themes developed above in relation to opportunity theories, Clarke stated that (1997, p. 2):

> Situational crime prevention departs radically from most criminology in its orientation ... proceeding from an analysis of the circumstances giving rise to specific types of crime, it introduces discrete managerial and environmental change to reduce the opportunities for those crimes to occur. Thus it is focused on the settings for crime, rather than upon those committing criminal acts. It seeks to forestall the occurrence of crime, rather than to detect and sanction offenders. It seeks not to eliminate criminal or delinquent tendencies through improvement of society or its institutions, but merely to make criminal action less attractive to offenders. Central to this enterprise is not the criminal justice system, but a host of public and private organisations and agencies – schools, hospitals, transit systems, shops and malls, manufacturing businesses and phone companies, local parks and entertainment facilities, pubs and parking lots — whose products, services and operations spawn opportunities for a vast range of different crimes.

More specifically, Clarke defined situational crime prevention as follows:

> Situational prevention comprises opportunity-reducing measures that (1) are directed at highly specific forms of crime, (2) involve the management, design or manipulation of the immediate environment in as systematic and permanent way as possible, (3) make crime more difficult and risky, or less rewarding and excusable as judged by a wide range of offenders. (1997, p. 4)

In addition, Clarke described four primary components of the broader situational prevention framework (1997, p. 6):

1. A theoretical foundation drawing principally upon routine activity and rational choice approaches.
2. A standard methodology based on the action research paradigm.
3. A set of opportunity-reducing techniques.
4. A body of evaluated practice including studies of displacement.

Opportunity theories explain crime in terms of a calculation of effort, risk and reward. From the point of view of prevention, a routine activity analysis of crime should lead to the introduction of 'routine precautions' to prevent crime (Felson, 1998, p. 139). This can involve simple and obvious actions by individuals, such as locking doors, keeping wallets out of reach of thieves, and avoiding dangerous areas. Routine precautions can also be adopted in a more systematic fashion by organisations, through the application of regular security risk assessments, security management interventions, and system tests (see Chapter 10 and Chapter 11).

Situational prevention is focused on fitting interventions to specific situations, and this can only be determined through primary research. The 'action research' component refers to practitioner-researcher collaboration, and the involvement of all relevant stakeholders in the applied research process. In that regard, Clarke sets out five stages required for the implementation of a situational prevention project (1997, p. 15):

1. Collection of data about the nature and dimensions of the specific crime problem.
2. Analysis of the situational conditions that permit or facilitate the commission of the crime in question.
3. Systematic study of possible means of blocking opportunities for these particular crimes, including analysis of costs.
4. Implementation of the most promising, feasible and economic measures.
5. Monitoring of results and dissemination of experience.

Monitoring should attempt to include all crime-related incidents pre- and post- intervention, stakeholder experiences and opinions, and financial costs. As noted in Chapter 1 of this book, in a model project the classic scientific method is followed with a matching control group to ensure changes in the experimental group are not wrongly attributed to the interventions. This is not always possible however. A number of instructive crime prevention case studies are 'natural experiments', where authorities make changes outside a scientific paradigm. In these cases, an association between interventions and outcomes can still be identified with good incident data and the presence of ad hoc 'controls' that review possible alternative explanations for project outcomes (Clarke, 1997, p. 35).

Finally, the 'set of opportunity-reducing techniques' is summarised in Figure 6.2. The original set of 16 techniques was enlarged in the early 2000s to 25, grouped under five strategic areas: 'increase the effort', 'increase the risks', 'reduce the rewards', 'reduce provocations' and 'remove excuses'. These approaches can also be structured in terms of a hierarchy of 'hard' and 'soft' approaches. Harder methods involve various forms of 'target hardening', denial of access, and threats of arrest and punishment. Examples include locks, fences, barriers, street closures, security guards and police. Softer approaches 'assist compliance' by communicating rules, reducing frustration, and making it easy for people to obey the rules. Examples include (Clarke, 1997):

- providing entertainment when people are queuing reduces irritability and conflict
- providing food and entertainment at licensed premises reduces boredom, intoxication and the likelihood of violence
- visible, accessible, free public toilets help prevent public urination
- the availability of rubbish bins helps prevent littering
- frequent and clear speed limit signs help prevent inadvertent speeding and remind wilful speedsters of the law and their obligations.

Intermediate measures include 'denying benefits', 'deflecting offenders' and 'assisting natural surveillance'.

Applications: Intervention Projects

Perhaps the greatest strength of situational crime prevention lies in its expanding 'body of evaluated practice'. The second edition of *Situational Crime Prevention: Successful Case Studies* included 23 studies where opportunity-based analyses of crime problems led to the successful introduction of situational interventions. A number of these cases are described in various amounts of depth in following chapters of this book. Below are brief summaries of three of Clarke's (1997) case studies.

- In the early 1990s, in the housing estate of Dudley in the United Kingdom, the local authority upgraded street lighting across a section of

Figure 6.2
Twenty-five techniques of situational prevention.

Increase the Effort	Increase the Risks	Reduce the Rewards	Reduce Provocations	Remove Excuses
1. Target harden • Steering column locks and immobilisers • Anti-robbery screens • Tamper-proof packaging	6. Extend guardianship • Take routine precautions: go out in group at night, leave signs of occupancy, carry phone • "Cocoon" neighborhood watch	11. Conceal targets • Off-street parking • Gender-neutral phone directories • Unmarked bullion trucks	16. Reduce frustrations and stress • Efficient queues and polite service • Expanded seating • Soothing music/muted lights	21. Set rules • Rental agreements • Harassment codes • Hotel registration
2. Control access to facilities • Entry phones • Electronic card access • Baggage screening	7. Assist natural surveillance • Improved street lighting • Defensible space design • Support whistleblowers	12. Remove targets • Removable car radio • Women's refuges • Pre-paid cards for pay phones	17. Avoid disputes • Separate enclosures for rival soccer fans • Reduce crowding in pubs • Fixed cab fares	22. Post instructions • "No Parking" • "Private Property" • "Extinguish camp fires"
3. Screen exits • Ticket needed for exit • Export documents • Electronic merchandise tags	8. Reduce anonymity • Taxi driver IDs • "How's my driving?" decals • School uniforms	13. Identify property • Property marking • Vehicle licensing and parts marking • Cattle branding	18. Reduce emotional arousal • Controls on violent pornography • Enforce good behavior on soccer field • Prohibit racial slurs	23. Alert conscience • Roadside speed display boards • Signatures for customs declarations • "Shoplifting is stealing"
4. Deflect offenders • Street closures • Separate bathrooms for women • Disperse pubs	9. Utilize place managers • CCTV for double-deck buses • Two clerks for convenience stores • Reward vigilance	14. Disrupt markets • Monitor pawn shops • Controls on classified ads • License street vendors	19. Neutralize peer pressure • "Idiots drink and drive" • "It's OK to say No" • Disperse troublemakers at school	24. Assist compliance • Easy library checkout • Public lavatories • Litter bins
5. Control tools/weapons • "Smart" guns • Disabling stolen cell phones • Restrict spray paint sales to juveniles	10. Strengthen formal surveillance • Red light cameras • Burglar alarms • Security guards	15. Deny benefits • Ink merchandise tags • Graffiti cleaning • Speed humps	20. Discourage imitation • Rapid repair of vandalism • V-chips in TVs • Censor details of modus operandi	25. Control drugs and alcohol • Breathalyzers in pubs • Server intervention • Alcohol-free events

Source: Center for Problem-Oriented Policing (2016). (Used with permission.)

residential roads (Painter & Farrington, 1997). A similar area physically and demographically was used as a control site. Approximately 70% of crime occurred after dark on both sites. The new white lighting at the experimental site doubled the amount of light, greatly enhancing natural surveillance. Resident surveys were undertaken in the year before and the year after installation. In the experimental site, victimisation was reduced by 23% from the 42.0% of survey respondents to 32.3%. In the control site, victimisation fell by 3% from 39.1% to 38.0%. In terms of the incidence of crime, there was a 41% reduction at the experimental site from 114.8 crimes per 100 households to 68.0. At the control site, crime fell 15% from 82.1 incidents per 100 households to 69.8.

- In the early 1980s, the Finsbury Park area of London experienced a significant problem with street prostitution; 'curb crawling' by male customers; and associated problems of disorder, harassment, crime and traffic congestion. In 1983, 666 women were arrested for solicitation in an intensified crackdown. Pimps and brothel keepers were also arrested. This appeared to reduce the problem, although previous experience suggested the effects of police crackdowns were not sustained. A series of meetings between police, local residents and the local authority led to agreement on modifications to a traffic management plan that would limit access to the area. In 1985, the introduction of restricted access through road closures led to 'a remarkable transformation ... Soliciting and curb-crawling virtually disappeared, and the area was transformed from a noisy and hazardous "red-light' district into a relatively tranquil residential area', with no evidence of displacement (Matthews, 1997, p. 78). The overall crime rate fell by 42% in one year.

- A US study by DiLonardo (1997) measured the impact of electronic article surveillance (EAS) by comparing inventory shortage rates. In the apparel sections of eight stores without EAS, losses increased 30% over five years. In stores that installed EAS, losses decreased by 17%. In a separate nine-year study with one store, in one year following the installation of EAS losses fell from 7.0% to 1.4%. The system was then removed and losses went up to 7.7%. Reinstallation resulted in an immediate fall to 2.9%. The 7.7% loss was put at US$616,000 and the 2.9% loss put at US$238,000 — a difference of US$378,000. EAS installation was costed at US$105,000, which allowed for a substantial overall saving of US$273,000.

It is clear from these examples that situational crime prevention techniques are highly adaptive. The relevance of situational measures is also evidenced in the case study chapters (see Chapter 8 and Chapter 9).

Related Approaches

Situational crime prevention overlaps with a number of other approaches to crime reduction. Four of these are briefly outlined below

Crime Prevention Through Environmental Design

Crime Prevention Through Environmental Design (CPTED) is a form of situational prevention focused on physical settings. The CPTED method is concerned with designing open malls, parks, streets, buildings, entrances and rooms in ways that facilitate 'defensible space' and 'territoriality' (Crowe, 1991). CPTED is expanded on in the next chapter.

Problem-Oriented Policing

Problem-Oriented Policing (POP) was developed by Herman Goldstein and articulated in a 1979 journal article 'Improving Policing: A Problem-Oriented Approach' and a 1990 book *Problem-Oriented Policing* (Goldstein, 1979, 1990). Like 'community policing', POP involves police adopting a consultative and cooperative approach to solving crime-related problems, rather than simply reacting to crime by attempting to arrest offenders. POP advocated an information-driven approach, and the process aspects of situational crime prevention can be seen in the problem-solving SARA model: 'Scan, Analyse, Respond, Assess' (Eck & Spelman, 1987), including continuous monitoring and improvement.

Crime Mapping

Computer aided crime mapping is useful to show graphically how crime patterns occur across space and time; including stable, fluctuating and evolving patterns (Anselin, Griffiths, & Tita, 2011). Situational crime prevention operates on the assumption that the more crime is concentrated at particular times or places, the more amenable it is to effective interventions. 'Hot spot analysis' is a related term that targets highly concentrated areas of crime.

Product Design Against Crime

There is also work focused on building crime prevention features into products (Ekblom, 2011). Examples include fixed hanger tops in hotel wardrobes that prevent pilfering of hangers, wetsuit pockets for car keys, nonreusable syringes preventing sharing of needles, backpacks made from cut-resistant materials, table hooks for handbags at cafés and restaurants, and personal identification number (PIN) access to mobile phones and computers.

Issues

It seems that few innovations are introduced without complications and controversy. Situational crime prevention has its share of detractors, potential pitfalls and drawbacks that need to be taken seriously. The following sub-sections briefly analyse these issues and provide some rejoinders and possible solutions.

Displacement

Displacement presents as a potential problem with situationally based interventions. Making crime more difficult in one place may simply drive offenders to nearby areas or other types of crime. Displacement makes situational interventions unfair as well as unproductive from a wider social perspective. Research has shown that displacement can occur in some cases (Clarke, 1997). However, it is more often the case that there is no evidence of displacement, as offenders are often limited in their scope and easily discouraged from further attempts at crime. Research has also shown the existence of a 'multiplier' or 'halo effect' in some cases, where the crime reduction effects of an intervention are extended to neighbouring areas due to the broader deterrent effect on would-be offenders (Clarke, 1997; van Dijk, 2012, p. 17).

An Inconvenient Fortress Society?

Another concern is that situational crime prevention will produce a 'fortress society' of high walls, barbed wire and vicious guard dogs, with annoying and inconvenient security devices (Clarke, 1997, p. 37). It is true that many manifestations of crime prevention can be annoying, frustrating, ugly, and even threatening and oppressive. However, other security innovations, such as entry-phone systems and transparent fencing, can be unobtrusive and enhance convenience. In residential complexes, CPTED principles, discussed in the next chapter of this book, usually emphasise the importance of aesthetics and convenience in developing territoriality, 'image' and manageable space that create crime-prevention outcomes from an improved sense of community.

Inequality

Situational crime prevention has also been criticised for failing to address the deep causes of crime in social inequality, poverty and unemployment (Clarke, 1997). It is probably true to say that statements about the focus of situational crime prevention sometimes appear to exclude other crime prevention methods. However, early childhood interventions aimed at improving school performance, family integration and social capital can generate large reductions in crime; and some offender rehabilitation and management programs have also shown significant reductions in reoffending rates (see Chapter 3 to Chapter 5). The obvious point must be that crime is multi-dimensional and needs to be addressed from a variety of directions. The many successes of situational prevention underscore the large contribution it can make within a comprehensive approach. Situational interventions are particularly suitable for agents that have a mission for crime prevention but face challenges in changing dispositional factors in the potential offender population. A store owner can do little about the long-range motivations of shoplifters and burglars, but they can do a lot to prevent crime on their premises.

Of course, successful situational interventions reduce the demand on the public justice system. Primary prevention also reduces the negative experiences of potential offenders (and their families) with the criminal justice system. Van Dijk has emphasised the role of security in preventing the escalation of crime and the development of criminal careers. This includes a social justice outcome for potential offenders as well as victims. Car theft and burglary, for example, often serve as 'stepping stones' to more serious crimes for young males (van Dijk, 2012, p. 17). The idea that relatively minor crimes like joy riding in stolen vehicles and domestic burglary are the gateway to more serious crimes and criminal careers is a commonplace of criminology. However, what has received much less attention is the fact that the prevention of these crimes can steer young people away from a criminal lifestyle. Property crime prevention by security services therefore has an often unacknowledged role in preventing more serious property crimes, and also preventing crimes of violence such as robbery and armed robbery.

The cost of security can cause significant disadvantage for some. However, governments can address the problem of capacity to pay through subsidised security; as well as security in government housing, public transport, public hospitals and public schools. Van Dijk has emphasised the widening gap worldwide between victimisation of the rich and poor in relation to their ability to afford security. With little or no prospect of the public police bridging the gap:

> The results of the International Crime Victim Survey (ICVS) show that across twelve western nations the lowest income groups have stepped up their household security to a lesser extent than the middle and upper classes. They cannot afford to. As was expected, the survey also shows that the lowest quartile have benefitted less from the falls in burglary victimisation than the rest of the population (van Dijk, 2012, p. 17).

With this phenomenon in mind, van Dijk argues that 'situational crime prevention is not just a matter of efficiency. It is also a matter of social justice' (p. 17).

Conclusion

This chapter has outlined the main claims of situational crime prevention to generate large reductions in a wide range of crimes. The benefits for prevention of an opportunity perspective on crime are developed in more detail in the following chapters of this book. It should be clear from the evidence presented so far that situational crime prevention has a great deal of untapped potential. A multi-pronged approach to crime reduction — criminal justice, developmental, social and situational — has the potential to make enormous inroads into the large problem of criminal victimisation in modern society.

References

Anselin, L., Griffiths, E., & Tita, G. (2011). Crime mapping and hot spot analysis. In R. Wortley & L. Mazerolle (Eds.), *Environmental criminology and crime analysis* (pp. 97–116). Abingdon, England: Routledge.

Bates, L., Soole, D., & Watson, B. (2012). The effectiveness of traffic policing in reducing traffic crashes. In T. Prenzler (Ed.), *Policing and security in practice* (pp. 90–109). Houndmills, England: Palgrave-Macmillan.

Bowers, K., Hirschfield, A., & Johnson, S. (1998). Victimization revisited: A case study of non-residential repeat burglary on Merseyside. *British Journal of Criminology, 39,* 429–452.

Center for Problem-Oriented Policing (2016). *Twenty five techniques of situational prevention.* Retrieved from http://www.popcenter.org/library/25%20techniques%20grid.pdf

Clarke, R. (Ed.). (1997). *Situational crime prevention: Successful case studies.* Guilderland, NY: Harrow and Heston.

Clarke, R. (1999). *Hot products: Understanding, anticipating and reducing demand for stolen goods.* London, England: Home Office.

Clarke, R. (2012). Opportunity makes the thief. Really? And so what? *Crime Science, 1*(3), 11–19..

Clarke, R., & Eck, J. (2003). *Become a problem solving crime analysis in 55 small steps.* London, England: Jill Dando Institute for Crime Science, University College London.

Cohen, L., & Felson, M. (1979, August). Social change and crime rate trends: A routine activity approach. *American Sociological Review, 44,* 588–608.

Cornish, D., & Clarke, R. (Eds.). (1986). *The reasoning criminal.* New York, NY: Springer-Verlag.

Crowe, T. (1991). *Crime prevention through environmental design.* Boston, MA: Butterworth-Heinemann.

Curran, D., & Renzetti, C. (2001) *Theories of crime.* Boston, MA: Allyn & Bacon.

DiLonardo, R. (1997). The Economic benefit of electronic article surveillance. In R. Clarke (Ed.), *Situational crime prevention: Successful case studies* (pp. 74–82). Albany, NY: Harrow and Heston.

Eck, J., Clarke, R.V., & Guerette, R. (2007). Risky facilities. *Crime Prevention Studies, 21*, 225–264.

Eck, J., & Spelman, W. (1987). *Problem-solving: Problem-oriented policing in Newport News.* Washington, DC: National Institute of Justice.

Ekblom, P. (2011). Designing products against crime. In R. Wortley & L. Mazerolle (Eds.), *Environmental criminology and crime analysis* (pp. 195–220). Abingdon, England: Routledge.

Felson, M. (1994). *Crime and everyday life.* Thousand Oaks, CA: Pine Forge Press.

Felson, M. (1998). *Crime and everyday life.* Thousand Oaks, CA: Pine Forge Press.

Gabor, T. (1994). *Everybody does it! Crime by the public.* New York, NY: Macmillan.

Goldstein, H. (1979). Improving policing: A problem-oriented approach. *Crime and delinquency, 24*, 236–258.

Goldstein, H. (1990). *Problem-oriented policing.* New York, NY: McGraw-Hill.

Macintyre, S. (2001). *Burglar decision making.* Doctoral dissertation. School of Criminology and Criminal Justice, Griffith University, Brisbane, Australia.

Makkai, T., & Prenzler, T. (2015). The nature and prevalence of crime. In H. Hayes & T. Prenzler (Eds.), *An introduction to crime and criminology* (pp. 59–77). Sydney, Australia: Pearson.

Martinson, R. (1974). What works? — Questions and answers about prison reform. *The Public Interest, 35*(Spring), 22–54.

Matthews, R. (1997). Developing more effective strategies for curbing prostitution. In R. Clarke (Ed.), *Situational crime prevention: Successful case studies* (pp. 74–82). Albany, NY: Harrow and Heston.

Painter, K., & Farrington, D. (1997) the Crime reducing effect of improved street lighting: The Dudley Project. In R. Clarke (Ed.), *Situational crime prevention: Successful case studies* (pp. 209–226). Albany, NY: Harrow and Heston.

Sutherland, E. (1947). *Principles of criminology.* Philadelphia: J. B. Lippincott.

van Dijk, J. (2008). *The world of crime.* Thousand Oaks, CA: SAGE.

van Dijk, J. (2012, June). *Closing the doors: Stockholm Prizewinners lecture 2012.* Paper presented at the Stockholm Criminology Symposium, Stockholm.

Walker, J. (1994) Trends in crime and criminal justice. In D. Chappell & P. Wilson (Eds.), *The Australian criminal justice system: The mid-1990s* (pp. 1–36). Sydney: Butterworths.

Chapter 7

Crime Prevention Through Environmental Design: Evolution, Theory and Practice

Mateja Mihinjac and Danielle Reynald

This chapter provides a brief overview of the theoretical framework of crime prevention through environmental design (CPTED — pronounced *sep-ted*). As a proactive crime prevention approach that relies on manipulation of physical and social environments, CPTED strategies are aimed at minimising criminal opportunities and motivation while simultaneously enhancing desirable behaviour. These strategies are focused on reducing victimisation at specific places, increasing detection of suspicious behaviour, and minimising fear of crime at places. The chapter sketches the evolution of CPTED, outlines related theoretical developments, overviews CPTED components, and briefly depicts their practical application. Despite some limitations and critiques related to its conceptual framework and implementation, the empirical literature demonstrates CPTED techniques can be highly effective when sufficient attention is paid to implementation and when intricacies of the processes are considered. Most significantly, we conclude that continued development of CPTED rests on the more explicit incorporation of place managers and guardians and encouraging their active engagement in realising the intended function of CPTED.

CPTED: Definition and Description

CPTED is a crime deterrence and fear reduction approach aimed at influencing the behaviour of space users through manipulating physical and social elements in the environment. It is aimed at addressing opportunity and motivational factors of both potential offenders and those who guard against crime. More specifically, CPTED involves protection of people, objects and places by using environmental design and social strategies to increase crime control prospects while supporting the intended use of space and positive social interaction. Concurrently, by manipulating cues from the environment that affect the perception of risks and rewards from committing a crime, it intends to discourage illegal and antisocial behaviours. While the name implies its crime prevention focus, the International CPTED Association's mission statement advocates CPTED as a vehicle for improving safety and quality of life beyond its explicit crime-prevention orientation: 'to create safer environments and improve the quality of life through the use of CPTED principles and strategies'[1].

CPTED principles operate at specific places through manipulation of the design, materials and layout of places, buildings, streets and cities, and through social and cultural activities. CPTED strategies can function effectively at both larger spaces (residential neighbourhoods, entertainment districts), and at more specific locations (dwellings, bars, schools, parks, public transport). It also has applicability for reducing robberies and violence, property crime, for managing public events, and for addressing terrorism threats. This suggests the utility of CPTED as a viable and cost-beneficial alternative to more intrusive and traditionally offender-focused interventions. A context-specific understanding of places, their dynamics and social milieu, and underlying characteristics of crime problems, are crucial for tailoring effective (and specific) CPTED strategies.

CPTED also importantly functions as a fear reducing measure. Well designed and managed places increase aesthetic quality and reduce uncertainty by eliminating concealment areas through landscaping and building design, improving visibility through lighting, or removing advertising material from windows. While such physical surroundings influence perception of safety, often the presence of people and the surrounding social environment (where social ties are strong) plays an even larger role in reducing fear (Loukaitou-Sideris, 1999).

With the potential for providing such safety outcomes, CPTED has become a viable intervention that rests on a premise of two dimensions: environment and design. While the *environment* focuses on 'people and their physical and social surroundings', *design* is concerned with 'physical, social, management, and law enforcement directives' (Crowe, 2000, p. 35). The core components that comprise CPTED are borne out of unification of these two dimensions, and will be presented later in this chapter.

CPTED also requires a number of procedural considerations that include a well-designed and effectively implemented policy, departmental coordination and cooperation, and political will. Managerial considerations are equally essential and should encourage proactive integration of CPTED into the intended functioning of place. Thus, while CPTED engages informal users, owners and managers to make spaces safer, it equally relies on policymakers and crime prevention professionals to develop strategic frameworks.

Evolution of CPTED

Original Environmental Theorists

The roots of contemporary CPTED can be traced back to the pioneers who wrote about urban planning. The most influential was Jane Jacobs, a jour-

---

[1] www.cpted.net

nalist with knowledge of architecture and urban design. Jacobs' (2011/1961) criticisms of car-oriented city developments following the Great Depression culminated in her calls for diverse city ecosystems where a steady flow of activity would promote vibrancy and safety while increasing opportunities for meaningful social interaction. Her concept of 'eyes upon the street' became a synonym for the CPTED concept of 'natural surveillance' (Jacobs, 2011, p. 45).

Urban planner Elizabeth Wood (1960, 1961) was equally critical of the sprawling neighbourhood and housing developments that failed to account for people's needs and desires. Her calls for 'balanced neighbourhoods' and 'design for social fabric' saw the confluence of effective design and social capital as an answer to urban renewal. In 1968, Shlomo Angel empirically explored and pioneered the association between urban design and crime patterns (Angel, 1968). He further compared these findings to the intensity of land uses (concentrations of people in spaces) and called for integration of social deterrents with crime prevention through physical design.

Influenced by his predecessors, an American architect Oscar Newman advocated 'defensible space' principles for increasing safety in private and communal residential spaces (Newman, 1972). Newman's theory evolved from the New York public housing research which showed disproportionately lower crime in low-rises with clearer territorial proprietorship compared to high-rises characterised by areas with ambiguous ownership (hallways, elevators, stairwells, lobbies). Newman concluded such 'undefended' areas should be avoided in favour of 'defensible' spaces through incorporation of 'natural surveillance', 'territoriality' and 'image/milieu' principles.

Despite some criticisms this theory and the proposed principles were influential for future crime prevention and housing policy. The defensible space theory also laid foundations for CPTED demonstration projects (Westinghouse studies) that tested implementation in a school, commercial and residential setting (Kaplan, Bickman, Pesce, & Szoc, 1978). The tested principles are intimately related to contemporary CPTED techniques, namely 'access control', 'surveillance' and 'activity support', while 'motivation reinforcement' substituted territoriality to demonstrate applicability beyond the residential setting and to account for motivational factors of both offender and nonoffender communities (Kaplan et al., 1978, p. 8). Contemporary CPTED is, owing to its practical applicability, largely based upon Newman's original conceptualisation (see Figure 7.1 for a timeline of CPTED developments and theoretical influences).

Figure 7.1
Timeline of CPTED developments and theoretical influences.

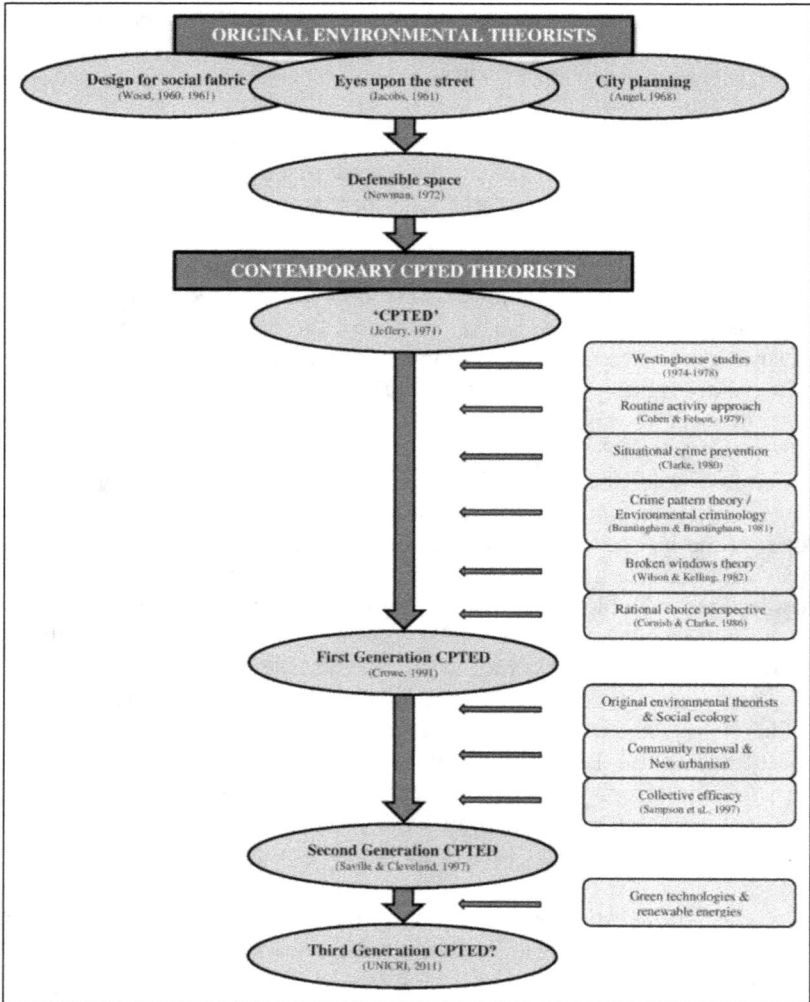

Contemporary CPTED Theorists

The original environmental theorists laid foundations for the development of contemporary CPTED. In 1971 an American criminologist C. Ray Jeffery first coined the term 'crime prevention through environmental design', advocating for environmental engineering of criminal behaviour (Jeffery, 1971).

Jeffery later expanded this deterministic view into an integrated systems perspective of reciprocally interactive relationship between the internal (brain) and external environment (Jeffery & Zahm, 1993).

Having been influenced by early CPTED and related developments in crime prevention (see Figure 7.1), in 1991 an American criminologist Timothy Crowe conceptualised CPTED as a space management approach (Crowe, 2000). Crowe's approach employs 'natural access control', 'natural surveillance' and 'territorial reinforcement' principles and is synonymous with the first generation CPTED that prioritises opportunity reduction. Advances in modern technology and expansion of the private security industry have broadened these concepts beyond their 'natural' roots, to include organised and mechanical/technological dimensions.

Criticisms that CPTED promoted a fortress-like mentality, in 1997 culminated in its second generation (Saville & Cleveland, 2008). Emphasising essentiality of previously neglected social milieu espoused by the original theorists, the second generation encompasses four components: 'social cohesion', 'connectivity', 'community culture', and 'threshold capacity' (Saville & Cleveland, 2008, p. 81). Such 'social' CPTED envisions the confluence of physical and social components, and has been practically applied in the neighbourhood capacity building approach called 'SafeGrowth' (Saville, 2017). The ultimate goal is the residents' ownership over preventing and solving social problems.

Technology enthusiasts have already begun thinking about further developments by introducing the third generation CPTED. They proposed employing modern and environmentally sustainable green technologies to foster safer living environments (United Nations Interregional Crime and Justice Research Institute [UNICRI], 2011). While this conception does not yet have any theoretical basis, such innovative strategies may help achieve intended crime prevention outcomes while improving spaces. Despite ongoing developments, CPTED in practice remains heavily reliant on the principles collated under the umbrella of 'first generation'.

Theoretical Foundations

CPTED draws from multiple disciplines including architecture and urban planning, criminology, and psychology. The environment and design dimensions of CPTED speak to these influences and their interaction needed for effective prevention of crime and facilitation of desirable behaviour.

Architecture and Urban Planning

CPTED emerged from architecture and planning. Original theorists observed the interplay between social and physical environments in influencing crime. More recently, the influence of 'new urbanism' has seen integration of infrastructure for work, entertainment, movement and transportation with the goal of designing safe, sustainable and enjoyable contemporary cities (Australian Council for New Urbanism, 2006). CPTED remains intrinsically connected to the design and organisation of cities and neighbourhoods.

Criminology

Criminological thinking postulates opportunity and motivational aspects of offending. The opportunity perspective stemming from environmental criminology outlines (a) offenders' search patterns characterised by geography ('crime pattern theory'; Brantingham & Brantingham, 1981); (b) offenders' decision-making influenced by environmental cues ('rational choice perspective'; Cornish & Clarke, 1986); and (c) the effect of place management and guardianship on crime ('routine activity approach'; Cohen & Felson, 1979). Amalgamation of this knowledge has been effectively applied in situational crime prevention (see Chapter 6) and CPTED.

The social (human) ecology branch rejects deterministic viewpoints in favour of the wider social and cultural context. Originating from the Chicago school of urban sociology in 1920s, social ecology extrapolates from social disorganisation, urban sprawl and socio-economic conditions to explain crime (Wikström, 2009). As these effects produce weak social ties, they disrupt the balance and fuel criminal motivation. Jacobs' and Wood's thinking strongly resonated with these ideas, while the second generation CPTED has renewed this interest.

Psychology

Environmental psychology explains human behaviour as a response to environmental cues. It draws specifically on the 'environment–organism(mind)–behaviour' interactive model (Jeffery & Zahm, 1993, p. 339). Jeffery's psychobiological understanding of CPTED further expanded this model to account for the uniqueness and distinctiveness of individuals' behaviour (Robinson, 1996). This psychobiological perspective has been largely neglected in CPTED and deemed lacking in practical value.

Key CPTED Components

Two schools of thought have emerged from cross-pollination of ideas stemming from these theoretical foundations: one sees criminal behaviour resulting from opportunity (first generation CPTED); the other explains criminal motivation stemming from socioecological conditions (second generation CPTED).

Figure 7.2

First generation CPTED components.

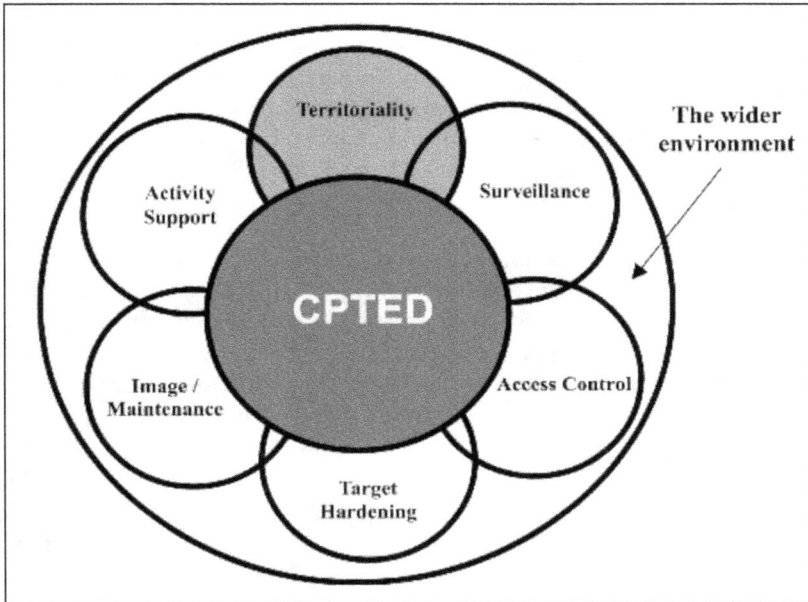

Source: Adapted from Moffatt (1983, p. 23) in Cozens, Saville, & Hillier (2005, p. 330).

First Generation CPTED (Opportunity)

Crime deterrence in first generation CPTED is achieved through disrupting opportunity elements within the built and natural environment. The principles align closely with the 25 techniques of situational crime prevention (see Chapter 6, Table 6.1). Although CPTED authors have presented distinct conceptual frameworks, the five principles discussed below are most consistently cited. These are 'surveillance', 'territoriality', 'access control', 'activity support', and 'image/maintenance'.

Territoriality

As a central concept, territoriality focuses on control of places using boundaries and clear signs of ownership. Newman defined territoriality as 'capacity of the physical environment to create perceived zones of territorial influences' and suggested this increases their defensive capacity (Newman, 1972, p. 51). Effective design provides clear territorial cues through demarcation of public, semi-public and private spaces.

Clear signs of ownership may help prevent residential burglary. For example, Brown and Altman (1983) assessed 306 houses in Salt Lake County to distil the most influential markers for preventing burglary. A series of statistical analyses using police records and visual inspections of the houses showed that territorial markers conveying cues of ownership (such as symbolic and actual barriers, signs of ownership, and design supporting supervision) were associated with reduced victimisation. Excessive territoriality measures, however, may counteract opportunities for natural surveillance and social interaction (Brown & Altman, 1983; Reynald, 2011).

Surveillance

Surveillance signifies the ability *to see* and *be seen*. Newman (1972, p. 78) defined natural surveillance as 'the capacity of physical design to provide surveillance opportunities for residents and their agents'. Such opportunities can be created through open layouts, clear sightlines, windows overlooking spaces, or improving night-time visibility. These promote supervision by relying on formal and informal guardians for protection of people and property. Reynald's (2011) 'guardianship in action' model supports the idea that lower residential property crime levels can be explained in part by enhanced opportunities for supervision. She empirically tested the underlying mechanisms that facilitate active guardianship by residents (their availability, monitoring and intervention) in two successive studies in The Hague, which included observations of 814 and 2,847 residential properties respectively. The results showed that opportunities for surveillance — when unobstructed by territorial markers — could predict active guardianship. The developments in security industry (Chapter 10 to Chapter 12) have extended surveillance to organised and mechanical forms, which encompass allocation of security guards, lighting and CCTV. Such security management practices are often implemented in commercial settings and at public events with frequent public-private partnerships (Prenzler & Sarre, 1998).

Access Control

This technique directs or restricts access to places or facilities. Cozens and colleagues (2005, p. 335) explained that opportunities for crime can be reduced by 'denying access to potential targets and creating a heightened perception of risk in offenders'. Restricting street accessibility may, for example, reduce residential burglary (Johnson & Bowers, 2010). This UK-based study from Merseyside looked at burglary frequency of 118,161 homes in relation to their street segments. A multilevel analysis of the segment attributes (type of road and level of connectedness to road) demonstrated a positive association between street permeability and burglary risk suggesting cul-de-sacs and local roads may reduce burglary victimisation.

While access control tends to employ subtler strategies that include informal surveillance and territoriality at a broader place-based level, target hardening operates at a micro-target level and is concerned with restricting access through (typically) highly visible approaches such as locks and reinforced materials. These may promote 'fortressing' (Ellin, 1997). From this perspective, Cozens and colleagues (2005) have questioned the inclusion of target hardening under the CPTED umbrella.

Activity Support

As an underlying principle of effective place management, activity support facilitates desired activities and discourages unwanted conduct (Cozens et al., 2005). Conjoining activities in the same place encourages informal surveillance and, in turn, fosters a sense of safety. For example, juxtaposing an ATM along highly used spaces, entertainment districts mixed with shopping areas, or a children's play area in the vantage point of cafes, provides opportunities for guardianship (Crowe, 2000). Thus, this principle relies on strategic design and effective place management to create, and maintain, facilities that promote intended use while increasing opportunities for informal surveillance.

Image/Maintenance

Effective place management also entails the upkeep of places (Newman, 1972). Places emanating a positive image devoid of signs of damage and incivilities attract users of desirable activities while discouraging illegitimate ones. Inviting places also prompt attitudes of pride and care. In this way social disorder can be reduced and community cohesion promoted (Saville, 2017). The 'broken windows theory' (Wilson & Kelling, 1982) similarly emphasises how spaces emanating a positive image are less likely to become targeted for crime as they elicit perceptions of ownership and control.

For example, regular maintenance of public transportation services in the Victorian Travel Safe Program in Australia increased use of services and in turn reduced negative perception and fear of victimisation (Carr & Spring, 1993). The program was introduced in 1990 in response to vandalism, assaults and associated continuous cancellation of services. In addition to the rapid repair of vandalised property, the program also enhanced security features across the system and mobilised community participation, resulting in crimes against persons to decrease by 42%, and availability of services increasing from 65% to 70% to 98% within two years.

Second Generation CPTED (Motive)

Revising the original CPTED ideas about motivational propensity behind offending, the second generation theory expanded this premise to include socio-cultural and community aspects grounded in social ecology (Saville &

Cleveland, 2008). The aim was to encourage thinking beyond the physical determinism that has come to characterise the opportunity-reduction approach. While motivation is most successfully addressed in a neighbour-hood or other community with shared values and expectations, social techniques are also effectively applied in diverse smaller settings. The concepts include 'social cohesion', 'connectivity', 'community culture', and 'threshold capacity' (see Figure 7.3).

Social Cohesion

As a central concept, social cohesion hinges upon community involvement in pro-social behaviours (Saville & Cleveland, 2008). Inclusive environments generate a strong social fabric and foster interactions that increase informal surveillance and kinship. Under such atmosphere, the effect of opportunity techniques can be sustained and optimised. As Saville (2017, p. 302) noted, it is not simply the eyes on the street that have power to prevent crime but rather the '*caring* eyes'.

Figure 7.3
Second-generation CPTED components.

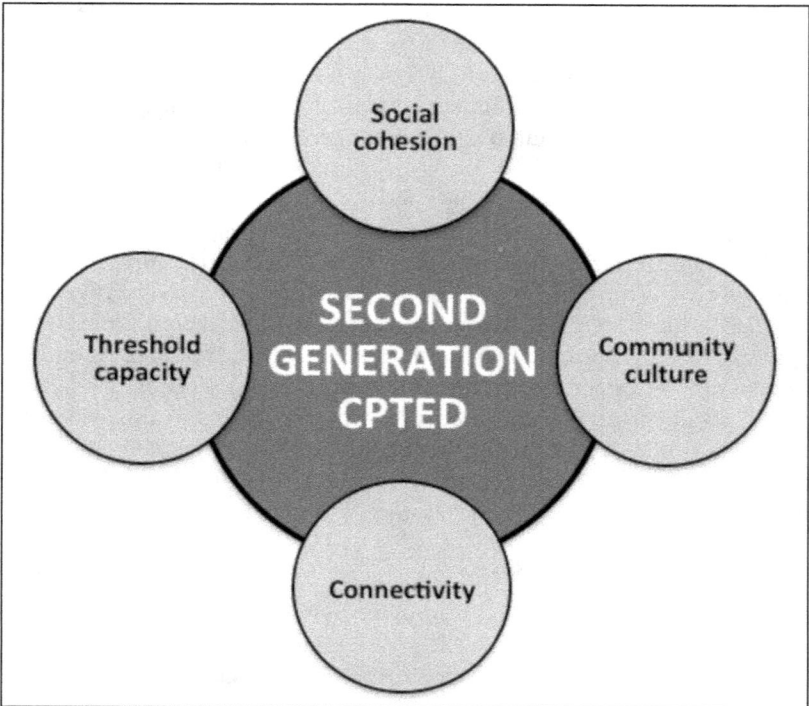

The original CPTED authors prioritised people and encouraged their interaction as a prerequisite for establishing meaningful connections. This is echoed in Newman's (1972, p. 3) sentiment: 'when people begin to protect themselves as individuals and not as a community, the battle against crime is effectively lost'. Such neighbourhood qualities build on social capital and enhance resilience to social disorganisation which may, according to Brown (2016), also reduce homicide. Brown's qualitative study explored the factors that impacted homicide in a socially disadvantaged and homicide-ridden neighbourhood Hollygrove in New Orleans. He conducted semi-structured interviews with 25 residents, community representatives and public servants to obtain qualitative accounts of the conditions impacting social cohesion and consequently homicide. This led him to realise the importance of increasing social capacity for reducing homicide: 'when the community embraced countercultural values, experienced social marginalization, and retrenched from relationship with outsiders, homicides increased' (p. 229).

Connectivity

'Connectivity' refers to both transportation networks and to high-level connectivity amongst neighbourhoods and internal/external authorities and organisations. Maintaining positive relations with these entities is essential for addressing neighbourhoods' specific needs (Saville & Cleveland, 2008, p. 82). As Jacobs (2011, p. 160) symbolically explained: 'nothing is more helpless than a city street alone, when its problems exceed its powers'.

Dickout (2006) demonstrated the power of partnership between the residents, businesses and the police in addressing violent crime in one of Calgary's nightlife entertainment areas. With an understanding that preventing violence was a shared responsibility, the stakeholders formed an 'Operation Street Sweeper' to allow effective collaboration under the culture of mutual respect. Appreciation for different perspectives fostered a sense of commitment where the parties would work together to proactively address the issues rather than rely on enforcement strategies to treat recurring symptoms. For example, while regular communication between business owners and residents helped identify mutually beneficial solutions to problems bar staff cooperated closely with the police who would diffuse situations before escalating into violence. An eight-man patrolling task force was also established. These partnerships created a sense of equality and control that fostered commitment, and thus helped to change reputation of the area as inherently dangerous. Within six months of the program, violent crime dropped by 67%.

Community Culture

This is the idea of 'bringing people together in a common purpose' (Saville & Cleveland, 2008, p. 83). The concept strongly relates to social cohesion and capacity building, as it is often the culture that drives a sense of community and local pride that strengthen social ties, and catalyse positive social change. Conversely, 'a neighbourhood cannot forge a culture if the people living there feel powerless to instigate change' (Dickout, 2006, p. 31). Collectivism can be built through activities such as local events and festivals, music and art or through some shared mission.

Activities promoting local culture have been particularly effective in reducing youth antisocial behaviour. One of such activities was a participatory arts program from Leicester, England, led by the community development organisation Soft Touch (National Culture Forum & Chief Cultural & Leisure Officers Association [NCF & CLOA], 2011, p. 13). Every Friday and Saturday night Soft Touch would position itself in designated areas with the highest levels of youth antisocial behaviours to facilitate arts, crafts and music activities from their mobile studio. Within 18 months 470 young people partook in the activities, while within the first 12 months of the program the police detected a 15% reduction in crime and antisocial behaviour as well as a significant reduction in calls for police service.

Threshold Capacity

This concept borrows from social ecology and asserts the importance of healthy and balanced neighbourhoods and city centres for preventing crime (Saville & Wong, 1994). Balanced land uses increase community resilience by ensuring that 'social stabilisers' (cohesion and inclusion-promoting activities) outweigh 'destabilisers' (too many pubs, pawn shops, abandoned buildings). The 1993 Vancouver study empirically measured the relationship between one of such potential 'destabilisers': bars, and crime incidents to determine acceptable concentrations of premises before they might lead to disorder requiring police attention (Saville & Wong, 1994). The dependent variable measuring disorder was operationalised as calls for police service. This included one month of data for five neighbourhoods. The independent variable measuring bar density was operationalised as a number of bar seats per neighbourhood. Following a series of statistical analyses, the theoretical model revealed calls for police service grew exponentially as the number of bar seats increased. While the authors could not determine the exact tolerable levels of bar density, they recalled that several existing planning practices mandated a minimum of 45 to 50 metres distance between the bars before exceeding the capacity.

CPTED as a Socio–Physical Approach

While most commonly associated with attempts to 'design out crime', CPTED roots originate from the idea of inclusive social environments. Successful environments are characterised by a synergy between social and physical measures, with opportunity and motivation reinforcing each other to holistically reduce crime (Saville, 2017). While opportunity reduction measures may sometimes need to be prioritised (e.g., commercial settings), in other situations social programming strategies are favourable (e.g., residential neighbourhoods). Above all, the main focus of CPTED and other crime prevention measures should be on facilitating prosocial behaviours:

> CPTED is truly a misnomer because, when it is applied well, the concepts focus not on crime prevention, but on building positive environments, motivating desirable attitudes and behaviours, and reinforcing primary intended functions. The focus is not on what should *not* happen, but on what *should* happen. (Schneider, 2006, p. 7)

Criticisms

A common criticism of CPTED is that of displacement, where crime prevented in one setting may move to other places, times or targets (Barr & Pease, 1990). Criminologists have largely dispelled this claim in terms of inevitability, and, conversely, shown how the opposite phenomenon can occur: the 'diffusion of benefits'. This occurs when the positive effects of the intervention extend beyond the target area (Eck, 2002). To mitigate the risk of displacement and other negative consequences, CPTED strategies need to undergo a well thought-out implementation process and prioritise social measures that address motivational aspects. Moreover, crime prevention strategies and programs need to be monitored and accordingly managed.

Another criticism refers to over-emphasising the deterministic role of physical environment and neglecting the social context. This may be due to the perceived difficulty in addressing motivational factors and regarding opportunity as the root cause of crime (Clarke, 1980). This criticism stimulated the development of second generation CPTED, which perceives crime as a social problem needing effective social solutions (Saville & Cleveland, 2008). The original environmental theorists contended places could not be defended without capable and willing guardians regardless of their physical properties. Social CPTED therefore rejects environmentally deterministic practices while providing more lasting crime prevention effects.

CPTED as Part of a Holistic Crime Prevention Approach

Although a distinct approach, CPTED is often applied as part of a suite of crime prevention initiatives. These include 'problem-oriented policing' (POP), 'community policing' and public–private partnerships (PPPs). This is beneficial considering the complexity of crime problems and the need for tailored approaches. POP, as an analytical policing strategy, devises solutions that correspond to particularly defined crime problems (Goldstein, 1990). Community policing fosters partnerships with communities and relevant agencies outside law enforcement to provide solutions to community-concerning problems (Office of Community Oriented Policing Services, 2012). PPPs are often established to supplement public policing in commercial and public settings (Prenzler & Sarre, 1998). CPTED therefore easily fits within each of these strategies and assists in realising public safety. Being subsumed under the umbrella of larger prevention strategies, however, sometimes makes it difficult to disentangle the distinct effects of CPTED.

Conclusions: CPTED for the Future

Looking back at the origins of CPTED, in conjunction with the developments that have been made since, one of the paths forward is to more clearly define the role of people as crime controllers. Good physical design, achieved through effective place management, needs to support and encourage informal guardianship and intended use of space. Equally important is advancing 'responsibilisation' strategies to encourage citizens to exercise care and control over shared spaces (Reynald, 2011). In light of this, one of the critical steps forward in the continued development of CPTED is better integration of physical and social elements in the delivery of CPTED strategies (Armitage, 2014), with the realisation that passive physical design is contingent upon active participation of people.

Future developments also need to pay more attention to the intricacies of implementation processes. Cozens and Love (2015) cautioned against oversimplifying CPTED theory and its implementation, and advocated moving away from the one-size-fits-all approach. This necessitates deepened analysis of the problem and contextual factors, and multi-stakeholder involvement in projects to incorporate relevant concerns and increase a sense of ownership. Moreover, this process needs to move beyond the traditional risk assessment checklists to also account for space users' perceptions of safety by employing tools such as safety audits (Wekerle & Whitzman, 1995). This may necessitate looking at the disciplines beyond criminology: the attitude that had characterised early developments of CPTED (Robinson, 1996). Only by rejecting a reductionist approach can we generate the environment conducive to advancement of the theory and reinforce the practical value of CPTED.

References

Angel, S. (1968). *Discouraging crime through city planning*. Berkeley, CA: Institute of Urban and Regional Development.

Armitage, R. (2014). Crime prevention through environmental design. In G. Bruinsma & D. Weisburd (Eds.), *Encyclopedia of criminology and criminal justice* (pp. 720–731). New York, NY: Springer.

Australian Council for New Urbanism. (2006). *Australian new urbanism: A guide to projects*. Melbourne: Ecologically Sustainable Design Limited.

Barr, R., & Pease, K. (1990). Crime placement, displacement, and deflection. *Crime and Justice, 12*, 277–318.

Brantingham, P.L., & Brantingham, P.J. (1981). Notes on the geometry of crime. In P.J. Brantingham & P.L. Brantingham (Eds.), *Environmental criminology* (pp. 27–54). Beverly Hills, CA: SAGE.

Brown, B., & Altman, I. (1983). Territoriality, defensible space and residential burglary: An environmental analysis. *Journal of Environmental Psychology, 3*, 203–220.

Brown, K.J. (2016). *You could get killed any day in Hollygrove: A qualitative study of neighborhood-level homicide* (Unpublished doctoral dissertation). University of New Orleans, Louisiana.

Carr, K., & Spring, G. (1993). Public transport safety: A community right and a communal responsibility. In R.V. Clarke (Ed.), *Crime prevention studies* (pp. 147–155). Monsey, NY: Criminal Justice Press.

Clarke, R.V. (1980). 'Situational' crime prevention: Theory and practice. *The British Journal of Criminology, 20*(2), 136–147.

Cohen, L., & Felson, M. (1979). Social change and crime rate trends: A routine activity approach. *American Sociological Review, 44*(4), 588–608.

Cornish, D., & Clarke, R. (1986). Introduction. In D. Cornish & R. Clarke (Eds.), *The Reasoning criminal: Rational choice perspectives on offending* (pp. 1–16). New York, NY: Springer-Verlag.

Cozens, P., & Love, T. (2015). A review and current status of crime prevention through environmental design (CPTED). *Journal of Planning Literature, 30*(4), 393–412.

Cozens, P., Saville, G., & Hillier, D. (2005). Crime prevention through environmental design (CPTED): A review and modern bibliography. *Property Management, 23*(5), 328–356.

Crowe, T. (2000). *Crime prevention through environmental design: Applications of architectural design and space management concepts*. Oxford, England: Butterworth-Heinemann.

Dickout, D. (2006). A community based approach to creating safer nightlife spaces: 2nd generation CPTED in action. *The CPTED Journal, 2*(1), 25–32.

Eck, J. (2002). Preventing crime at places. In L. Sherman, D. Farrington, B. Welsh & D. Layton MacKenzie (Eds.). *Evidence-based crime prevention* (pp. 241–294). New York, NY: Routledge.

Ellin, N. (1997). Shelter from the storm or form follows fear and vice versa. In N. Ellin (Ed.), *Architecture of fear* (pp. 13–45). New York, NY: Princeton Architectural Press.

Goldstein, H. (1990). *Problem-oriented policing*. New York, NY: McGraw-Hill.

Jacobs, J. (2011). *The death and life of great American cities (50th anniversary ed.)*. New York, NY: Modern Library. (Original work published 1961)

Jeffery, C. (1971). *Crime prevention through environmental design*. Beverly Hills, CA: SAGE.

Jeffery, C., & Zahm, D. (1993). Crime prevention through environmental design, opportunity theory, and rational choice models. In R. Clarke & M. Felson (Eds.), *Routine activity and rational choice: Advances in criminological theory* (pp. 323–350). New Brunswick, NJ: Transaction.

Johnson, S., & Bowers, K. (2010). Permeability and burglary risk: Are cul-de-sacs safer? *Journal of Quantitative Criminology, 26*(1), 89–111.

Kaplan, H., Bickman, L., Pesce, E., & Szoc, R. (1978). *Crime prevention through environmental design: Final report on schools demonstration, Broward County, Florida.* Arlington, VA: Westinghouse Electric Corporation.

Loukaitou-Sideris, A. (1999). Hot spots of bus stop crime: The Importance of environmental attributes. *Journal of the American Planning Association, 65*(4), 395–411.

National Culture Forum & Chief Cultural & Leisure Officers Association ([NCF & CLOA). (2011). *The role of culture and sport in reducing crime and anti-social behaviour.* Retrieved from http://www.cloa.org.uk/images/stories/The_role_of_Culture_and_Sport_in_reducing_crime_and_anti_social_behaviour.pdf

Newman, O. (1972). *Defensible space: Crime prevention through urban design.* New York, NY: Macmillan.

Office of Community Oriented Policing Services. (2012). *Community policing defined.* Washington, DC: US Department of Justice.

Prenzler, T., & Sarre, R. (1998). Regulating private security in Australia. *Trends and Issues in Criminal Justice, 98*(1–6).

Reynald, D. (2011). Translating CPTED into crime preventive action: A critical examination of CPTED as a tool for active guardianship. *European Journal on Criminal Policy and Research, 17*(1), 69–81.

Robinson, M. (1996). The theoretical development of 'CPTED': Twenty-five years of responses to C. Ray Jeffery. In S. William & F. Adler (Eds.), *The criminology of criminal law: Advances in criminological theory* (pp. 427–462). New Brunswick, NJ: Transaction.

Saville, G. (2017). The missing link in CPTED theory. In B. Teasdale & M. Bradley (Eds.), *Preventing crime and violence* (pp. 297–307). Cham, Switzerland: Springer International.

Saville, G., & Cleveland, G. (2008). Second-generation CPTED: The rise and fall of opportunity theory. In R. Atlas (Ed.), *21st Century security and CPTED* (pp. 79–90). Boca Raton, FL: CRC Press.

Saville, G., & Wong, P. (1994). *Exceeding the crime threshold: The carrying capacity of neighborhoods.* Paper presented at the 53rd Annual Meeting of the American Society of Criminology, Miami, Florida.

Schneider, T. (2006). Violence and crime prevention through environmental design. In H. Frumkin, R. Geller, I. Rubin & J. Nodvin (Eds.), *Safe and healthy school environments* (pp. 251–269). Oxford, England: Oxford University Press.

United Nations Interregional Crime and Justice Research Institute (UNICRI). (2011). *New energy for urban security: Improving urban security through green environmental design*. Retrieved from http://www.unicri.it/news/files/2011-04-01_110414_CRA_Urban_Security_sm.pdf

Wekerle, G., & Whitzman, C. (1995). *Safe cities: Guidelines for planning, design, and management*. New York, NY: Van Nostrand Reinhold.

Wikström, P. (2009). *Social ecology of crime*. Retrieved from http://www.oxfordbibliographies.com/view/document/obo-9780195396607/obo-9780195396607-0027.xml

Wilson, J., & Kelling, G. (1982). Broken windows. *The Atlantic Online*. Retrieved from http://www.lantm.lth.se/fileadmin/fastighetsvetenskap/utbildning/Fastighetsvaerderingssystem/BrokenWindowTheory.pdf

Wood, E. (1960). *A New look at ... the balanced neighborhood*. New York, NY: Citizens' Housing and Planning Council.

Wood, E. (1961). *Housing design: A social theory*. New York, NY: Citizens' Housing and Planning Council.

Chapter 8

Reducing Property Crime and Fraud: Twelve Case Studies

Tim Prenzler

The case studies in this chapter illustrate large reductions in crime through a range of situational interventions. Many of the cases involve collaboration between stakeholders, including police, security providers, business groups and residents. A number also illustrate the value of an experimental approach and running pilots before full implementation. The chapter concludes by drawing out lessons from the case studies, including the benefits of diagnostic research and the need for comprehensive impact measures.

Background

Many of the big gains in the global downturn in crime have been in property crime; in areas such as theft, burglary and motor vehicle theft. Much of this can be attributed to the expansion of situationally based security measures, or 'securitization' (Chapter 6 and Chapter 12). A good deal occurred through market-driven private-sector adoptions of security. In other cases, governments intervened in the market by mandating security. Examples include legislated standards for home security and vehicle security.

The case study summaries in this chapter include seven in the area of property crime reduction, selected to indicate something of the range of possible approaches and settings. The variety of cases available on the record is now extensive, including some highly inventive interventions (Center for Problem-Oriented Policing, 2016). For example, a project in New York City in the 1980s was successful in eliminating graffiti on subway trains through a systematic cleaning program. The approach included a commitment to keeping defaced carriages out of circulation, thereby removing the rewards for offenders (Sloan-Howitt & Kelling, 1990). It is sometimes the case that very simple changes have large effects on crime. In a UK study, for example, thefts from bags at a busy market were significantly reduced by widening aisles to improve surveillance (Poyner & Webb, 1997).

This chapter also includes five case studies on fraud reduction. Unfortunately, there were very few cases to choose from. This is surprising given that fraud appears to be one of the few areas of crime that is increasing globally — partly because of increased opportunities via the internet —

and fraud often represents the largest category of dollar losses attributed to crime (Prenzler, in press). Nonetheless, there are some studies showing potential for large gains; and simple measures, applied systematically, are sometime very effective. One example is 'proof of purchase' requirements to stop refund fraud (Challinger, 1996). Blais and Bacher (2007), in a study of insurance fraud, found that suspected 'claim padding' was reduced by simply including warnings about prosecution policy on company letters.

The focus of the present chapter is on property crime and fraud, but it must be said that crime prevention projects are often aimed at reducing these and other crimes simultaneously. This is especially the case with place-based projects, with success measured across both violent and property crimes.

Property Crime

Collective Security on Dutch Industrial Estates

In the late 1980s, at the 300 hectare Enschede-Haven industrial site, the Area Entrepreneur Association requested police increase patrols to reduce crime. Police analysed the offence profile for the area and suggested a partnership in which the police would support on-site private security. From that point, the following steps occurred (van den Berg, 1995):

1. The association formed a cooperative from the majority of the 410 companies.
2. Police established a Project Agency, which coordinated the cooperative, the police and local government.
3. A successful submission was made to a national government crime prevention body to subsidise the start-up costs of the project.
4. A government employment agency supported the recruitment of unemployed persons as security guards.
5. Police provided the guards with training.
6. Sufficient funds were collected to station a security guard on the estate outside business hours.
7. All alarm activations were channelled through one security firm's monitoring station.
8. The on-site guard checked activations before contacting police, thereby minimising false call outs.
9. The project was advertised on signage around the site.
10. The local council improved lighting and the general appearance of the area.

Van den Berg's (1995) evaluation does not describe how the project worked in terms of arrests or deterrence. However, security incidents were reduced by 72%, from 90 per month in the year-and-a-half before the project began to 25 per month in the year-and-a-half after it was established. The partnership continued as a self-funded project once the initial subsidy expired. A similar partnership on the Vianen industrial estate produced a 52% reduction in burglary (van den Berg, 1995).

The Kirkholt Project

One of the most famous anti-burglary initiatives on the record is the Kirkholt Project in the United Kingdom (Forrester, Frenz, O'Connell, & Pease, 1990). The project targeted repeat victimisation on a housing estate, and involved several strategies. Within a few days of a burglary, a crime prevention officer would conduct a security survey of the premises, with security hardware upgrades funded by the local Council's Housing Department. Another measure involved the removal of coin operated fuel meters, which attracted burglars. A specific form of Neighbourhood Watch — 'cocoon watch' — was also introduced. This involved asking victims' immediate neighbours to report suspicious activity. Cocoon watch participants were also given free security upgrades. Cocoon surveillance was based on a finding that 70% of burglary entry points were visible to neighbours. Burglary rates declined by 75%, from 44 per month before the project began to 11 per month in the third year after implementation, with no observable displacement. In fact, burglaries in neighbouring areas declined by 24%. In addition, multiple victimisations in the experimental site were reduced almost to zero. When savings from reduced burglaries were set against costs, the project produced an estimated overall saving of £1.2 million.

The Leicester Small Business and Crime Initiative

This initiative was focused on commercial burglary (Tilley & Hopkins, 1998). It was managed by a committee, with representatives from the city council, police and chamber of commerce. Funding was provided by a bank charity. Initial survey research informed a focus on repeat or 'chronic' victims. Security audits were carried out by a project officer following a police incident report. A mix of security devices was usually installed, including alarms and CCTV. Portable alarms were installed in some cases. These could be shared with other premises once risk periods for repeat offences had expired. Silent alarms were also used, with a view to capturing and incapacitating offenders after research found numerous offenders could complete a burglary following the activation of an audible alarm. The project resulted in very few arrests. However, burglary was reduced by 41%, from 735 incidents in the year before the project to 433 in the second and final year of evaluation. Criminal damage was reduced by 36%.

Stopping Prolific Burglars in Boggart Hill

A project targeting prolific burglars in Boggart Hill, in the United Kingdom, was successful in arresting repeat offenders in an initial 'crackdown' period, using profiling techniques that matched known offender methods with offence characteristics. In a traditional police operation, 'the response to the burglary problem would have ended there' (Farrell, Chenery, & Pease, 1998, p. 7). In the case of the Boggart Hill project, a 'consolidation phase' saw the installation of security hardware on burgled homes. The approach generated a 60% reduction in burglaries, from an average 44.9 per month pre-project to 18.5 in the consolidation phase. A 'hallow effect' or 'diffusion of benefits' was evident in a 36% drop in burglaries in adjoining areas.

Operation Identification in Wales

This operation was a UK Home Office demonstration project involving the large-scale application of property marking as a defence against domestic burglary in a small community (Laycock, 1991). Police and special constables visited residences offering free use of property marking equipment. On a second visit, officers took an inventory of the marked property. Window and door decals advertised the fact that property inside the home was marked. There were further visits and letters, and participation extended to 72% of households. The project received extensive media coverage, and known burglars were included in the home visits. In the 12 months before Operation Identification, participating households were the victims of 91 burglaries. This fell 61% to 35 burglaries after the operation began, with no evidence of displacement. For nonparticipants, the victimisation rate was stable, with 37 incidents before and 39 after the operation.

CCTV in Newcastle upon Tyne

The Newcastle upon Tyne City Centre Partnership Security Initiative is one of the few open space CCTV programs showing significant reductions in crime (Brown, 1995). The system was set up in 1992 with a combination of local private sector money and a government grant. Sixteen cameras were installed with zoom, pan and tilt capability. Police managed the system, with the CCTV control room linked by radio to patrol officers and retailers. Data about the concentration of crimes was used to locate cameras.

According to Brown (1995, p. 26), the system had a 'strong deterrent effect'. Cameras assisted rapid interventions by police, and the rate of arrests per criminal incidents increased. The system also assisted with convictions: 'Almost all of the 400 people arrested as a direct result of the scheme admitted guilt after being shown video footage' (in Brown, 1995, p. 26). The evaluation reported the average number of incidents across a range of crime types for 26 months before the program was fully implemented, and compared these with the average number for 15 months after implementation. Major findings for the area within the CCTV system were as follows (Brown, 1995, p. 17):

- Burglary was reduced by 57% from 40 incidents per month to 17 per month.
- Theft from motor vehicles declined 50% (18 to 9).
- Theft of motor vehicles declined 47% (17 to 9).
- Criminal damage declined 34% (32 to 21).
- Other theft declined 11% (223 to 198).

While the rate of arrests increased relative to the number of recorded offences, the overall number of arrests decreased as offences decreased. In addition, a diffusion of benefits was observed in adjoining areas, which experienced substantial, albeit smaller, reductions in crimes.

Strike Force Piccadilly: Combating ATM Ram Raids and Bam Raids in Sydney

Strike Force Piccadilly was set up in 2005 by the New South Wales' Police Property Crime Squad to counter a dramatic upsurge in ATM ram raids in the greater Sydney area. The Strike Force won two Australian Crime and Violence Prevention Awards and the 2013 international Herman Goldstein Award for Excellence in Problem-Oriented Policing.

Police were initially overwhelmed by the attacks on ATMs (see Figure 8.1). In some of the more destructive raids, gangs smashed through shopping centres in stolen vehicles and knocked over ATMs in central atriums. In mid-2006, the Piccadilly team convened a stakeholder forum, which led to the establishment of an ongoing partnership between police and security managers from the ATM Industry Association, the Australian Bankers' Association, cash-in-transit firms, and the Shopping Centre Council of Australia (Prenzler, 2011). Research and information sharing identified vulnerabilities around machines, including easy vehicle access and frequent false alarm activations that delayed police responses. The analysis led to a commitment to implement the following measures:

1. a police priority response 1800 number (based on multiple alarm activations)
2. the installation of situational prevention measures, including ATM relocations, specialist bollards (with anti-cutting technology) and anti-ramming devices (such as flexible base plates)
3. e-mail circulation of intelligence reports

4. publication of an ATM risk assessment and reduction guide

5. on-site CPTED-based advice by police crime prevention officers.

These changes were effective in producing large reductions in 'successful' raids (where cash was obtained) and 'unsuccessful' raids (involving considerable property damage). The rapid response system closed the raiders' timeframe, the relocations reduced access, and the bollards and anti-ramming devices increased target hardening. The reduced time frames assisted investigations, which led to the arrest and incapacitation of 97 persons between August 2005 and June 2007. Figure 8.1 shows the number of successful and unsuccessful ram raids on a three-month (quarterly) basis from October 2005 to March 2013. Over the longer term, there was a 100% reduction in successful raids, with no cases after August 2009. Unsuccessful raids declined by 84% from the initial peak period.

However, in 2008 criminal gangs adopted a new technique, which had spread overseas (Prenzler, 2011). Explosive gas attacks — or 'bam raids' — involve pumping combustible gases into ATMs and setting them alight, destroying the machine and allowing access to the cash canister. The outbreak of bam raids included 19 attacks in November 2008. Strike Force Piccadilly 2 was formed in July 2008. The strategies used in Piccadilly 1 were maintained, including the stakeholder meetings and 1800 hotline. In addition, ATM operators installed gas detection equipment. The detectors would trigger:

• a back-to-base alarm that alerted police on the priority system

• an audible alarm and release of smoke designed to act as deterrents

• release of a gas that mixed with the explosive gas, making it inoperable.

Figure 8.1

ATM ram raids and bam raids, Greater Sydney Area, October 2005 to March 2013.

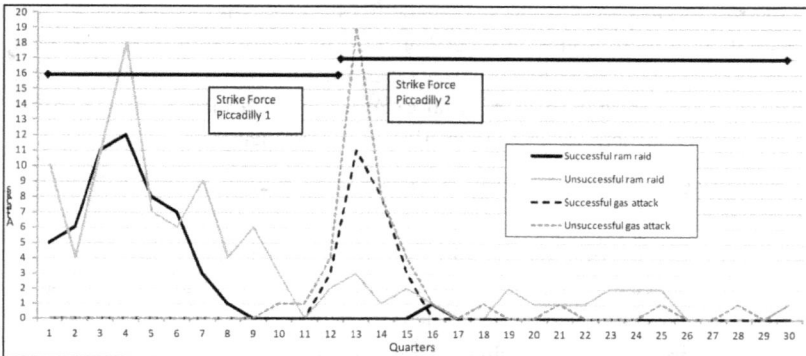

Source: Data provided by the New South Wales Police, August 2013. (Used with permission.)

The capture and incapacitation of a small group of specialist offenders was facilitated by CCTV footage and assistance from commercial partners in the preservation of crime scenes. Figure 8.1 shows there was a 100% reduction in successful bam raids, with no cases recorded after April 2009. Unsuccessful attacks declined by 95% from the peak period.

Fraud

Combating Fare Evasion on Public Transport in the Netherlands

Increases in 'fare dodging' (as well as 'vandalism, and aggression') on public transport in the Netherlands from the 1960s to the 1980s were attributed to cost-cutting measures, including removing the position of conductor (van Andel, 1989, p. 47). Opportunities for fare evasion were also enlarged by the introduction of additional doors on trams. In response to escalating problems, in 1984 the Ministry of Transport and Public Works supported the employment of 'Safety, Information and Control' officers — or VICs — on the tram and metro services in three cities to provide patrols and check tickets. In addition, from 1985, bus drivers were required to check all tickets as passengers boarded through the front door.

Evaluation of the fare evasion component of the project occurred through random checks on passengers; and a survey of passengers and staff. The results were complex, across three cities and three modes of transport. Overall, large reductions were found in the first year, with further drops in most cases in following years. The largest estimated declines in fare evasion in the first year were on the Amsterdam Metro, from 23.5% of passengers to 6.5% (-17%), and Rotterdam buses, from 14.1% to 2.4% (-11.7%) (pp. 50–51). The Hague tram system, where VICs could not impose fines, had an initial drop but without subsequent falls. Surveys showed that passengers noticed more inspections and were strongly supportive of the changes because they improved the fairness of the system. Staff were also supportive.

The new boarding procedures on buses involved a delay factor, which necessitated the assignment of extra buses. In two cities, the savings were estimated to almost completely cover the costs. The VIC program cost about three times the money that was saved, but the goals were not exclusively financial.

Reducing Cheque Fraud in Sweden

Knutsson and Kuhlhorn (1997) illustrate the relative ease of some forms of crime — and crime prevention — with the example of cheque fraud in Sweden. In the 1960s, banks would honour losses from fraudulent cheques up to 300 kronor without identification. This created an almost perfect opportunity for fraud, especially for large numbers of minor forgeries. Stockholm saw the proliferation of a trade in stolen cheques, where cheque crimes grew by 500% from 2,663 cases in 1965 to 15,817 in 1970. Banks and retailers were resistant to change until the scale of the problem forced them to negotiate with police. In 1971, the bank guarantee was withdrawn and proof of identity was required for all cheque transactions. The measure had a dramatic effect. Across Sweden, the number of reported cheque crimes fell 82% from 1970 to 1972. In Stockholm, offences fell 86% to 2,198. These reductions were sustained over subsequent years at between 10 and 20% of the peak levels.

Data-Matching Against Welfare Fraud in Sweden

Kuhlhorn (1997) reported on the introduction of a data-matching program for housing subsidies in Sweden. One database consisted of income estimates for recipients of housing subsidies (the target group). The other contained income estimates for recipients of sickness insurance. In the first database, applicants were motivated to understate their income with a view to increasing their subsidy. In the second database, applicants were motivated to overstate their income to increase their sickness benefit. The data-matching system was introduced in 1979. In the first year of operation, 39,408 households lost all or part of their subsidy (6.1% of checked households). Over two years there was a large increase in voluntary corrections. Kuhlhorn's study did not describe any prosecutions, nor were there any data on cost–benefit ratios. The study did, however, report the findings of an opinion poll on the program. The survey found that 94% of respondents thought the checks were appropriate, and 87% of housing subsidy clients in the sample supported the checks.

Chip and PIN Security and Plastic Card Fraud in the United Kingdom

In the United Kingdom, the replacement of signature and magnetic stripe security with 'chip and PIN' technology began with a trial in 2003 (Levi, 2008). (The computer chip on the card authenticates the personal identification number [PIN] entered by the customer.) The trial was initiated in response to the growing problem of card misuse, including forging signatures, theft of cards, and skimming and cloning. A survey of consumers in the trial area showed 83% supported the new technology. A national roll out, funded by the card companies, began later in 2003, which involved issuing approximately 140 million cards to 42 million customers, and upgrading hundreds-of-thousands of ATMs and retail terminals.

An evaluation by Levi (2008) covered two years of data across a number of categories. In relation to UK-issued cards in UK retail 'face-to-face' transactions, losses from fraud declined by 67%, from £218.8 million in 2004 to £72.1 million in 2006. The fraud category 'mail non-receipt' (mainly misuse of cards stolen from letters) saw an 81% fall from £79.9 million to £15.4 million. Other categories saw less dramatic falls. 'Counterfeit (skimmed/cloned) card fraud' fell by 23% and ATM fraud by 17%. Victimisation of UK cardholders abroad, where the new system did not operate, increased 43%.

Early Intervention Against Welfare Fraud in Australia

In 2011 to 2012, Australia's main welfare distributor, Centrelink, introduced a system of personal contact with clients to identify error and embryonic fraud. Introduction of the system was prompted by a legal case that reduced the criminal liability of customers who failed to inform Centrelink of changes in their eligibility. A set of pilot projects, mainly involving telephone communication, supported the roll out of a system that included SMS and e-mail 'reminders' about obligations to report changes in circumstances that might affect payments (Department of Human Services, 2012, p. 222). Centrelink already had a complex array of antifraud measures in operation — including identity verification procedures, covert surveillance and data-matching. However, the rates of detected fraud and prosecutions had been trending upwards, and Centrelink was losing tens of millions of dollars each year (Prenzler, 2016). Part of the problem was that administrative processes allowed 'non-compliance' to go undetected and unremedied for too long. Losses built up, and cases were then treated criminally as fraud. Clients drifted from what might have started as 'error' into 'full-blown' fraud.

When the new program was introduced, several antifraud strategies were also stepped up. However, direct contact was the main innovation in the period. The government reported that, in a five-month period, there were over 120,000 contacts under the 'front-foot initiative', saving an estimated A$37 million (Carr, 2012). The legal case also prompted a major downgrade of criminal matters. Overall, as Figure 8.2 shows, the number of fraud cases referred by Centrelink to the Commonwealth Director of Public Prosecutions (CDPP) declined by 80%, from a peak of 5,312 in 2007 to 2008 to a low of 1,071 in 2013 to 2014, the number of defendants declined by 78% from a peak of 4,684 in 2009 to 2010 to 1,008 in 2014 to 2015, while the number of convictions declined by 80% from a peak of 4,019 in 2009 to 2010 to 814 in 2014 to 2015.

Figure 8.2

Centrelink referrals to the CDPP, defendants and convictions, 1999–2000 to 2014–2015.

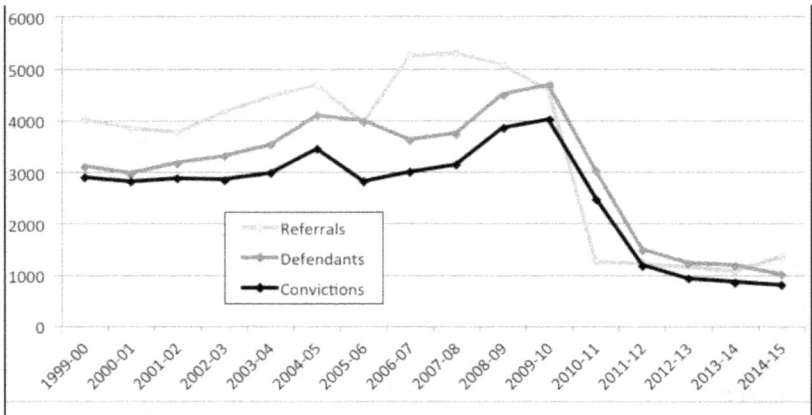

Source: Prenzler 2016, p. 193. (Used with permission.)

Implications

The case studies outlined above demonstrate the benefits of introducing situational prevention methods into diverse opportunity structures for crime. Techniques included target hardening, target removal, property identification, reducing anonymity, enlarged surveillance and guardianship, removing excuses, and rule setting and communication. These techniques were often implemented in various combinations. Benefits were also apparent from focusing on repeat victimisation, repeat offenders (to a lesser extent), and crime hot spots. The benefits of focused geographical place management were evident in the property crime cases. For example, one of the main explanations for the success of the Newcastle upon Tyne CCTV project, in comparison to similar but less successful projects, was that business activity was highly concentrated in the town centre, and camera coverage of likely crime locations was high. Industrial estates and small communities also included a defined area of responsibility, with limited access and reduced anonymity.

A number of the case studies were notable for using start-up funds to employ security officers, or to fund or subsidise security upgrades. Sources included taxpayer monies from government, business collectives where each member paid a small share, or charitable trusts. Initial success then led to self-sustaining programs. The Dutch cases were part of a wider crime prevention program facilitated by the national government, with planning and financial support. In that regard, the antiburglary cases can be compared with an unsuccessful Australian project. The Beenleigh Break and Enter Reduction Project, set up in the late-1990s, sought to apply lessons from the successful UK projects, but interventions were largely limited to free security advice and encouragement of property marking (National Crime Prevention, 2001). The lack of financial support most likely explained the failure to install security hardware. While the evaluation identified a decrease in repeat victimisations, overall incidents of burglary increased.

Another important lesson from the case studies concerns the role of police. The final chapter in this book refers to research showing the limited impact of police on crime prevention. However, this assessment was done at an international comparative level. A good number of the cases analysed in the present chapter showed local police in leadership and coordinating roles; and also playing a role in providing rapid response and arrests in association with actions taken by private sector partners. While the cases illustrate the common view that 'police cannot prevent crime on their own', they also show police are often essential partners on successful projects.

Readers will recall that situational crime prevention has been accused of lacking a social justice dimension. Clearly, however, there was a general public benefit in all of the case studies, whether in reduced victimisation across a wide range of persons or reduced costs to taxpayers. The Dutch crime prevention programs also provided social benefits through enhanced employment. The VICs project gave work to approximately 1,200 persons: '50 per cent had been unemployed, 30 per cent were women, and 25 per cent came from ethnic minorities' (van Andel, 1989, p. 49). Reduced crime opportunities also help potential offenders stay out of the criminal justice system.

Another lesson concerns the relative simplicity of many interventions, even when they involve advanced technology. In the case of mandated identification requirements for cashing cheques, Knutsson and Kuhlhorn describe how an 'expensive and ineffective system of formal control' — involving police investigations and prosecutions — was superseded by 'an inexpensive and effective situational control' based on reducing anonymity (1997, p. 116). Antifraud data-matching, on the other hand, involves sophisticated computing technology, but via a very simple principle of comparing records to identify inconsistencies. Kuhlhorn described the cross-referencing capacity of data-matching technology as 'a crime prevention Eldorado' (1997, p. 238). His analysis did not include cost–benefit estimates, but early research on data-matching against welfare fraud in the United States found savings were approximately twice the costs (Greenberg, Wolf, & Pfiester, 1986).

Democratic accountability is also a value implicit in these case studies. This is particularly important where public-sector resources are involved. Accountability is also relevant more generally, because criminal victimisation has wide-ranging effects and crime prevention interventions often entail issues about privacy and civil liberties. The case studies in this chapter, in the main, represent efforts to take an honest and scientific approach to program evaluation, including stakeholder experience and opinion surveys. However, this approach tends to be the exception rather than the rule. In many jurisdictions, millions of dollars are spent on crime prevention projects without proper evaluation and accountability (see Chapter 1). At the same time, most of the case studies in the chapter do not 'tick all the boxes' in terms of model practice. Post-intervention data were often limited to one or two years, leaving open the question of sustainability. Financial data were often missing entirely. Although, it is not essential for crime reduction projects to show a profit (see Chapter 1), financial data are important to full accountability.

Conclusion

Many of the cases summarised in this chapter showed exciting and quite extraordinary reductions in crime, with good evidence linking interventions to successful outcomes. Many of the projects exemplify democratic values of consultation and collaboration. Property crime and fraud remain significant problems around the world, with many millions of victims each year. The small number of case studies selected for this chapter show that large reductions in these crimes can be achieved through determined efforts, including systematic program development and implementation.

References

Blais, E., & Bacher, J. (2007). Situational deterrence and claim padding: Results from a randomized field experiment. *Journal of Experimental Criminology, 3*, 337–352.

Brown, B. (1995). *CCTV in town centres: Three case studies.* London, England: Home Office.

Carr, K. (2012, December 18). *Prevention better than cure for social security system.* Retrieved from http://pandora.nla.gov.au/pan/65939/20130322-1615/www.mhs.gov.au/media/media_releases/2012/12/18_dec_2012_-_prevention_better_than_cure_for_social_security_system.html

Center for Problem-Oriented Policing. (2016). *Situational crime prevention evaluation database.* Retrieved from http://www.popcenter.org/library/scp/

Challinger, D. (1996). Refund fraud in retail stores. *Security Journal, 7*(1), 27–35.

Department of Human Services (2012). *Annual report, 2011–12.* Canberra, Australia: Author.

Farrell, G., Chenery, S., & Pease, K. (1998). *Consolidating police crackdowns: Findings from an antiburglary project.* London, England: Home Office.

Forrester, D., Frenz, S., O'Connell, M., & Pease, K. (1990). *The Kirkholt Burglary Prevention Project: Phase II.* London, England: Home Office.

Greenberg, D., Wolf, D., & Pfiester, J. (1986). *Using computers to combat welfare fraud*. Westport, CT: Greenwood.

Knutsson, J., & Kuhlhorn, E. (1997). Macro-measures against crime: The example of check forgeries. In R. Clarke (Ed.), *Situational crime prevention: Successful case studies* (pp. 113–121). Guilderland, NY: Harrow and Heston.

Kuhlhorn, E. (1997). Housing allowances in a welfare society: Reducing the temptation to cheat. In R. Clarke, (Ed.), *Situational crime prevention: Successful case studies* (pp. 235–241). Monsey, NY: Criminal Justice Press

Laycock, G. (1991). Operation Identification, or the power of publicity? *Security Journal, 2*(2), 67–72.

Levi, M. (2008). Combating identity and other forms of payment fraud in the UK. *Crime Prevention Studies, 23*, 111–131.

National Crime Prevention. (2001). *Lightning strikes twice: Preventing repeat home burglary*. Canberra, Australia: Attorney-General's Department.

Poyner, B., & Webb, B. (1997). Reducing theft from shopping bags in city centre markets In R. Clarke (Ed.), *Situational crime prevention: Successful case studies* (pp. 83-89). Guilderland, NY: Harrow and Heston.

Prenzler, T. (2011). Strike Force Piccadilly and ATM security: A follow-up study. *Policing: A Journal of Policy and Practice, 5*(3), 236–247.

Prenzler, T. (2016). Welfare fraud prevention in Australia: A follow-up study. *Crime Prevention and Community Safety, 18*(3), 187–203.

Prenzler, T. (in press). Fraud victimisation and prevention. In A. Deckert & R. Sarre (Eds.), *The Australian and New Zealand handbook of criminology, crime and justice*.

Sloan-Howitt, M., & Kelling, G. (1990). Subway graffiti in New York City: "Gettin' up" vs. "Meanin' it and Cleanin' it". *Security Journal, 1*(3), 131–136.

Tilley, N., & Hopkins, M. (1998). *Business as usual: An evaluation of the Small Business and Crime Initiative*. London, England: Home Office.

van Andel, H. (1989). Crime prevention that works: The care of public transport in the Netherlands. *British Journal of Criminology, 29*(1), 47–56.

van den Berg, E. (1995). Crime prevention on industrial sites: Security through public-private partnerships. *Security Journal, 6*(1), 27–35.

Chapter 9

Reducing Violence and Disorder: Seven Case Studies

Tim Prenzler and Mateja Mihinjac

This chapter reports on evaluated situationally oriented intervention projects designed to reduce problems of violence and disorder. As in the previous chapter on property crime and fraud, the case studies are selected on the basis of evidence of substantial reductions in targeted offences. The question of evidence is important when looking for exemplar cases with lessons than can be applied in other locations. Consequently, the summaries include attention to issues of impact measurement, as well as key process aspects of the projects — including diagnostics, stakeholders, collaboration, community responses and, in some cases, factors contributing to the breakdown of projects. The chapter begins with a brief outline of the global problem of violence and dimensions of victimisation. The scale of the problem is enormous, creating a major and urgent policy challenge for prevention science.

Background

Cases studies showing large-scale and sustained reductions in violence and disorder are difficult to find. In fact, of the seven case studies summarised in this chapter, only one fulfils both these criteria. The small number of case studies on effective reductions in violence in the scientific literature internationally stands in marked contrast to the enormous size of the problem (UNODC, 2014; START, 2016; also see 'violence' at Center for Problem-Oriented Policing[1]). Some countries, particularly in Central and South America, Africa and the Middle East, suffer chronic rates of murder, kidnappings, robberies, assaults, gang violence and terrorist attacks, which cause enormous personal suffering, debilitate civil life, and stymie economic and political development. In many other countries, the personal risks of violence may be lower but consciousness of risk has a negative effect on citizens' feelings of safety and freedom, especially more physically vulnerable sections of the population (van Dijk, 2008). In the area of domestic violence, research indicates that approximately one third of women will experience

---

1 www.popcenter.org/library/scp/

some form of domestic violence in their lifetime, and this seems to be fairly consistent around the globe (World Health Organization [WHO], 2014).

It also appears to be the case that, internationally since the 1990s, violent crime has not seen the same types of large reductions in rates as occurred with property crimes (Australian Institute of Criminology [AIC], 2016; van Dijk, Tseloni & Farrell, 2012). This is possibly because the 'securitization' process that lies behind much of the 'international crime drop' is either more effective against property crime or more targeted towards property crime through corporate applications. Property crimes such as burglary, theft and motor vehicle theft tend to occur in large volumes and have been reduced in relatively large numbers through the application of increasingly sophisticated security technologies that make crime more difficult to commit (van Dijk, 2012). Violence often involves an opportunity structure that is less amenable to manipulation. For example, incidents might be infrequent, highly dispersed and difficult to predict. A good deal of violence also occurs between intimates or acquaintances in situations where it is difficult for third parties, such as police or security services, to intervene. One exception to this pattern is robbery, which is a kind of violent property crime and has seen substantial reductions in many cases, most likely as a result of securitization (van Dijk, 2008).

Violence has diverse adverse effects, and international surveys indicate support services are generally inadequate (van Dijk, 2008). There are the obvious tangible harms involving loss of life, as well as injuries across a spectrum from minor pain, cuts and bruises to major physical trauma and permanent disability. There are also numerous indirect impacts, such as post-traumatic stress disorder, including elevated fear of crime. Many victims of violence, including the love ones of homicide victims, simply never recover from their loss. Direct and indirect forms of victimisation represent a major public health problem and a large financial cost, mainly to health systems and emergency services. One example concerns traffic crashes, which should be considered a type of violent crime. In Australia in recent years there has been a fairly static rate of approximately 1,500 fatalities and 40,000 injured persons requiring hospitalisation per annum, costing the community at least $18 billion (Prenzler, Manning & Bates, 2015, p. 93; Productivity Commission, 2016). Economic analyses of terrorism indicate that repeat attacks have highly damaging effects on national economies through reduced business confidence and reductions in tourism (Prenzler, et al., 2015, p. 91).

Overall then there is a very strong case for greater investment in experiments to reduce violence. The following cases studies have been selected both to instruct and inspire. They illustrate forms of success against diverse crime types, and the format involves an honest reportage of weaknesses and failures in project design, implementation and outcomes.

Case Studies

Operation Cul-de-Sac: Preventing Gang Crime in Los Angeles

Operation Cul-de-Sac was an initiative of the Los Angeles Police Department targeted at gang crime in South Central Los Angeles, particularly drive-by shootings, following the failure of traditional arrest strategies (Lasley, 1996). A preliminary analysis found that shootings and other criminal activities, such as assaults and drug trafficking, were concentrated in thoroughfares that allowed easy vehicular and pedestrian access to targets and quick escape routes. To address the problem, in 1990, 14 major roads leading to and from the hotspots were blocked off with road barriers. The barriers, installed in a ten block area, consisted of fixed iron fences, with a lock that could only be opened for emergency vehicles, as well as some planter boxes.

The project evaluation employed a variety of data from one year before the intervention to two years following the intervention. The main pre-intervention numbers were for 1989, while 1990 was a phase-in year when the barriers were installed and intensified police patrols, including foot and bicycle patrols, were activated alongside the barriers. In 1991 the barriers were the only innovation that continued. In 1992 the program was discontinued and many of the gates were vandalised and rendered ineffective. A comparison area was chosen to account for other potential factors that might have contributed to outcomes and to identify possible displacement effects.

The following major changes were identified in the evaluation (Lasley, 1996):

- The number of drive-by shootings recorded by police in the target area reduced from 38 in 1989, the year prior to the intervention, to one in 1990, the year of the implementation of the intervention (-95%). No data were available for the second and main year of the program because the police withdrew their support for the evaluation.
- The number of murders averaged 5+ per year prior to the intervention, and five in 1989. There was then one murder in the following two years (-90%).
- The totality of selected 'predatory' crimes ('murder, rape, street robbery, aggravated assault and purse snatching') fell from 332 the year before the intervention to 307 in the first year post-intervention and then to 243 in the second year (1992); making for a total reduction of 27% (pp. 54–56).
- Within that figure, the number of aggravated assaults fell from approximately 191 the year before the intervention to 171 in the first year post-intervention and then to 139 in the second year (1992); also making for a total reduction of approximately 27%.
- Overall crime in the area fell by 20%.

- Displacement was not detected. Most crimes were stable in neighbouring areas. There was a possibility of some 'positive displacement,' with reductions in murders and drive-by shootings in neighbouring areas (p. 48).

- There was also no evidence of 'adaptation effects', involving offenders finding alternative means of committing offences (p. 49).

- 81% of 42 residents interviewed about the barrier system felt it had a positive effect, 98% believed it had reduced drive-by shootings, and 86% felt safer in the area and in their homes. Furthermore, 63% said the barriers 'restored order' and 71% said they went out more (p. 79). These effects were primarily attributed to the barriers reducing the 'flow of strangers', perceived as a threat to locals (p. 80). There was also a perceived 'defensible space' effect through reduced fear of retaliation when reporting crimes to police. At the same time, the barriers were also seen as ugly and inconvenient.

- There was a small increase in school attendance, which was attributed to students and parents feeling that travel to and from school was safer.

Soon after the program ended and the barriers were removed, the overall crime rate returned to the levels before the intervention, while homicide rates went higher as a result of renewed and intensified drive-by shootings by gangs from both sides of the barriers.

Staying Home Leaving Violence: Preventing Repeat Domestic Violence in New South Wales

'Staying Home Leaving Violence' is a large domestic violence reduction program in New South Wales, Australia, managed by the Department of Family and Community Services (DFCS, 2016). A range of individual support services is provided to combat homelessness, harassment and violence. Security measures include maintenance or upgrading of fences, trimming shrubs, sensor lights, padlocks on electricity boxes, door and window locks, security doors and screens, 'SOS' personal alarms ,and CCTV (Breckenridge, Walden, & Flax, 2014).

An evaluation by Breckenridge et al. (2014) employed 12 months of data from 2012 to 2013 covering 22 sites. An exit survey of 100 female clients was supplemented by in-depth interviews with 21 clients, interviews and focus groups with 36 service providers, and police dispatch data post-intervention. It was not possible to create a control group for comparative purposes; however, the findings were extremely positive. For example, the survey data showed the following (pp. 7 and p. 58):

- 93.3% of respondents said they were living in a home they believed was safe over the long term,

- 52.5% were still living in their home,
- of those who moved, 84.7% said they had chosen to move,
- 87% felt safer at home than when they entered the program, and
- 83% said their children were safer (only 8% disagreed).

Two-thirds of interviewees had experienced harassment or a breach of an order, although these incidents were not considered a major threat. Typical comments in the interviews regarding the alarms included (in Breckenridge et. al., 2014, p. 102):

> ... it changed a lot ... that little alarm made me feel so much better. I was able to sleep knowing that it's there.

> I feel relief ... Everywhere I go it's with me, even night time ... not just for me, it's for my kids too. They know this alarm ... my children they feel safe.

Professional service providers agreed the program was crucial in ensuring safe and stable housing (Breckenridge et. al., 2014). This laid the foundation for participants to pursue their legal rights and address education and employment needs. The service providers also considered CCTV systems particularly useful in enhancing security by allowing clients to surveille the exterior of their residence and document any breaches of orders. The evaluation of police dispatch data for two years post-intervention showed 14 genuine dispatches, with police action leading to charges against three men.

The Kansas City Relighting Program: Targeting Night-time Street Crime

This initiative involved a partnership between the Kansas City Department of Public Works and the United States National Institute for Law Enforcement and Criminal Justice (Wright, Heilweil, Pelletier, & Dickinson, 1974). The institute had been interested in exploring the relationship between street lighting and crime, and the Kansas City government agreed to participate and accept a proposed evaluation process. A grant was provided to support the program, with the evaluation carried out by the University of Michigan. Rising crime rates in the city provided the context for the project. Work began with exploratory studies of crime locations and optimal levels of lighting. A number of commercial and residential areas were selected for lighting upgrades. The focus was on violent 'street' crime occurring at night, especially robbery. The 'relighting' process was described as follows (Wright et al., 1974, p. 1):

> Between October 1971 and March 1972, 1800 mercury and sodium streetlights were installed in approximately 500 blocks in the downtown business district and a mixed residential/commercial

neighbourhood. These lights replaced the older incandescent illumination in these blocks.

The project evaluation involved a complex design with diverse findings. The main positive impact was in the target area of violent crime occurring at night, mainly robbery. In the 12 months prior to the lighting upgrade, night-time street robberies had increased by 32% in the target blocks (Wright et al., 1974, p. 49). In the 12 months post-installation, robberies in this category decreased by 52%, from 67 to 32. Street assaults at night had increased by 40% prior to the upgrade, and then decreased by 41%, from 37 to 22. There was a small reduction in robbery in the 'non-relit blocks' and a very small increase in assaults. While there did not appear to be any displacement of robberies to relit streets during the day (temporal displacement) and also 'nonstreet locations' (such as alleyways, parks and schoolyards) in relit blocks (spatial displacement), there were large increases in assaults in these areas (+67% for night-time nonstreet locations, from 21 to 35, and +78% for daytime street locations, 21 to 35). Overall, despite these negatives, the researchers saw the project as a success: 'The crimes of primary interest in this study – night street crimes of violence, which are the crimes that most terrorise people – showed dramatic and significant responsiveness to upgraded street lighting' (p. 58).

Reducing Robbery in Gainesville Convenience Stores

The City of Gainesville Florida is famous in the crime prevention literature for a bold approach to preventing robberies in convenience stores. The prevention program came out of a crime crisis. Across the period 1981 to 1986 there were 234 robberies of convenience stores, mainly armed robberies. Of 47 stores, 96% were victimised at least once, 81% twice or more, and 47% five or more times (Clifton, 1987). In 1985, the police department engaged with the convenience store industry to identify possible solutions. Criminologists and security consultants were also involved in a detailed situational analysis of the robberies. This revealed that the majority of offences occurred between 7pm and 5am (74%), and that stores with visible security cameras and time-release safes had lower victimisation rates. Interviews with offenders revealed that they targeted stores with poor visibility inside and outside, and preferred times when there was only one clerk on duty.

In response to the findings, stores agreed to a voluntary program to reduce these risk factors. However, implementation was poor and police successfully lobbied for the introduction by the city of the Gainesville Convenience Store Ordinance. The 1986 legislation mandated the following security features in stores (Clifton, 1987, p. 12):

- removal of window signs to allow a clear view of the sales area
- location of the sales area for visibility from outside

- cash minimisation ($50 in the till) through the use of time release drop safes
- signage informing of limited cash
- lighting standards in parking lots to remove hiding places
- installation of visible CCTV
- mandatory 'robbery prevention training' for night-time staff.

Following a six-month trial period that failed to achieve desirable outcomes, the Ordinance was amended in early 1987 to mandate two clerks on duty at high-risk times between 8 pm and 4 am.

There are a number of different accounts of the impacts of the interventions, although sources indicate an overall long-term reduction in offences of approximately 80% from the peak year of 1986. An initial report by the Police Chief stated there was a 64% reduction in robberies, from 55 to 20, across comparable nine month periods in 1986 and 1987 before and after the full intervention package (Clifton, 1987, p. 14). For the same period, there was a 75% reduction in robberies in the 8 pm to 4 am time period, from 36 down to nine. Subsequently, Hunter and Ray Jeffrey (1997) reported reductions in convenience store robberies in Gainesville from 97 in 1986 to 39 in 1987 (-60%), and continuing downward to 18 in 1990, the final year of their study (-81%) (p. 198; see also Schmerler, Perkins, Phillips, Rinehart & Townsend, 2006, pp. 33–34).

However, a study commissioned by the National Association of Convenience Stores — which opposed the two clerk ordinance — argued that the decline in offences began in the months before the two-clerk rule came into effect and that that the reductions were largely attributable to the arrest of three prolific offenders (Erickson, 1998). It was also argued that the 1986 offence rate was an abnormality attributable mainly to prolific offenders. Clifton (1987) had reported 30 offences in 1984 and 33 in 1985, prior to the spike to 97 in 1986. At the same time, another subsequent study reported that the convenience store lobby successfully influenced state government to override the Gainesville ordinance, beginning with actions in 1990 that diminished the effect of the ordinance (Schneider & Kitche, 2002, p. 143). By 1995 and following years, offences had risen to rates similar to those before the ordinance was enacted at approximately 28 per year. In addition, there appears to be support from a range of convenience store robbery studies for the benefits of appropriate combinations of the CPTED measures in the Gainesville package (e.g., Erickson, 1998; Hunter & Ray Jeffrey, 1997).

The Australian National Firearms Agreement and Mass Shootings

At around 9.30 am on December 14, 2012, 20-year-old Adam Lanza walked onto the grounds of the Sandy Hook Elementary School in Newtown

Connecticut. He carried a military-style semi-automatic rifle and two semi-automatic handguns that belonged to his mother, whom he had shot dead earlier. Lanza started shooting, eventually killing 20 children aged between six and seven, and killing six staff members, before fatally shooting himself (Australian Broadcasting Commission [ABC], 2012). This mind-boggling act led to renewed calls for gun control legislation in the United States, with references to the 1996 Australian National Firearms Agreement (NFA) as an exemplar. The issue prompted a study by Lemieux, Bricknell, and Prenzler (2015), which was the first to make direct comparisons of mass shootings between the two countries.

The study made use of two databases: one private and one public sector. The absence of an official government source in the United States meant that the researchers had to use a private database, derived largely from Media reports. This meant that it was likely that many cases were missed, especially domestic violence cases that received much less attention than 'spree killings' in public or semi-public places. The Australian data were drawn from the Australian Homicide Monitoring Program, managed by the federal government agency the Australian Institute of Criminology. Based on police records, this is a comprehensive and reliable source. There were a number of other constraints. The researchers were obliged to adopt a US Federal Bureau of Investigation definition of mass shootings, involving four or more fatalities. This meant that attacks involving three or less fatalities were not counted, and injuries were not included. Consequently, the data represented just the 'tip of the iceberg' of the problem.

The study obtained data for 33 years from 1981 to 2013. A very complicated legislative picture applied in the United States involving state and federal regulations. Overall, US legislation was extremely liberal and allowed ordinary citizens to own arsenals that included military-style assault weapons. The Australian NFA, introduced in late 1996, was developed in response to the killing of 35 persons in a spree shooting at Tasmania's Port Arthur tourist park. Prime Minister John Howard was able to seize the moment and persuade all the states and territories to sign up to a regulatory framework with the following key elements (Lemieux et al., 2015, pp. 132 and 133):

- a ban on automatic weapons and very limited access to semi-automatic weapons
- comprehensive licensing for all firearms
- licensed ownership of mainly low calibre weapons permitted for work purposes (e.g., removing feral animals) and sport (including mandatory membership of a club)
- self-defence not an acceptable reason
- 28 days waiting period

- training requirements
- secure storage requirements
- discretion for regulators around 'fit & proper person' criteria, with exclusions and revocations for disqualifying offences (e.g., violence, drugs) and domestic violence protection orders
- a 12 months prosecution amnesty and large-scale buy-back for weapons deemed illegal (approximately 700,000 weapons were surrendered).

Table 9.1 shows the number of mass shooting incidents and deceased victims (excluding offenders) identified in the Lemieux et al. (2015) study. While the datasets could not accurately map all dimensions of the topic, the table shows a marked contrast between the two countries. Australia had 13 mass shootings, with 104 fatalities, leading up to and including the Port Arthur Massacre, but the problem was eliminated — within the framework of the study — following the NFA. In the United States, a major problem worsened, with 24 incidents and 190 fatalities up to 1996, and 49 incidents and 386 fatalities after 1996.

The Surfers Paradise Safety Action Project and Alcohol-fuelled Disorder

This project was established in 1993 as a multipartner initiative designed to reduce violence within and around licensed venues in the major tourist area of Surfers Paradise, Australia. Periodic police crackdowns had proven unsuccessful, and mounting community and business concern forced authorities to take action. The initiative came from a criminologist, who obtained a cooperation from key stakeholders and a federal grant to support the work as a 'demonstration project' (Homel, Hauritz, Wortley, McIlwain, & Carvolth, 1997, p. 44). It was managed through a steering committee involving the Gold Coast City Council, state health department, police, the local chamber of commerce, a tourist promotion body, the liquor regulator and a university research team. A project officer coordinated the day-to-day oper-

Table 9.1

'Mass Shootings'*, Australia and the United States, 1981 to 1996 and 1997 to 2013

	Incidents		Fatalities	
	Australia	United States	Australia	United States
1981 to 1996 (16 years)	13	24	104	190
1997 to 2013 (17 years)	0	49	0	386
Total	13	73	104	576

Note:

* Four or more fatalities excluding the shooter.

Source: Adapted from Lemieux et al. (2015).

ations and stakeholder liaison. An initial assessment of the nature and causes of the problem led to the development and implementation of the following interventions (Homel et al., 1997):

- enlarged responsible service practices to reduce drinks discounting and service of alcohol to intoxicated individuals and underage clients
- publication of responsible service policy
- reduced noise levels
- improved cleanliness
- availability of lower alcohol drinks
- upgraded entertainment
- more professional, less aggressive, security staff
- more rigorous identification checks
- improved availability of food
- improved access and reduced crowding around bars to reduce situational precipitators of conflict
- more public transport.

The evaluation involved multiple sources including field observations of 18 nightclubs over two summers in 1993 and 1994 (pre- and post-intervention). The observation data revealed significant reductions in incidents of verbal abuse (-82%, from12.5 to 2.3 per 100 hours of observation) and arguments (-68%, from 7.1 to 2.3 per 100 hours) (Homel, et al., 1997, p. 70). Physical assaults declined by 52% as a rate per 100 hours. However, this was not statistically significant given the small numbers involved: 11 and 4 incidents. Police records showed reductions in incidents of 'drunk and disorderly' conduct across comparable five month periods pre- and post-implementation — from 258 to 146 (-43%); and assaults — from 50 to 33 (-34%). There was no evidence of displacement of violence or disorder to neighbouring areas. In 1994 the approach was replicated in three cities: Cairns, Townsville and Mackay – with similar positive outcomes (Hauritz, Homel, Mcllwain, Burrows & Townsley, 1998).

In Surfers Paradise, the project plan included an 'intensive intervention' period with a major role for the project officer (Homel et al., 1997, p. 76). The idea was then to move from this 'person-dependent' form of management to 'process-dependent' program maintenance by stakeholders, including venue management and the regulator. However, data for 1996 showed that aggression, conflict and violence had largely returned to pre-intervention levels. Stakeholder testimony indicated that 'many licensees were flaunting its provisions in order to secure short-term profits' and that the liquor licensing regulator 'failed to discipline the errant operators' (p. 77).

Victoria's Travel Safe Program

A Travel Safe program in Victoria, Australia, was introduced in late 1990 to address problems of assaults, vandalism, and intimidating and offensive behaviour on the public transport system (buses, trains, trams), along with associated problems of cancelled services, negative media and reduced patronage (Carr & Spring, 1993). The program was initiated from within the Public Transport Corporation, with better data for diagnostics, community consultation (mainly through a 'consultative community forum') and consultation with experts (p. 149). Out of this process the following interventions were implemented:

1. Rapid removal of graffiti and litter, and rapid repair of vandalised property, to improve positive perceptions of the transport system and deny benefits to graffiti offenders.
2. Installation of security devices such as security phones, better lighting (including at bus and tram shelters) and CCTV.
3. High security in stabling yards.
4. Greater circulation and visibility of staff amongst passengers.
5. Increased security guard presence, and increased guards and police at higher risk times and places.
6. A personal escort service for passengers to parked cars.
7. Community volunteers involved in the removal of physical signs of incivilities and in landscaping in order to increase a sense of ownership.

The results after two years of the program included a reduction of crimes against the person, mainly assaults, by 42% from an average of 57.3 to 33.1 incidents per month. At one stage during 1990 the number of broken train windows averaged 700 per week. This declined to 110 per week in 1992 (-84%). Graffiti 'hits' also declined significantly. Services were more reliable and the availability of trains increased in peak periods from 65% to 70% to 98%.

Implications

These case studies illustrate the potential efficacy of a variety of mainly situationally based measures to reduce violence and disorder. These included target hardening (e.g., street barriers to prevent gang-related violent crime, and home security to protect victims of domestic violence), enlarged guardianship (increased staffing to prevent convenience store robberies), assisting natural surveillance and increased formal surveillance (better lighting to prevent street robberies at night, and increased security patrols on public transport), restricting access to tools for crime (licensing firearms and prohibiting military-style assault weapons to prevent mass shootings), denying benefits (graffiti removal to reduce vandalism), and reducing frustrations (less crowding, more food and better entertainment to prevent violence in nightclubs).

As in the previous chapter on reductions in property crime and fraud, the case studies in the present chapter highlighted the importance of diagnostics in the design of programs. Prevention strategies need to suit the specific types of opportunities that occur within program parameters, and this can only be achieved through an initial study of as many factors as possible that may be facilitating crime. In most of the case studies, success was also associated with place-based interventions concerned with specific geographical locations or hot spots for crime. A big advantage of this approach is that there is a clear focus on a manageable area, and resources can be targeted where they are most likely to have the largest effect.

Another feature of the case studies in this chapter, as in the previous chapter, was the role of partnerships. This ensures 'buy in' from all the main groups who need to make contributions within their sphere of influence in order to optimise outcomes. This is usually best managed through a steering committee, with open and honest dialogue within a respectful environment.

The case studies on violence and disorder also exhibited a variety of evaluation methods, including consistent pre- and post-intervention measures. Most involved more than one measure of crime, and in most cases this allowed for reinforcement of the findings. A number allowed for forms of experimental controls through the inclusion of comparison groups, which also allowed for consideration of possible displacement effects. Nonetheless, a number of the case studies suffered from limitations in their evaluation protocols. None had detailed financial cost–benefit data, and most had fairly short pre- and post-intervention periods.

In three case studies with longer follow-up periods — Operation Cul-de-Sac, the Surfers Paradise Safety Action Project, and the Gainesville robbery ordinance — it appeared that the interventions were abandoned and crime rebounded. In the case of Operation Cul-de-Sac, this was attributed to the disengagement of the Los Angeles Police Department in the highly charged political environment that developed at the time — particularly in regard to alleged police racism, highlighted in the Rodney King beating of 1991. The road barriers were seen by some as an imposition by police on black communities, creating a 'living prison' (in Lasley, 1996, p. 27). The evaluation report concluded that police should have engaged in community consultation about the barriers, and responded to community preferences and concerns. In the Surfers Paradise case, the loss of the project officer in the context of a weak government enforcement culture meant that private operators reverted to irresponsible alcohol serving practices in the interests of maximising profits. In the Gainesville case, it was reported that opposition from the convenience store industry, concerned about costs, led to a dilution of the interventions.

The one case study that showed a sustained positive impact was the Australia National Firearms Agreement in preventing mass shootings, and this, at least in part, related to the persistence of a cross-party, cross-jurisdictional, consensus on the package of controls and consistent application across the country (Lemieux, et al., 2015). The NFA represents a legislated solution to a crime problem. This was also allegedly the case with the Gainesville robbery ordinance. The impact of legislation is, of course, always dependent on the clarity of wording and the level of enforcement.

Only one of the case studies — The Kansas City relighting program — included evidence of possible significant adverse displacement effects. In contrast, the Los Angeles road closure project included a possible 'positive displacement' effect. However, in both these cases there was essentially one intervention — lighting or road closures — and the negative displacement problem simply highlights the fact that crime has multiple causes and therefore usually requires multiple forms of prevention. Personality, family and social background can create determined offenders who will seek alternative crime opportunities when ones readily to hand are shut down (Chapter 2 to Chapter 5). The author of the Project Cul-de-Sac evaluation emphasised how opportunity reduction through street closures was 'focused on a proximate cause rather than a 'root cause' of crime (Lasley, 1998, p. 2). The root cause was located in the economic decline, rapid population growth, high unemployment and poverty that were allowed to develop in South Central Los Angeles in the 1970s.

Conclusion

Drawing from a selection of case studies, this chapter has demonstrated the potential of a variety of situationally based crime prevention strategies to reduce violence and disorder. The chapter focused on 'successful' case studies, although some failed following initial successes and others involved some elements of failure as well: small reductions in some crimes and/or apparent displacement. However, both the success and the failures provide important lessons about diagnostics in design, multiple measures, partnerships, consultation and maintenance. Overall, the case studies demonstrate the crucial role of leadership in both the public and private sectors in making crime prevention happen — or not happen.

References

Australian Broadcasting Commission (ABC). (2012). *School massacre victims shot multiple times.* Retrieved from http://www.abc.net.au/news/2012-12-16/gunman-who-killed-26-27forced27-his-way-into-us-school/4430128.

Australian Institute of Criminology (AIC). (2016). *Australian crime: Facts & figures 2014*. Canberra: Author.

Breckenridge, J., Walden, I., & Flax, G. (2014). *Staying Home Leaving Violence evaluation*. Sydney, Australia: Gendered Violence Research Network, University of New South Wales.

Carr, K., & Spring, G. (1993). Public transport safety. *Crime Prevention Studies, 1*, 147–155.

Clifton, W., Jr. (1987). *Convenience store robberies in Gainesville, Florida: An Intervention strategy by the Gainesville Police Department*. Gainesville, FL: Gainesville Police Deparment.

Department of Family and Community Services (DFCS). (2016). *Staying Home Leaving Violence*. Retrieved from http://www.community. nsw.gov.au/parents,-carers-and-families/domestic-and-family-violence/staying-home-leaving-violence.

Erickson, R. (1998). *Convenience store security at the millennium*. Alexandria, VA: National Association of Convenience Stores.

Hauritz, M., Homel, R., Mcllwain, G., Burrows, T., & Townsley, M. (1998). Reducing violence in licensed venues. *Trends and Issues in Crime and Criminal Justice, 101*, 1–6.

Homel, R., Hauritz, M., Wortley, R., Mcllwain, G., & Carvolth, R. (1997). Preventing alcohol-related crime through community action: The Surfers Paradise Safety Action Project. *Crime Prevention Studies, 17*, 35–90.

Lasley, J. (1996). *Using traffic barriers to 'design out' crime: A Program evaluation of LAPD's Operation Cul-de-sac*. Washington, DC: US Department of Justice.

Lasley, J. (1998). *'Designing out' gang homicides and street assaults*. Washington, DC: National Institute of Justice.

Lemieux, F., Bricknell, S., & Prenzler, T. (2015). Mass shootings in Australia and the United States, 1981-2013. *Journal of Criminological Research, Policy and Practice, 1*(3), 131–142.

National Consortium for the Study of Terrorism and Responses to Terrorism (START). (2016). *Annex of statistical information, Country reports on terrorism 2015*. Baltimore, MD: Author.

Prenzler, T., Manning, M., & Bates, L. (2015). The implications of a harm perspective on terrorism, road safety, tobacco, alcohol, illicit drugs, and workplace health and safety. *Journal of Policing, Intelligence and Counter-Terrorism, 10*(2), 88–101.

Productivity Commission. (2016). *Report on government services 2016: Chapter 6, Police services, Attachment tables*. Canberra, Australia: Author.

Schmerler, K., Perkins, M., Phillips, S., Rinehart, T., & Townsend, M. (2006) *A Guide to reducing crime and disorder through problem solving partnerships*. Washington, DC: US Department of Justice.

Schneider, R., & Kitchen, T. (2002). *Planning for crime prevention*. London, England: Routledge.

United Nations Office on Drugs and Crime (UNODC). (2014). *Global study on homicide 2013*. Vienna, Austria: Author.

van Dijk, J. (2008). *The world of crime.* Thousand Oaks, CA: SAGE.

van Dijk, J. (2012, June). *Closing the doors: Stockholm Prizewinners lecture 2012.* Paper presented at the Stockholm Criminology Symposium, Stockholm, Sweden.

van Dijk, J., Tseloni, A., & G. Farrell (Eds.), (2012). *The International crime drop.* Basingstoke, England: Palgrave.

World Health Organization (WHO). (2014). *Intimate partner and sexual violence against women.* Geneva, Switzerland: Author.

Wright, R., Heilweil, M., Pelletier, P., & Dickinson, K. (1974). *The impact of street lighting on crime.* Ann Arbor, MI: University of Michigan.

Chapter 10

Principles of Security Management

Rick Draper, Jessica Ritchie, and Tim Prenzler

The effective management of security related risks relies on three basic principles: (1) understanding what may be at risk of loss or compromise, from whom, and in what context; (2) successfully assessing the range of factors that may make a risk event more likely and/or more harmful to stakeholders; and (3) making informed and defensible decisions about responses that may be appropriate in the circumstances. This chapter considers established security management practices and their theoretical underpinnings, drawn from the science of crime prevention. In doing so, the chapter explores the application of international standards in the assessment and management of security related risks.

Fundamental Security Questions

Irrespective of context, the fundamental questions that need to be answered in understanding and effectively managing security-related risks are:

1. What are we trying to protect?
   - What is it that might be 'at risk'?
   - What makes it attractive to a potential source of threat?
   - What is its importance to concerned stakeholders?
   - What is the full range of consequences for all stakeholders, given a specific threat scenario?

2. From what/whom are we trying to protect it?
   - What is the nature of the source of threat?
   - What are their objectives?
   - What are their capabilities?
   - What is their motivation?

The nature of what needs protecting in any given situation is going to be context-dependent and may span a number of specialised areas. For example, in the area of information security there are four aspects of information that may require separate consideration:

1. Protection from unauthorised access.
2. Protection from unauthorised disclosure.

3. Protection from alteration or change.

4. Protection from loss or destruction.

While in this example the asset being protected may be one specific piece of information, it is clear that depending on the potential source of threat, very different strategies may be needed to effectively protect that information from the different modes of potential compromise. Understanding the nature of the asset being protected, and the potential threats to that asset, is fundamental to being able to develop and implement effective security risk management strategies.

In considering 'what we are trying to protect', the following general categories should always be considered:

- People (not just limited to staff)
- Information (known, printed, digital-storage, transit and destruction)
- Property
- Activities/Operations
- Reputation/Goodwill.

The process of deriving answers to these fundamental security questions involves assessing the strategies in place to reduce the likelihood of a threat being realised and/or mitigate the consequences. This is discussed in practical terms in Chapter 11 where the concept of a 'security survey' is introduced. However, before considering how to undertake a security survey it is important to understand the concepts of risk and risk management.

Risk and Risk Management

The origins of structured approaches to managing security-related risks can be traced back to the late1970s and early 1980s — the same period during which the initial work on opportunity based crime prevention was being done. Walsh and Healy (1982, p. 2–1) noted that '[no] security plan or program can be effective unless it is based upon a clear understanding of the actual risks it is designed to control'. This language differs a little from that used in published risk management standards (e.g., Standards Australia, 1995, 2006; Canadian Standards Association [CSA], 1997; International Organization for Standardization [ISO], 2009a, 2009b). Nonetheless, Walsh and Healy (1982, p. 2–1) highlighted the need for a clear understanding of:

1. The kinds of threats or risks affecting the assets to be safeguarded.

2. The likelihood or probability of those threats becoming actual loss events.

3. The impact or effect upon the asset or upon the enterprise responsible for the asset if the loss occurs.

Despite having published standards and reference documents for decades now, there is still a lack of consistency in the terms and definitions used by practitioners, as well as in security related texts and articles (Garcia, 2006, pp. 509–510). To the casual observer, Walsh and Healy (1982) may appear to use the words 'threat' and 'risk' interchangeably in their reference to the assets to be safeguarded. However, while these two terms are related, they have clear and separate meanings when describing security related matters.

The ISO defines 'risk' as the 'effect of uncertainty on objectives' (ISO, 2009a, p. 1). This implies that risk is the combination of the likelihood or probability that something will happen, and the outcomes of that occurrence. The Standards Australia handbook, *HB 167: Security risk management,* presents a range of formulaic approaches to quantifying or qualifying the level of risk, but consistently highlights the key parameters of 'likelihood' and 'consequences' as essential to describing risk (Standards Australia, 2006, pp.163–168). Similarly, the Canadian Standard defines risk as 'the chance of injury or loss as defined as a measure of the probability and severity of an adverse effect to health, property, the environment, or other things of value' (CSA, 1997, p.3).

The term 'threat', in a security risk management context, is often used to describe the risk event; that is, what might happen (e.g., robbery, theft of stock, assault on staff, information compromise,. The likelihood of a given threat being realised can be assessed by identifying and understanding the factors relevant to a 'source of threat'; that is, in crime prevention terms, the 'potential offenders'. These factors for consideration may be similar for some threat sources, but differ significantly for others. For example, there will be different factors to consider in assessing the likelihood of theft of stock where the source of threat is managerial staff — compared to an external criminal threat source.

The term 'vulnerabilities' is used to refer to weaknesses that increase the likelihood of a threat source successfully realising a threat against a specific asset, resource or function (Federal Emergency Management Agency [FEMA], 2005 pp. 1–3); for example, aspects of 'target suitability' and 'capable guardianship' in terms of opportunity theory. However, it must also be noted that the term 'vulnerability' is also applied to factors that increase the potential consequences arising from a risk event. Whether or not a particular weakness represents a vulnerability is directly related to the nature of the threat source. A threat source making rational choices will logically weigh up the effort required and potential risk involved, against the perceived reward (Clarke, 1997). The capability and motivation of an offender to target a specific asset, resource or activity will be key factors in identifying vulnerabilities.

In summary, vulnerabilities contribute to an increased likelihood that a threat to a given asset, resource or activity will be realised and/or the consequences arising from such an event will be worsened. The actual risk can be defined by describing the nature of the threat in combination with a foreseeable consequence; that is, if the 'threat' is robbery, a risk arising from robbery may be described as 'loss of cash through robbery'. Note the two parts to the description of the risk: consequences (loss of cash) and threat (robbery).

There are, however, a range of potential consequences that may arise from any given risk event (Standards Australia, 2006, p. 72). For example, in a robbery of a convenience store, the range of consequences might include:

- physical injury to staff
- physical injury to customers
- psychological injury to staff
- psychological injury to customers
- loss of cash
- loss of merchandise
- loss of personal property belonging to staff
- loss of personal property belonging to customers
- disruption of operations
- reduced productivity (e.g., police and court time)
- damage to reputation (e.g., affecting staff recruiting).

The degree to which any of these consequences may be experienced will be influenced by the risk management strategies in place. For example, the risk of loss of cash through robbery may be mitigated by insurance; and the risk of harm to staff through robbery may be reduced by store layout, staff training and/or physical barriers. There may also be some potential for financial and productivity losses arising from civil litigation or prosecution for workplace health and safety breaches. For example, Sarre and Prenzler (2009) note that, in the case of *Derrick v. ANZ Banking Group*, the New South Wales Industrial Relations Commission fined the bank $156,000 'for not maintaining a safe workplace and failing to carry out adequate risk assessments' (p. 209). While in this case the fine was not insignificant, the direct and indirect costs of being prosecuted added substantially to the overall consequences arising from the original robbery.

Clearly, it is impractical to attempt to assess in detail all consequences that may arise from every conceivable threat to every asset. The *HB 167: security risk management* notes that a 'criticality assessment is a vital step in the identification of risk as it provides a starting point for consideration of the pertinent threats.... and vulnerability to those threats' (2006, p. 46). Criticality refers to the likely harm from a threat being realised. Care needs to be taken not to focus too much on events with highly damaging consequences but an extremely low likelihood. This might distract from other assessments of risk to assets, resources and activities that are vital to an organisation. In addition, the criticality of any asset should not be assessed only in terms of its direct financial value. Consideration may also need to be given to its social value and the time and resources that may be needed to recover from its loss or destruction.

The lead-time to recovery following a risk event may be a key factor in considering criticality. For example, in gold mining the two critical inputs, besides ore and human resources, are power and water. If power and/or water supply are lost for a significant period of time, the processing of crushed ore will cease. There is in fact a finite period of time for disruption of either of these services after which the costs of resumption of production at the facility may simply not be financially viable.

The steps in the overall risk management process are now well defined and provide a sound basis for developing an understanding of security-related risks and the treatment of those risks (see ISO, 2009a). Terminology can be important in ensuring that there is no scope for misinterpretation. The steps listed below summarise the standard risk management process as defined by the ISO (2009a, p. 14).

1. Establish the context
2. Risk assessment
2.1 Risk identification
2.2 Risk analysis
2.3 Risk evaluation
3. Risk treatment

Note: All steps should involve 'communication and consultation' and 'monitoring and review'.

It should be noted that the term 'risk assessment' is the collective term embracing the separate steps of risk identification, risk analysis and risk evaluation. It is in the risk analysis phase that the likelihood and consequences of the risk event are estimated within the given contexts applicable to the risk assessment.

Sources of Threat

The potential sources of threat are very much dependent upon the context within which the at-risk asset, resource or activity may be found. Some references categorise sources of threat according to the type of threat, although some sources of threat should in fact be considered under multiple types. Some of the motivating factors influencing sources of threat, as defined in *HB 167: Security risk management*, include the following (2006, p. 53):

- Malicious acts
- Greed or personal gain
- Terrorism
- Incidental acts.

The sources of threat for malicious acts may include disgruntled personnel, contractors or customers. They may also include general sources of threat such as vandals or propagators of computer viruses who might not have specifically targeted the owner of the asset per se, but rather exploited an opportunity that was available to satisfy their own malicious objectives. The other categories of threat are somewhat self-evident, with incident threats frequently arising through acts of negligence or as byproducts of some other action.

Walsh and Healy (1982, p. 2–3) place risk events that security managers should consider into eight categories:

1. Nuclear War
2. Natural Catastrophe
3. Industrial Cisaster
4. Civil Cisturbance
5. Crime
6. Conflicts of Interest
7. Terrorism
8. Other Risks.

Whatever categorisation method is used, it is important in considering sources of threat to understand their likely objectives as far as may be practicable. For example, an easy-to-identify source for the threat of robbery is external criminals (i.e., not a staff member). Their objectives in committing a robbery would appear to be to gain money or goods. However, they may also include, for example, satisfying an initiation test to join a gang. Understanding threat source objectives can be a vital contributor to developing risk management plans. If the threat source perceives that they will not be able to satisfy their objectives without undue risk or effort ('rational choice'), they may be deterred from prosecuting the threat.

At the centre of any determination of threat likelihood is an understanding of the potential capability and motivation of the threat source. The level of motivation for a threat source to prosecute the threat at any given *time and place* is likely to be contributed to by (a) the underlying rationale for pursuing the threat, and (b) the level of expectation regarding achieving the intended objectives — that is, why? and will the expected outcomes for the threat source be achieved?

For example, a staff member committing theft will want to have a reasonable expectation that they will not be detected and identified. The underlying rationale for theft may be to gain money to satisfy a gambling addiction. This might be a powerful motivation. However, if controls are such that the would-be criminal has no reasonable expectation of getting away with the theft, they are unlikely to proceed. They may be deterred by the potential shame of identification, loss of their job or a criminal conviction, fine or imprisonment. This can be contrasted with the risk entailed in suicide terrorism. A suicide bomber will have little or no concern about shaming, loss of employment or criminal justice processes. However, if it is possible to limit their expectation of achieving their objectives in prosecuting a threat against a given target, the target logically becomes less desirable.

Threats, Vulnerabilities and Layered Protection

Farrell and Pease (2006, p. 181) summarise Cohen and Felson's routine activity theory in the following terms: 'A crime occurs when a suitable target and a potential offender meet at a suitable time and place lacking capable guardianship' (see also Chapter 6). In security risk management terms, this may be re-drafted as: 'A risk event will occur when a source of threat is able to exploit vulnerabilities to adversely affect an asset, resource or activity'. The concept of 'capable guardianship' does not inherently require the physical presence of a human protector for the asset (Farrell & Pease, 2006, p. 182). However, the keyword here is 'capable', and this needs to be considered in the context of the applicable source of threat. For 'guardianship' to be capable in a protective security context, it will necessarily involve multiple layers of protection. This layering of protection has its origins in military strategy and is referred to as 'defence-in-depth' or 'security-in-depth' (see van Maanengerg, 1995, pp. 83–84, Standards Australia, 2006, p. 59; also Kovacich & Halibozek, 2013, p. 340).

The basic principle of defence-in-depth is that the security of the asset is not reliant on any one layer of protection. The layers of protection can be physical or mechanical in nature, such as fences, walls, and security enclosures. Examples of situational techniques here include target hardening, and controlling access and egress. Protections can also be procedural, such as policies and procedures, codes of conduct, pre-employment screening and supervision (van Maanengerg, 1995, pp. 83-84). Situational examples include rule setting and alerting conscience. They can be technical, such as alarm systems, CCTV, firewalls, and analytics – involving strengthened surveillance and access control. Protections can also involve greater human guardianship, such as static security officers and response teams. These layers of protection should also be derived from design elements or usage characterises that are incorporated to support operational and behavioural objectives (Crowe, 2013, p. 28).

As noted in *HB 167: Security risk management*, the goal in assessing the vulnerability of any given asset to a range of possible sources of threat is to consider the vulnerabilities in each layer of protection for that asset (Standards Australia, 2006, p. 59). The fact that one security strategy is not

100% effective does not mean there is automatically an increase in the likelihood that the threat will be realised. An unlocked door is not automatically a vulnerability (Johnston, 2010, p. 38.). The role and contribution of each strategy needs to be considered. A key question here is: does the combination of strategies represent capable guardianship for the subject target (asset) for a given category of offender (threat source) at a given time and place?

Risk Analysis and Risk Assessment

The international standard, *ISO 31010: Risk management — Risk assessment techniques*, presents an expansive range of risk assessment techniques and guidance regarding their selection and use (see ISO, 2009b). It is important to note that risk assessment techniques can vary significantly in terms of complexity and applicability to particular types of risk. For example, the 'Bow Tie' analysis (ISO, 2009b, pp. 64–66) — focused on a single adverse event in the centre of a flow chart of causes and consequences — is found more commonly in health and safety risk assessments than in security, as it is has limitations in dealing with multiple interrelated causation factors. In contrast, the 'Layers of Protection Analysis' technique (ISO, 2009b, pp. 59–60) appears to align more closely with the defence-in-depth approach, commonly found in security applications, and the 25 techniques of situational prevention (see Chapter 6). In practice, the most common technique found in security risk assessments in Australia and New Zealand is the 'Consequence/Probability Matrix' (ISO, 2009b, pp. 82–86). This is largely due to the presentation of this technique as an example in the original risk management standard (see Standards Australia, 1995, Appendix E).

Quantitative and qualitative versions of the Consequence/Probability Matrix have been used to varying extents to analyse security-related risks. An example of a qualitative matrix is shown in Figure 10.1. One of the keys to successfully using this technique is ensuring that the rationale for assessed levels of likelihood and consequences are well documented. Notwithstanding that subjectivity in assessments is a limitation of this technique, it can be used to deliver useful and consistent risk analyses across multiple facilities (Draper & Rose, 2006). The more granular and refined the inputs, the more consistent and reliable the output.

Drawing on routine activity theory (Cohen & Felson, 1979) and the rational choice perspective (Cornish & Clarke, 2011) as a theoretical base for evaluation, it is possible to make an estimate of the level of likelihood of a specific location being a target for a robbery. The relative 'attractiveness' of the location will be influenced by the perceived level of reward available and the opportunities to commit the crime with the least effort and least risk to the offender. For example, if there is likely to be a low level of cash held at the facility and the perceived guardianship at the location is high, the 'attractiveness' of the location may be assessed as being 'very low' (see Figure 10.2).

It is somewhat self-evident, and supported by Cohen and Felson's routine activity theory, that irrespective of how attractive a target may be for a crime, such as robbery, there will be no likelihood of the crime occurring if there is no offender. Figure 10.3 illustrates how consideration of the level of similar crime in the area (base crime weighting) can be overlaid on a measure of 'attractiveness' to derive the likelihood of a location being targeted for robbery.

Risk Treatment

A range of physical security strategies is discussed in more detail in Chapter 11. However, it should be noted that regulatory requirements and guidelines

Figure 10.1
Example of a qualitative consequence/probability matrix.

Risk		Potential Consequences				
		Insignificant	Minor	Moderate	Major	Catastrophic
Likelihood	Rare	Low	Low	Moderate	High	High
	Unlikely	Low	Low	Moderate	High	Extreme
	Possible	Low	Moderate	High	Extreme	Extreme
	Likely	Moderate	High	High	Extreme	Extreme
	Almost Certain	High	High	Extreme	Extreme	Extreme

Source: Draper a Rose, 2006, p. 463. (Used with permission.)

Figure 10.2
Determining the relative attractiveness of a target for robbery.

Example

Attractiveness		Opportunity				
		Very Low	Low	Moderate	High	Very High
Cash Level	Very Low	Very Low	Very Low	Very Low	Very Low	Very Low
	Low	Very Low	Very Low	Low	Low	Low
	Moderate	Very Low	Low	Moderate	Moderate	High
	High	Very Low	Low	Moderate	High	Very High
	Very High	Very Low	Low	High	Very High	Very High

Low	Low	=	Very Low
Robbery Opportunity Descriptor	Cash Level Descriptor		Attractiveness Descriptor

Source: Draper & Rose, 2006, p. 463. (Used with permission.)

Figure 10.3
Determining likelihood based on attractiveness and availability of offenders.

Likelihood	Base Crime Weighting				
	Very Low	Low	Moderate	High	Very High
Very Low	Rare	Rare	Rare	Rare	Rare
Low	Rare	Rare	Unlikely	Unlikely	Unlikely
Moderate	Rare	Unlikely	Possible	Possible	Likely
High	Rare	Unlikely	Possible	Likely	Almost Certain
Very High	Rare	Unlikely	Likely	Almost Certain	Almost Certain

Source: Draper & Rose, 2006, p. 465. (Used with permission.)

exist in some sectors and these must be taken into account when developing risk treatment plans (Draper, 2013, p. 283). Notwithstanding any statutory obligations, there are other risk management options beyond seeking to reduce the likelihood of a risk event and/or reduce the consequences. These other options include:

- Accepting the risk (an informed cost–benefit decision)
- Avoiding the risk (eliminating all exposure)
- Redistributing the risk (decentralising the target/loss potential)
- Transferring the risk (though insurance or transferring functions).

While some authors opt for other terms, it is generally accepted that strategies to reduce exposure to security related risks fall into three categories of control or 'sub-systems' (Garcia, 2013, p. 18; Standards Australia, 2006, p. 64):

- Delay strategies
- Detection strategies
- Response strategies.

Some sources add 'deterrence' and 'recovery' strategies to this list (Standards Australia, 2006, p. 64). Marier (2012, pp. 1–2) refers to the '5 Ds' of perimeter security: 'deter, detect, deny, delay, and defend'. However, it can be argued that the three categories in the dot-point list above may act as a deterrent to a potential threat source, either individually or in combination. Similarly, during the recovery phase following a risk event, strategies falling into one or more of the three generally accepted categories will be used.

Irrespective of how risk treatment strategies may be categorised, it is important that the objectives for those strategies be well defined and documented. For example, a CCTV camera may be used to either provide wide area detection capability or images to enable clear identification of persons entering the field of view. These are very different objectives, and if both are required this may require the use of two cameras or a high-resolution megapixel camera and supporting software capable of delivering both requirements.

Security Risk Management in Practice

Managing security-related risks involve a range of considerations that are anchored in the various contexts within which the applicable risks arise. For example, large corporations and government agencies will routinely have senior personnel in dedicated security management roles and may have mandated risk management requirements that must be followed (Attorney-General's Department, 2012). Smaller organisations, such as a small business, will not have the capacity or risk profile to justify the appointment of dedicated staff. In these cases, security management responsibilities will be formally or informally assigned within other roles. In any case, the successful management of security related risks relies on all staff, and potentially other stakeholders, understanding and accepting their individual roles and responsibilities with respect to security. A key principle of security management therefore involves integrating all staff into appropriate security roles, and this involves clarifying those roles in policy statements, and providing suitable training and supervision (see Chapter 11).

The practice of security management is able to draw on the theoretical foundations and substantial body of applied crime prevention research arising from the work of criminologists including Ronald V. Clarke, Marcus Felson, Paul and Patricia Brantingham, and others (McCrie, 2004). In a protective security context, Clarke's (1997) situational crime prevention and Cohen and Felson's (1979) routine activity approach both present practical hypotheses that can be applied in understanding specific security related risks, and in making decisions about strategies that may reduce the likelihood that a risk event will occur (Draper & Rose, 2006). The applicability of situational crime prevention theory to security risk management is further evidenced by the number of case studies illustrating the effectiveness of such measures (e.g., Clarke, 1997; see Chapter 6, Chapter 8 and Chapter 9). Similarly, the theoretical principles of CPTED (see Chapter 7), as originally described by C. Ray Jeffery (1971), have been shown, along with other environmental factors, to reduce the likelihood of specific security risks being realised (see Hunter & Jeffery, 1992, p. 201).

Clarke's matrix of 25 situational crime prevention techniques is divided into five broad strategies (see Chapter 6; Center for Problem-Oriented Policing[1]):

1. 'Increase the effort' the offender needs to make in order to succeed.
2. 'Increase the risk' to the offender.
3. 'Reduce the rewards' to the offender.
4. 'Reduce provocations' that may encourage, facilitate or precipitate offending.
5. 'Remove excuses' available to the offender.

These five strategies are directly relevant to managing security-related risks. For example, fences, locks, safes and other 'target hardening' strategies are routinely associated with security to make it harder for a threat source to compromise an asset (i.e., increase the effort — see Chapter 11). Similarly, CCTV systems and intruder alarms are intended to increase the likelihood of the threat source being detected and disabled, thereby increasing the risk to the offender. Examples that reduce the rewards available to potential offenders include property marking and cash minimisation, which reduce the attractiveness of the target. Effective security policies and procedures for dealing with disgruntled customers or staff are intended to reduce potential provocations that may lead to violence. Likewise, awareness programs, which communicate security policies and procedures, reduce the range of excuses available for potential offenders in areas as diverse as fraud and embezzlement through to harassment and incident reporting.

Whatever the size of the organisation, senior executives across all areas must ensure that security-related risks associated with their area of influence are identified and understood. Effective security risk management requires informed decisions to be made in relation to planning for proactively addressing security needs as well as to support appropriate responses to threats that may be realised. Senior executives must be seen to not only be setting security policy, but also leading by example in the implementation of key principles of security management; including: clearly assigning security responsibilities and ensuring accountability, integrating security across all aspects of the organisation, conducting regular risk assessments, assessing the impacts of protective measures, and maintaining a flexible approach to changing threats. Security strategies also need to be compatible with the organisation's goals and philosophy. They need to be operationally appropriate and workable, and they need to represent fiscally responsible choices.

---

1 http://www.popcenter.org/25techniques/

Conclusion

The main principles upon which effective security management are based include developing a clear understanding of the assets and resources that may be exposed to loss or compromise; identifying the potential sources of threat to those assets and resources; and having an informed and defensible approach to managing the identified risks. The chapter has also shown how the concepts involved in situational crime prevention and routine activity theory can be used to enhance traditional security management practices through a clearer focus on opportunity factors in crime and opportunity reduction techniques. The application of international standards for risk management and risk assessment also provide a useful method for assessing crime risks and designing protective measures. This involves identifying assets, threats and vulnerabilities, and using a criticality matrix to apply layered security measures. This approach can also be systematised through the use of a security survey (see Chapter 11).

References

Attorney-General's Department (2012). *Protective security policy framework: Securing government business.* Retrieved from http://www.protectivesecurity.gov.au/pspf/Pages/default.aspx

Clarke, R.V. (1997). *Situational crime prevention: Successful case studies.* Albany, NY: Harrow & Heston.

Cohen, L., & Felson, M. (1979). Social change and crime rate trends: A routine activity approach. *American Sociological Review, 44,* 588–608.

Cornish, D., & Clarke, R. (2011). The rational choice perspective. In R. Wortley & L. Mazerolle (Eds.), *Environmental criminology and crime analysis* (pp. 28–47). Abingdon, England: Routledge.

Crowe, T. (revised by L. Fennelly). (2013). *Crime prevention through environmental design.* Waltham, MA: Butterworth-Heinemann

Canadian Standards Association. (1997). *CAN/CSA-Q850-1997 Risk management: Guideline for decision makers.* Ottawa, Canada: Author.

Draper, R. (2013). Standards, regulations, and guidelines: Compliance and your security program. In L. Fennelly (Ed.), *Effective physical security* (pp. 283–291). Waltham, MA: Butterworth-Heinemann.

Draper, R., & Rose, E. (2006). Development of robbery risk analysis tools: Using the Australian and New Zealand Standard. *International Journal of Risk Assessment and Management, 6,* 456–471.

Farrell, G., & Pease, K. (2006). Risk management. In M. Gill (Ed.), *The handbook of security* (pp. 179–199). Houndmills, England: Palgrave Macmillan.

Federal Emergency Management Agency. (FEMA). (2005). *FEMA 452 risk assessment: A how-to guide to mitigate potential terrorist attacks against buildings*. Washington, DC: Author.

Garcia, M. (2006). Risk management. In M. Gill (Ed.), *The handbook of security* (pp. 509–531). Houndmills, England: Palgrave Macmillan.

Garcia, M. (2013). Introduction to vulnerability assessment. In L. Fennelly (Ed.), *Effective physical security* (pp. 11–39). Waltham, MA: Butterworth-Heinemann.

Hunter, R., & Jeffery, C. (1992). Preventing convenience store robbery. In R.V. Clarke (Ed.), *Situational crime prevention: Successful case studies* (pp. 194–204). Albany, NY: Harrow & Heston.

International Organization of Standardization (ISO). (2009a). *ISO 31000:2009 – Risk management – Principles and guidelines.* Geneva, Switzerland: Author.

International Organization of Standardization (ISO). (2009b). *ISO 31010:2009 Risk management – Risk assessment techniques.* Geneva, Switzerland: Author.

Jeffery, C. (1971). *Crime prevention through environmental design.* Beverley Hills, CA: SAGE.

Johnston, R. (2010). Changing security paradigms. *Journal of Physical Security, 4*(2), 35–47.

Kovacich, G., & Halibozek, E. (2013). Physical security. In L. Fennelly (Ed.), *Effective physical security* (pp. 339–353). Waltham, MA: Butterworth-Heinemann

Marier, K. (2012). The 5 D's of outdoor perimeter security. Retrieved from http://www.securitymagazine.com/articles/82833-the-5-d-s-of-outdoor-perimeter-security.

McCrie, R. (2004). The history of expertise in security management practice and litigation. *Security Journal, 17*(3), 11–19.

Sarre, R., & Prenzler, T. (2009). *The law of private security in Australia.* Sydney: Thomson Reuters.

Standards Australia. (1995). *AS/NZS 4360:1995 Risk management.* Sydney: Standards Australia and Standards New Zealand.

Standards Australia. (2006). *HB 167:2006 Security risk management.* Sydney: Author.

van Maanengerg, D. (1995). *Effective retail security.* Melbourne, Australia: Butterworth-Heinemann

Walsh, T., & Healy, R. (1982). The protection of assets manual. Santa Monica, CA: Merritt.

Chapter 11

Best Practice in Physical Security and People Management

Rick Draper, Jessica Ritchie, Eric Wilson, and Tim Prenzler

Physical security involves those aspects of protective security focused on tangible measures for the protection of assets. The strategies cover structural, mechanical and technical security. This chapter outlines best practice in the area through the security survey process, as part of a larger security risk assessment process, including the presentation of findings within a structured report format. The remainder of the chapter discusses the importance of developing and implementing security policies and procedures as part of managing people. This applies to people within, and external to, organisations. It concludes by highlighting the importance of effective communication and the integration of strategies around security awareness.

Physical Security

Physical security is one of four overlapping categories of what is more broadly known as 'protective security'. This is defined in the Australian Attorney-General's Department publication *Protective Security Policy Framework: Glossary of Security Terms* (2014, p. 16) as:

> A combination of procedural, physical, personnel, and information security measures designed to protect people, information and assets from security threats.

There is some debate about which security strategies should or should not be included within the area of 'physical security', and variations in definition can even be found within the one organisation (e.g., Attorney-General's Department, 2014; Garcia, 2007, pp. 1–11). However, for our purposes, physical security encapsulates tangible security strategies used in combination with the design, layout and orientation of structures and spaces to reduce the likelihood of specific threats and/or reduce the potential consequences should the associated risks be realised. This includes physical security strategies that are intended to prevent, delay, detect and/or respond to security-related threats to people, information and property assets, as well as threats to the activities or reputation of the individuals or organisations at risk.

In the rest of this chapter, the term 'resources' will be used to collectively describe those things that may be exposed to security related risks: including staff, clients, visitors, contractors, information in its various forms, physical property, cash, the activities and operations of an organisation, as well as reputation and goodwill.Many physical security strategies are highly visible and easily recognised, while others may be overlooked by the novice. A primary task for security management in this area is to find the most appropriate mix of strategies to suit the particular location and assets they are protecting. When considering different strategies, and likely cost-benefit ratios, the fundamental questions that underpin security risk management should apply (see Chapter 10):

1. What are we trying to protect?
2. From what or whom are we trying to protect it?

Depending on the setting, physical security considerations may include the following (Fennelly, 2013a; Standards Australia, 2006):

- site selection and site layout
- fences and barriers
- projectile and blast protection
- signage and rules
- sightlines and buffer zones
- operational and defensive/offensive lighting
- vehicular and pedestrian traffic controls
- building design and layout
- personnel and mail screening
- X-ray and metal detectors
- structural material selection and concealed obstacles
- vaults and secure rooms
- glazing materials and protective films
- doors and other portal design
- mechanical and electronic locking
- keying and electronic access control
- location selection for higher risk activities
- service counter design and barriers
- alarm systems and CCTV
- annunciation and system monitoring
- automated and electronic response systems
- uniformed and covert security patrols
- static guards and response capabilities

- security training and drills/exercises
- personal protective security equipment
- safes and protective enclosures
- property marking and asset management
- ID cards and visitor management
- cash and asset handling
- tamper-evident enclosures and security seals
- transport of cash and valuables
- incident recording and reporting
- incident notification and response.

Physical security strategies are 'tangible' or otherwise procedurally related to a tangible security strategy (e.g., standing operating procedures for staff, key control procedures). Some further strategies that can be utilised include pre-employment screening (personnel security strategy), antivirus software (information security strategy) or encrypted telecommunication (communications). Overlaps are evident across all categories of protective security, and the operation of one strategy is often dependent on protection from another in a different category. For example, data protection on a computer server is an information security strategy that is dependent on physical security strategies to prevent the server from being physically disconnected or stolen.

Defence-in-depth

The previous chapter referred to the key security principle of defence-in-depth. This approach is particularly applicable to physical security through the use of barriers and controlled entry/exit points to create concentric rings of protection against intruders. The best way to picture this is to think of a medieval fortress with an open area outside, moat and drawbridge, portcullis, outer and inner walls, ramparts, turrets, courtyards and a keep. This facilitates operation of the '5 Ds' of perimeter security: 'deter, detect, deny, delay, and defend' (Marier, 2012, pp. 1–2). Each protective layer — beginning with the outer perimeter — should work to block or impede the progress of intruders towards their targets, as well as making it more difficult for them to exit with stolen assets. More obvious outer layers should serve to initially deter intruders. Where these fail, delays at each stage should allow sufficient time for a detection system to alert guardians who can intercept the intruder and 'defend' the premises.

A basic CPTED principle is that in most cases a front entrance should be as open as possible to allow for natural surveillance and surveillance by employees (Prenzler, 2009). This can be achieved through low shrubbery and 'see through' fencing, with as few hiding places as possible. The rear and sides of buildings usually afford less visibility and should be fortified as much as possible. The use of grills and shutters to target harden facilities is especially important for locations that have easy public access and lack guardianship outside opening hours — such as sporting clubs on public land and school buildings. Generally speaking, the less guardianship there is the more target hardening is required.

Spaces between the outer perimeter and the walls of buildings should be cleared of obstructions to optimise surveillance. Wherever possible, all loose objects should be removed so they cannot be used to break through walls, doors or windows. Doors, windows and cladding need to be constructed from sturdy material, with high quality frames and locks. Intruder alarm systems, including CCTV, should be advertised to deter offenders, and they can assist in reducing the window of opportunity for crime. Back-to-base alarms assure absent owners that there will be a response by mobile security guards. Verification of alarm activations is now a key principle of efficient physical security management, especially if a police response is required (Prenzler, 2009). Verification is greatly facilitated by CCTV, with real-time visual monitoring over the internet, including relays from premises to mobile phones anywhere in the world. Of course, larger premises or group security arrangements can support on-site security personnel who provide a much shorter response time.

The idea of layered security includes the interiors of buildings. These areas should be compartmentalised as much as possible to prevent intruders moving between locations. For example, hung ceilings allows access points into locked rooms. In this situation, higher value targets — such as medications, cash, jewellery, tools, computers and audiovisual equipment — should be placed in high security rooms, cabinets or safes, or secured with chains or brackets.

Additional policies and procedures can be adopted to reduce physical security risks. These have been summarised by Prenzler (2009, pp. 24–25) in relation to the prevention of burglary in commercial and institutional premises:

1. The capacity of burglars to 'case' premises should be limited. Stock should be kept out of site of nonemployees as much as possible so offenders cannot appraise the value and vulnerability of goods.

2. Checks should be carried out at closing time to make sure no offenders have hidden themselves inside premises.

3. Cash minimisation through frequent banking can reduce losses from burglary, robbery, and theft. Signage stating 'no cash kept on premises' can reduce burglars' perceptions of potential rewards.

4. Damage done by thieves when searching for high value items can also be minimised by strategies such as leaving open empty cash registers.

5. Efforts should also be made to enlarge guardianship by encouraging legitimate use of premises outside operating hours. Because of

extended holidays, schools in particular have long periods of time when they are unoccupied and vulnerable to attack. This can be countered by encouraging use by holiday care groups and other community groups, as well as providing subsidised accommodation on school grounds for teaching or maintenance staff.

The Physical Security Survey

A physical security survey is a systematic documented approach to identifying potential vulnerabilities that increase the likelihood that a security related risk will be realised, and/or the consequences will be worsened. Visual inspection of all resources, security plans and security devices is a key element of a survey. The primary objective is to identify deficiencies or vulnerabilities that increase risks and recommend modifications to mitigate the risks (Fennelly, 2013b, p. 41; Standards Australia, 2006, p. 59).

Physical security surveys should be undertaken within a defined scope. The scope can be set by geographical boundaries or specific functional areas within a site, the types of threats or risks to be considered, or any combination of these. For example, the scope of a physical security survey for a grocery store might be limited to the risk of theft from new self-serve checkouts. Other very specific examples include threats to employees, short-changing customers by staff, and short-delivery by suppliers.

Failing to adequately define the scope of a physical security survey can lead to misunderstandings and potentially expose the person undertaking the survey to legal claims of negligence (Sarre & Prenzler, 2009, pp. 198–200). If there are constraints on time and resources, it is better to focus on a specific set of related risks at one time, rather than to attempt to comprehensively cover all risks and not be able to adequately complete the task. However, in applying limitations in scope, anyone undertaking a security survey should be mindful that the effects of a security strategy may extend beyond the risks being considered. Consequently, care should be taken in making recommendations that may introduce vulnerabilities or displacement issues in other areas.

Similarly, there may be vulnerabilities associated with some strategies due to the need to use the most cost-effective approach for managing a range of risks. For example, the idea within defence-in-depth of overlapping strategies and their associated vulnerabilities has been described as resembling slices of Swiss cheese (Standards Australia, 2006, pp. 59–60). The objective is to arrange the slices of cheese in such a way that the holes (vulnerabilities) in one slice (strategy) do not overlap holes in the adjacent slices, thus preventing a path through the slices.

Stages of a Physical Security Survey

There are normally eight stages to a physical security survey (or audit), if a structured analysis of the level of risk is included. These are:

1. Definition of scope and approach
   - Preparation
2. Resource appreciation
   - What is to be protected, within the scope?
3. Threat assessment
   - From whom is it to be protected, within the scope?
4. Audit of current strategies
   - What strategies are documented to be in place?
   - What strategies are actually in place?
   - Are they relevant and appropriate?
5. Vulnerability identification
   - What might a threat source exploit and how?
6. Security risk analysis (if applicable)
   - Likelihood of specific threats being realised
   - Consequences arising from those threats
7. Formulation of recommendations
8. Presentation of findings (e.g., report).

Once the scope is determined, there are two general approaches or methods to undertaking the survey: 'inward-out' and 'outward-in'. The 'inward-out' approach begins by looking at the resource potentially at risk. With due consideration of the sources of threat and their likely objectives, it considers the physical security strategies radiating out from the resource. For example, if the resource is tablet computers that might be stolen by opportunist criminals breaking into a school after hours, the physical security strategies placed in layers outward from the computer might include the following:

- Property marking
- Locked heavy duty cabinet
- Intruder alarm system with off-site monitoring
- Locked classroom
- CCTV
- Movement activated security lights
- Perimeter fence with locked gates.

In an 'inward–out' survey, it may not be necessary to continue beyond the point at which effective protection has been achieved. An example is a heavily locked cabinet in a locked classroom, equipped with a monitored intruder alarm system. The property marking would deny maximum benefit to the offenders for resale and, as such, acts as a deterrent. The locked cabinet increases the effort required by the offenders, delaying access to the tablet computers. In combination with the monitored alarm system, this increases the offenders' perception of risk of detection and apprehension (see Chapter 6 on situational crime prevention).

The 'outward-in' approach differs by commencing at the outermost layer of protection likely to be encountered by a given source of threat in targeting a specific resource. This approach requires thinking like the 'threat source' and considering what effects various physical security strategies may have on decision making. One way of strengthening an 'outward–in' survey is through a 'penetration test', in which a proxy offender attempts to successfully access a resource from the outer perimeter. This technique can be very useful for identifying vulnerabilities. There are, however, a number of potential issues that may arise, such as inappropriate responses from staff or unintended calls to police, if the test is not properly managed.

In both approaches, security assessors often use a checklist of items to evaluate. This can be generic (see Fennelly, 2103b) or tailor-made. Organisations can start with a generic checklist and then modify it from experience so that each survey makes use of a more relevant and comprehensive one. However, it must be kept in mind that checklists can limit the scope of an assessment. It is essential that auditors remain alert to new and emerging threats.

The scope of the physical security survey will be defined in consultation with the owner of the premises or senior management. Due to the likelihood of identifying vulnerabilities that could cause harm to the organisation, the survey can be sensitive and there may be a need to apply protective security strategies to the findings themselves. It is important that the authority to undertake the survey and the agreed scope are documented in writing. Other matters to take into account before commencing a physical security survey include:

- Contextual factors relevant to risk (e.g., local area crime rates)
- Organisational structure and positions of authority
- Stakeholders, their interest in the risks, and availability for consultation
- Operational factors and potential access constraints
- Health and safety issues
- Potential sources of information
- Format for the presentation of findings.

The Security Survey Report

The structure and format for reporting should be determined prior to the commencement of the survey. Notwithstanding templates used within organisations, there are three elements that are routinely used in presenting findings:

1. The Brief: a short narrative that includes an introduction describing the scope, a body with the substance of the findings, a conclusion based on the findings, and the recommendations.

2. The Matrix: a tabulated summary presenting the location/functional area, risk-related issues, findings and recommendations.

3. The Narrative Report: a comprehensive report that provides complete details of the physical security survey, findings, discussion, conclusions, recommendations and attachments. The structure of a typical narrative report includes the following:

- Cover Page
- Contents Page
- Distribution List
- Disclaimer
- Executive Summary
- Introduction and scope
- Description of sites/areas reviewed
- Findings
- Threat Assessment
- Existing Security Strategies (including strengths and weaknesses)
- Vulnerabilities
- Risk Analysis (if applicable)
- Conclusions
- Recommendations.

The reader of the report should be able to clearly understand the scope of the review, the nature of threats and associated risks, the contribution of existing strategies to risk mitigation, and the rationale for all recommendations.

Drawings, diagrams and photographs can be included within the body of the text for immediate reference or be collected at the end of the report. The reader should be able to understand where any photos were taken and their significance. For example, a photograph of the front of a retail store may be taken for orientation purposes, to show the construction materials used or to highlight some specific vulnerability. This is often very helpful in understanding the site descriptions, threats and any relevant issues.

Subject to specified requirements by those authorising the review, all formats should include privacy markings — e.g., 'SECURITY-IN-CONFIDENCE' — and caveats as may be applicable for information security, along with a list of nominated recipients of the report.

People Management in Security

The effective mitigation of crime-related risks fundamentally relies on people via planning and implementation. For example, a safe may be an appropriate physical security strategy to protect cash from theft by external criminal sources. However, its effectiveness is partly dependent on how well staff with the relevant security clearance guards the combination. This highlights the human imperative in security risk management.

Security Planning

Within some industries and some sectors of government, there are regulatory controls and specified requirements for security planning that must be met (Draper, 2013, p. 283). However, irrespective of size, all companies, not-for-profit organisations and government agencies can benefit from a structured approach to managing security-related risks that exceed minimum legislated requirements. Security management plans do not necessarily need to be complex, but they do need to reflect a viable process for understanding and responding to the range of risks faced by an organisation. It is important that objectives and implementation strategies are clearly defined, responsibilities assigned, and processes established for ongoing monitoring and review. At the same time, security management plans must also be sufficiently flexible to respond to the dynamic nature of threats (Girard, 2004, pp. 418–419). In addition, as discussed in Chapter 10, security-related risks should not be considered in isolation from other risks, such as workplace health and safety, to ensure there are no conflicts in prevention strategies.

A typical Strategic Security Risk Management Plan might include the following:

- a foreword written by someone important that cares about the plan (e.g., CEO)
- an introductory section giving some background and history about the plan
- a vision statement or aim for the plan (it is important to have a succinct strategic outlook)
- a mission statement
- principles and values that underpin the implementation of the plan
- context statement or illustration
- a small number of strategic directions/themes/pursuits/goals
- assumptions that have been incorporated into the plan
- outline of stakeholders, roles, responsibilities, expectations
- guidance for implementation and review (e.g., year by year priorities).

Operational plans with much more detail are required to enable the strategic directions to be put into practice.

Dedicated Security and Non-security Personnel

Security management plans, and associated procedural policies must take into account differences in roles within the organisation. If the nature of the organisation is such that there is a need for a dedicated security function, the optimum position for the function within the organisational structure is a matter of some debate (Bamfield, 2006, pp. 496–497). Whatever the lines of reporting that may apply, from a management perspective the executives charged with the security function must clearly understand the priorities for the organisation and be in a position to influence decisions that have a bearing on security risks.

The dissemination of security related policies and procedures needs to be undertaken in accordance with need-to-know principles (Attorney-General's Department, 2014). There are very specific considerations that need to be applied to persons with dedicated security roles. For example, security personnel in management and operational positions will be assigned tasks and duties, the details of which do not necessarily need to be widely distributed.

Management of contracted security personnel is also an important consideration where 'outsourcing' is used to replace in-house security staff or supplement in-house staff for security functions. The primary advantages seen in outsourcing are cost and resource flexibility. However, some organisations have found that outsourcing security roles can result in lower quality of service delivery (Bamfield, 2006, p. 501). However, many of the same difficulties can be experienced with both in-house and contracted security — including lack of clarity around roles, responsibilities and expectations.

The obligations of both employers and employees with respect to occupational health and safety are enshrined in legislation. However, there is little legislative policy to require most organisations to proactively consider many of the security responsibilities that fall to 'nonsecurity personnel'. Challinger (2006, p. 589) notes that '[some] management view security as an impediment to good business and efficiency'. This may in part explain why inadequate attention is often paid to nonsecurity personnel when considering security.

Security Policies, Procedures, Rules and Standing Orders

Good policies and procedures are the key foundations of effective management. They provide the basis for governance, communicate organisational values, and establish ethical and legal frameworks within which all aspects of the organisation are managed (Armstrong, 2008, p. 4). Policies and procedures document the actions members need to take to fulfil organisational purposes, and they identify the appropriate authorities for managing and supervising tasks. In essence, they are a guide for decision-making, as well as a reference point for disciplinary issues.

In any organisation, there will be subjects for policy development that are uniquely security-related, which need to be drafted separately. However, in areas where there are overlaps it is important to avoid the creation of separate security policies. Where possible, security requirements should be incorporated into other policy areas so that the management of security risks associated with the function is seen as integral and not a separate function. For example, human resource policies deal with recruitment and termination of employment with the goal to locate and employ the best person for a given role. Security requirements, such as background checks and verification of qualifications, should be documented alongside what might be seen as the core aspects of the employment policy and procedures.

Security policies potentially impact all aspects of the operations of an organisation, including customers, suppliers, visitors and neighbours. Consequently, it is important that all policies and procedures are reviewed on a regular basis to ensure they remain relevant and cover all issues. Failure to adequately document, review and maintain appropriate security policies can expose an organisation to claims of negligence and litigation (Sarre & Prenzler, 2009, p. 201). Similarly, any failure to maintain currency in policy areas related to regulatory controls may also expose the organisation to elevated risks.

In a security context, there are some important distinctions that should be drawn with respect to policy, procedure, rules and standing orders. Appropriate definitions include the following:

- 'Policies' are succinct statements of the organisation's philosophy and requirements within a specific area of its operations.
- 'Procedures' support the implementation of policy through more comprehensive statements detailing required actions by nominated groups of people within the subject area of operations.
- 'Rules' are concise statements of specific requirements under given policies.
- 'Standing orders' — sometimes referred to as 'standard operating procedures' or SOPs — are consolidated sets of procedures and rules presented in a format that facilitates easy reference and execution by specific groups of personnel (e.g., Security Standing Orders).

It is important to note that while consistency is highly desirable as a general concept for written policies, care needs to be taken that the core policy statement is clear and not lost amongst lengthy and unnecessary supporting material. Well-drafted security policies should include straight-forward information that is both stakeholder- and user-friendly.

Policies and their related procedures must not require actions that are unlawful, outside the control or competence of those tasked with implementation, vague or simply impractical. Post and Schachtsiek (1986, p. 127) provide a sample policy statement applicable in a retail setting: 'All those who shoplift from the expensive department store will be prosecuted'. On the surface, the policy might seem appropriate, but not all individuals will be detected, and the police and prosecution have the ultimate say in who is prosecuted. A more workable policy might be drafted as follows: 'The expensive department store will support the prosecution of all those identified shoplifting'. This would translate in implementation to an obligation for store to provide personnel resources, such as CCTV footage, to support the prosecution of offenders by the relevant authorities.

Documenting the full range of security related policies and procedures applicable to any organisation may seem like a daunting task. However, to misquote the Chinese philosopher Laozi: a comprehensive approach to managing security risks starts with a single policy statement. There is no point in excessive delays waiting to publish an entire manual when core policies and procedures that have been drafted could be implemented and support the contribution of staff and others to effective security management.

Security Awareness

'Security awareness' is the means through which an individual is made conscious of, and accepts, his or her own role and responsibilities in the protection of the assets of an organisation (Draper, 1997). While the subject matter for security awareness programs will vary according to the organisation and the nature of the risks being managed, the goal of every security awareness program must be to engender protective attitudes and behaviours — both personally and on behalf of the organisation.

A common mistake in attempting to implement a security awareness program is failing to gain an understanding of how others in the organisation perceive security, before the program is developed. Interpretation of critical aspects of the 'security philosophy' or 'security message' may be influenced by:

- observation
- personal experience
- the experiences of others, and/or
- targeted communication.

It is important therefore that there is alignment between the content of the message and what people are experiencing. Personal experiences can positively or negatively influence the interpretation of security awareness messages, with past victimisation or offending behaviour having an influence.

Security awareness programs frequently include the use of strategies that could be variously described as 'education' or 'training'. Education is generally seen as conferring general understanding, while training develops specific skills. Both are needed to increase awareness of general security vulnerabilities and responsibilities across an organisation, and task-specific obligations. The key here for security risk management is to recognise that while gaining 'attention' is important, it is only part of the equation in creating and maintaining awareness of security related issues.

Figure 11.1 illustrates the security awareness cycle, with corporate goals and security risks the key drivers in defining the rationale for an effective security awareness campaign. The five overlapping elements in the cycle reflect the need for security awareness programs to be thought of in terms of finite campaigns — that is, they have a distinct preparatory phase before

Figure 11.1
Security awareness campaign cycle.

Source: Draper, 1997. (Used with permission.)

implementation and at a defined point the program is brought to a conclusion and evaluated. Lessons learnt should be fed back into future programs.

There is a danger that security awareness programs are overly inward-looking. For example, they might focus exclusively on employee dishonesty. This can have an extremely negative effect on the perceived role of security within the organisation. It is vital that awareness programs be deployed to enhance all aspects of security in an organisation, not merely as a means of warning that 'security is watching you'. Security risk management strategies within any organisation impact on everyone who come into contact with that organisation. Staff, contractors, suppliers, customers and visitors are affected by, or have a role in, the implementation of security policies. Consequently, all of these groups must be considered as potential targets for aspects of security awareness programs.

Conclusion

This chapter began by examining physical security and went on to include aspects of people and policy management. Physical security strategies are among the most visible in protective security, although not all may be obvious to the casual observer. Core strategies include the defence-in-depth approach and the conduct of regular structured security surveys. The management of security risks ultimately relies on the effective management of people, including persons who do not have dedicated security roles. All staff have roles and responsibilities related to security, as do contractors, and even customers and visitors in various ways. As with most aspects of business management, plans, policies and procedures are central to success. Clear definitions of roles and responsibilities are essential to address the range of security risks that an organisation may face. Equally important are the methods used to communicate requirements and obligations to those affected, and ensuring that processes are in place to facilitate compliance.

References

Armstrong, M. (2008). *How to be an even better manager*. London, England: Kogan Page.

Attorney-General's Department (2014). *Protective security policy framework: Glossary of security terms*. Canberra, Australia: Author.

Bamfield, J. (2006). Management. In M. Gill (Ed.), *The handbook of security* (pp. 485–508). Houndmills, England: Palgrave Macmillan.

Challinger, D. (2006). Corporate security: A Cost or contributor to the bottom line? In M. Gill (Ed.), *The handbook of security* (pp. 586–609). Houndmills, Egnaldn: Palgrave Macmillan.

Draper, R. (1997). *Developing and implementing a security awareness program — Course notes*. Brisbane, Australia: International Security Management and Crime Prevention Institute.

Draper, R. (2013). Standards, regulations, and guidelines: Compliance and your security program. In L. Fennelly (Ed.), *Effective physical security* (pp. 283–291). Waltham, MA: Butterworth-Heinemann.

Fennelly, L. (Ed.). (2013a). *Effective physical security.* Waltham, MA: Butterworth-Heinemann.

Fennelly, L. (2103b). Security surveys and the security audit. In L. Fennelly (Ed.), *Effective physical security* (pp. 41–76). Waltham, MA: Butterworth-Heinemann.

Garcia, M. (2007). *Design and evaluation of physical protection systems.* Waltham, MA: Butterworth-Heinemann.

Girard, C. (2004). Planning, management and evaluation. In L. Fennelly (Ed.), *Handbook of loss prevention and crime prevention* (pp. 418–430). Burlington, MA: Butterworth-Heinemann

Marier, K. (2012). The 5 D's of outdoor perimeter security. Retrieved from http://www.securitymagazine.com/articles/82833-the-5-d-s-of-outdoor-perimeter-security.

Post, R., & Schachtsiek, D. (1986). *Security manager's desk reference.* Stoneham, MA: Butterworth-Heinemann

Prenzler, T. (2009). *Preventing burglary in commercial and institutional settings: A Place management and partnerships approach.* Washington, DC: ASIS Foundation.

Sarre, R., & Prenzler, T. (2009). *The Law of private security in Australia.* Sydney, Australia: Thomson Reuters.

Standards Australia (2006). *HB 167:2006 Security risk management.* Sydney, Australia: Standards Australia/Standards New Zealand.

Chapter 12

The Security Industry and Crime Prevention

Tim Prenzler and Rick Sarre

The first part of this chapter briefly examines the functions, history and contemporary dimensions of the security industry internationally and in Australia. It appears that the number of security operatives now out-numbers police in many locations. Certainly, security technology can be said to be pervasive in people's everyday lives. The growth of the industry has brought with it a set of issues around equity, amenity and misconduct; and these challenges are examined in this chapter along with a 'smart regulation' model to minimise problems. The chapter also examines how the industry prevents crime and contributes to justice by the exercise of legal authority and the application of specific situational techniques, including target hardening and formal surveillance. The chapter concludes with a brief review of evidence regarding the role of the industry in the current downward trend in international crime rates.

The Security Industry

The 'security industry' is sometimes referred to in terms of 'security services', 'protective security', 'private police' or 'parapolice'. Related terms include 'loss prevention' and 'asset protection' services. Although the industry tends to be focused on primary prevention, its work includes law enforcement (bringing offenders to justice) and restitution (or loss recovery) after crimes have been committed (Strom et al., 2010). The industry can be categorised in different ways (Prenzler, 2005). The commercial contract sector is obviously a primary grouping. These are specialist businesses that sell security, including guarding and alarm services and investigations. Customers include other businesses (such as retail or industrial firms), governments, NGOs (non-government noncommercial organisations like charities or clubs) or private citizens (e.g., householders). The other main sector is 'in-house' or 'propri-etorial' security. This is where an organisation, such as a commercial retail chain or government department, directly employs its own security staff.

A Very Brief History

The long-range history of the industry has not been well documented. It is clear, though, that guarding and forms of 'target hardening' can be found in the earliest types of human society. Protection of property and persons was usually aimed at multiple threats, such as wild animals, and weather and temperature extremes; as well as thieves, robbers, rapists, murderers, bandits and militias. Ancient 'low-tech' protective devices included dogs, walls, fences, gates, trip wires and bells, strong boxes and secret compartments (McCrie, 2006). The use of locks has been traced back as far as ancient Egypt. In urbanised societies, town authorities would engage guards and night watchmen to provide collective security. With the rise of capitalism and world trade in the 16th century, docks and transport networks became targets for crime, and European-based trading companies began to engage their own security to guard warehouses (Johnston, 1992).

It has been argued that by the 18th century private means of protection and justice were dominant in the face of an entirely inadequate and often corrupt public criminal justice system (Johnston, 1992). This included the services in England of 'private prosecution and felons associations'. These collectives were engaged in various forms of protection of members' property, including recovery of stolen property (Johnston, 1992). Modern professional policing as we know it was advanced by the example of the 'New Police' in London in 1829. The model of trained uniformed public police was quickly adopted around the world. At the same time, private security often remained the main source of protection and recoveries (Johnston, 1992).

The invention of the burglar alarm in the mid-19th century drove developments on the technical side of security, while also stimulating growth in the 'manpower' sector (McCrie, 2006). In the United States, westward expansion and the lag in government services spawned a number of famous security firms, including Wells Fargo and Pinkertons. Security businesses received a further boost from the expansion of manufacturing during World War Two and the need for guarding of factories. However, it was during the postwar economic boom, mainly from the 1960s, that a 'rebirth of private security' occurred which resulted in the massive expansion of the industry (Johnston, 1992).

This modern expansion has been associated with numerous influences, including increased litigation for security failures, the introduction of workplace health and safety legislation, and the modern terrorist threat (Small Arms Survey, 2011). However, the strongest influence appears to have been the large upsurge in general crime that occurred in many countries from the 1960s to the 1990s — driven by rising prosperity and freedom, and the proliferation of targets and opportunities for crime (van Dijk, 2008). This period was marked by a decisive shift away from reliance on police towards the self-provision of protection. Crime rates began to decline in many locations from the turn of the century, especially property crime rates. Nonetheless, the 'securitisation' process continued, and it continues to drive down crime rates (van Dijk, 2008).

The 1985 *Hallcrest Report* in the United States found that private security officers began to outnumber police in the late 1960s or early 1970s, and by 1990 *Hallcrest II* put the ratio of private security personnel to police at 2.4 to 1. Expenditures on private security were estimated to have exceeded those for public police by 1977 (Cunningham, Strauchs, & van Meter, 1990, pp. 229–239). In other places, police continued to outnumber security guards into the 1990s and 2000s, although growth in the guarding sector tended to exceed growth in policing (van Steden & Sarre, 2007).

Ongoing growth in security was also stimulated by technical refinements. From the 1970s, simple circuit breaker alarm mechanisms were supplanted by motion detectors and other sensors. Despite major problems with false activations, by 2008, in the United States, 92% of retail firms used an alarm system (Hollinger & Adams, 2009, p. 23). Since the 1980s, alarms have increasingly been supplemented by CCTV. In 2013, the number of CCTV cameras in the United Kingdom was put at between 4 and 6 million (Reeve, 2013). Significant improvements have been made in recent years in picture quality, remote monitoring and interactivity (e.g., communication between monitoring station staff and persons on-site). Smart card technology has also become a more convenient alternative to mechanical entry control.

Contemporary Industry Dimensions and Trends

Different data sources produce different pictures of the industry. The following subsections report on three recent sources and areas of coverage, including one global report and data from Europe and Australia.

The Graduate Institute of International and Development Studies in Geneva operates a global 'small arms' survey concerned with issues related to violence and firearms. The 2011 survey targeted the private security industry, with information obtained from 70 countries. It was estimated that 19.5 million people were employed in the sector. This was projected to include 25.5 million across all countries (Small Arms Survey, 2011, p. 101). Across the 70 countries, private security personnel were estimated to outnumber police by a ratio of 1.8 to 1. The industry was also valued at US$100 billion to US$165 billion (turnover) per annum, with an annual growth rate of 7% to 8%. Worldwide, private security companies were estimated to hold between 1.7 and 3.7 million firearms.

The Confederation of European Security Services (CoESS) is an association that publishes periodic assessments of the industry. The 2013 report covered 34 countries and found that there was a total of 2,017,313 private security guards (CoESS, 2013, p. 251). The number of private guarding hours for the year was estimated at just under 2 billion. The financial turnover for the year was put at € 34.5 billion. The previous study for 2011 included a comparison of police and security officers to population. The average number of security providers per 10,000 inhabitants was 31.1, compared to 36.3 police (CoESS, 2011, pp. 143–144). One outstanding exception to this ratio was the United Kingdom, with an estimated security-to-population ratio of 1/170 compared to 1/382 for police.

In Australia, 'guards and security officers' were only introduced into the Australian census in 1986, with 22,975 persons identified in the category, compared to 33,881 police (Prenzler, 2005, p. 54). Since that time, security categories have gone through several changes, making trend analysis difficult. In addition, a limitation with the census is that it only measures a person's 'main occupation'. Prenzler, Earle, and Sarre (2009) accessed data from regulatory agencies and identified a total of 112,773 individuals who held one or more security licences in 2008. It was presumed that most of these were part-time positions, given the contrast with the 2006 census figure of approximately 39,000 individuals in core security functions. The 2009 study also found that, in 2006, there were 5478 security and investigative companies. Just under half were described as 'owner-operator' with no employees.

Table 12.1 shows data from the 2011 Australian census for security-related occupations, including debt collectors. If we combine the last four security categories, which are the ones closest to the original 'guards and security officers', we can see that there has been, over the time frame of 25 years, a jump from 22,975 personnel in 1986 to 40,314 in 2011, a 75% increase. Within the same time frame, the number of police increased by only 46%, and the general population by 39% (from 15.6 million).

Issues

The growth of the security industry, especially the private sector component, has thrown up a range of social issues. These overlap with the critiques of situational crime prevention discussed in Chapter 6. Issues focused more on private security are outlined below.

Inequality in Protection

Is the democratic principle of equal protection distorted by the growth of private security? The answer to this question is difficult to discern. One argument is that if the rich pay for security this frees up the public police to provide a better service to the poor (Prenzler, 2004). This is difficult to prove empirically, but it is reasonable to assume that the large reductions in property offences, resulting from increased security (see later), give police more time to devote to disadvantaged locations and also to pursue more serious violent offences. In addition, it could be argued that the solution to the gap between the security rich and security poor is not less security, but more — including better security provided by governments to disadvantaged sectors of society.

Table 12.1

Security Providers, Australian Census, 2011

Category	Number
Private investigator	728
Security consultant	874
Locksmith	2,574
Insurance investigator	444
Debt collector	8,487
Court bailiff or sheriff	639
Armoured car escort	535
Security officer	38,147
Alarm, security or surveillance monitor	766
Crowd controller	866
Police	49,546
Population	21,507,717

Source: Australian Bureau of Statistics, 2013.

Private Justice

Another area of criticism, closely associated with the inequality thesis, has been defined more narrowly as a 'justice critique' (Prenzler, 2004, p. 273; Shearing & Stenning, 1983). With the growth of private security, more offenders are likely to be apprehended by private security. This may benefit some in terms of decisions not to inform police. At the same time, accused persons might suffer from the denial of due process that is more likely to happen in private hands. For example, an employee might be dismissed because of suspected, but unproven, theft. This is another potentially problematic aspect of security, but the dimensions are largely unknown. The risk is certainly one that should be acknowledged, and government processes should be put in place to guard against such inequalities and injustices. Unfair dismissal laws are one example. Another example concerns mandatory disclosure laws, which require the reporting of suspected offences in the workplace, such as child abuse or misconduct. An important test will always be the harm done to victims, and the need to deter future offending, against the costs associated with a simple prosecute-and-punish model of justice.

Quality-of-life Impacts

Does security come at too high a price in terms of loss of convenience, privacy and freedom? Fears of a 'dystopian' future have been expressed in concepts such as the 'new surveillance' (Marx, 2002), related to growth in security guards, CCTV, X-ray scanning and data-matching. This is an area of potentially adverse outcomes from the enlargement of security, and the risks need to be managed through a democratically based regulatory system. Examples include privacy legislation and codes of conduct for security providers, including for operators of surveillance equipment. It should also be noted that convenience and aesthetics are marketable products. A few examples include attractive security lighting, wireless locking, punch-in PINs and plantings around bollards. Furthermore, available survey data suggest that people generally do not feel threatened by security, with a good proportion feeling safer as a result of visible security (van Steden & Nalla, 2010).

Relations With Police

How should police and private security personnel relate to each other? It would seem obvious that they should work closely together to reduce crime. However, they also operate on different principles, and cooperation entails a number of potential conflicts of interest. Table 12.2 lists differentials that pose barriers to cooperation. For example, if police work closely with security firms — through information sharing or priority communications — then the clients of those firms may benefit unfairly. Police 'moonlighting' in the industry has also been identified as a problem (Born, Caparini, & Cole, 2007). Police in this situation may be tempted to exercise specific police powers or make use of police resources. Certainly, these issues need to be managed in ways that prioritise the interests of the public. Banning police from the industry, or requiring permission (subject to conditions) for them to continue, are possible responses. More generally, the benefits of public–private partnerships in reducing crime have strengthened the case for closer cooperation. It appears that partnerships can be managed in a way that demonstrates a broad benefit (Chapters 8 and 9).

Table 12.2

Opposing Principles of Public Policing and Private Security

Taxpayer funded	Profit driven
Public interest	Client interest
Equal service (on triage basis)	Selective service
Offender oriented	Protection oriented
Reactive	Proactive
Specific powers	Agent and citizen powers
Centralised bureaucracy	Fragmented
Heavily regulated	Less regulated
Intensive training	Minimal (mandated) training

Source: Adapted from Prenzler and Sarre, 1998, p. 3.

Conduct Issues

As the security industry has grown, more and more people have become subject to the activities of security personnel and the impacts of security technology. While the industry has enormous potential to protect people from crime, there is also a dark side that has to be acknowledged. One of the earliest studies of the industry was conducted by the RAND Corporation in the United States in the early 1970s. Based on case studies, litigation and complaints, the researchers identified the following problematic areas (Kakalik & Wildhorn, 1971, pp. 57–61):

> Abuse of authority
>
> Dishonesty and poor business practices
>
> Access to confidential police records and gathering information from third parties
>
> Non-reporting of crime and the 'private' system of justice
>
> High false-alarm rates
>
> Personnel quality, training and supervision.

The RAND team also summarised complaints made to 17 regulatory agencies in one year in the following format (Kakalik & Wildhorn, 1971, p. 54):

- Violation of regulation (413)
- Improper uniform or identification (369)
- Shootings (55)
- Impersonating a police officer (34)
- Theft (29)
- Failure to serve as agreed (29)
- Misrepresentation of services or fees (28)
- Violation of gun regulation (22)
- Illegal access to police records (18)
- Assault or use of excessive force (13)
- Negligence (13)
- Operating an unlicensed business (13)
- Drunkenness (12)
- Conviction of a crime (9)
- Offensive language (8)
- Killings (8).

There were also cases of 'false arrest, improper detention, invasion of privacy, improper search, improper interrogation, bugging, wiretapping, and extortion' (Kakalik & Wildhorn, 1971, p. 54).

More recently, Prenzler and Sarre (2008) developed a security industry ethical 'risk profile', with 11 categories derived from government reviews, inquiries, court cases, media reports, and practitioner interviews and surveys. Some types of malpractice are common to business, such as fraud and the black economy, which mainly derive from the profit motive and temptations to cheat customers and avoid tax. In other cases, misconduct is similar to that observed in policing, including assaults. These behaviours derive in part from frustrations with the end–means disjunction and legal limits on the exercise of authority and gathering evidence. The 11 areas of misconduct risk are summarised very briefly below.

1. Fraud

Clients of security firms are vulnerable to fraud because the services are often outside their capacity for oversight. For example, a security firm contracted to conduct night-time inspections on a premise might falsify the number of checks they do in order to maximise profits.

2. Incompetence and Poor Standards

Prior to the introduction of industry regulation, it was possible for security firms to set up business with few protections for clients and the general public. Even with 'basic' regulation (described later), training programs are often limited to between one day and two weeks for operatives, with no qualifications required for security firm owners or in-house security managers. Basic security in areas such as transporting cash and valuables has often been deficient and highly dangerous.

3. Under-award Payments and Exploitation of Security Staff

Price competition and the profit motive also drove a black economy in labour, involving under-award 'cash-in-hand' payments to security staff — who then miss out on entitlements like holiday and sick pay, superannuation, and penalty rates.

4. Corrupt Practices

Security firms have been known to offer bribes to police and other agencies for preferential referrals for business. Graft can also occur in tendering for contracts, in purchasing of security equipment and in carrying out training.

5. Information Corruption

This type of corruption has primarily occurred among private investigators, debt collectors and process servers, who will pay corrupt officers (such as public servants) for confidential information about people's criminal records, location, contact details and assets.

6. Violence and Associated Malpractice

Assaults have constituted the most high profile and widespread problem in the industry, concentrated amongst security staff at entertainment venues. Failure to protect patrons is part of the mix. Poor training and management also contribute to the victimisation of security staff at the hands of unruly patrons.

7. False Arrest and Detention

Security officers are vulnerable to exceeding their legal powers and arresting persons without sufficient evidence. They can also misrepresent their powers to hold people in detention.

8. Trespass and Invasions of Privacy

Private investigators, process servers and debt recovery agents can trespass onto private property. Security officers can also engage in illegal searches of personal items. Other breaches of privacy can include illegally accessing mail or other forms of communication or data.

9. Discrimination and Harassment

Security officers are vulnerable to allegations that they have targeted minority groups in ways that are discriminatory, through intimidation and selective exclusion. Private agents have been known to exceed their powers by making threats and engaging in harassing tactics.

10. Insider Crime

Security providers have skills that can be used to commit crime because they have technical abilities and privileged knowledge about the vulnerabilities of their clients.

11. Misuse of Weapons

Security officers can carry an array of weapons — including firearms, if licensed — that can be mishandled to inflict harm, including serious injuries and fatalities.

Regulation

This section addresses the issue of the best way to 'regulate' security in terms of preventing misconduct and ensuring the competency of practitioners. Security providers are normally regulated in part by a range of general accountability mechanisms that apply across industries. For example, the threat of prosecution under criminal law, and a fine or imprisonment, should deter security providers who might engage in criminal offences such as homicide, assault, trespass, robbery, theft, fraud, harassment and threats. If security providers do break the law, the criminal courts should provide justice or recompense to victims, including through sanctions and financial compensation. Similarly, all security providers are subject to civil law in areas such as assault, false imprisonment, harassment, breach of confidence and negligence. Security clients and ordinary citizens have successfully sued security providers on many occasions and obtained financial compensation (Davis et. al., 2003; Sarre & Prenzler, 2009). Commercial law and market forces provide additional partial regulatory mechanisms.

Security work is also regulated by numerous other laws, including criminal law, workplace health and safety legislation, privacy legislation and employment law. Other examples include liquor licensing legislation that prescribes; for example, certain ratios of customers to security staff; and weapons licensing that allows security officers to carry firearms under certain conditions (Sarre & Prenzler, 2009). Finally, there is also a degree of self-regulation through professional industry associations. Members must meet standards of integrity and competency if they wish to remain members. They can then use the badge of membership to promote themselves as credible operators.

Basic Industry-specific Regulation

The regulatory mechanisms outlined above have all failed spectacularly on occasions. As a result, governments have been forced to introduce industry-specific regulation centred on a basic licensing model. This usually includes preservice training requirements and a set of disqualifying offences (in areas such as violence and fraud). In Australia, security industry regulation is state- and territory-based. Table 12.3 lists the relevant Acts in force in 2011, based on a comprehensive national study (Sarre and Prenzler, 2011). These Acts and accompanying regulations varied across almost every requirement. Examples include disqualifying offences, discretion concerning 'fit and proper' person criteria, fingerprinting, and drug and alcohol tests.

Table 12.3

Security Industry Regulation, Australia, 2011

Jurisdiction	Legislation
Australian Capital Territory	*Security Industry Act 2003*
New South Wales	*Security Industry Act 1997*
Northern Territory	*Private Security Act 1995*
Queensland	*Security Providers Act 1993*
South Australia	*Security and Investigation Agents Act 1995*
Tasmania	*Security and Investigations Agents Act 2002*
Victoria	*Private Security Act 2004*
Western Australia	*Security and Related Activities (Control) Act 1996 + 2007 Amendment Act*

Source: Sarre & Prenzler (2011, p. 36)

Australian legislation is consistent with a basic regulatory model that emerged around the world in the last few decades (Button, 2007). Security firms must hold a security business licence. Usually the owners are not required to have qualifications, but they must not be bankrupt, must have a physical address, must meet insurance requirements and must not have committed any disqualifying offences. Operative licences are usually issued in categories, along the lines of those shown in Table 12.1, based on competency and integrity criteria. The regulatory agencies which administer the licensing legislation are usually located within 'fair trading' departments or police departments. These agencies process applications and renewals, investigate and resolve complaints, and carry out inspections. They normally have the power to deny, suspend or revoke licences; and they can refer criminal matters to the police or public prosecutor.

Smart Regulation

The basic model of security industry regulation has attracted high levels of in-principle support in public opinion surveys and surveys of security practitioners. At the same time, there is often criticism of inadequate training and inaction against noncompliant firms and individuals; and recurring problems and conduct scandals still occur where the basic model is in operation (Australian Skills Quality Authority [ASQA], 2016; Sarre & Prenzler, 2011, White, 2015). A major part of the problem is that the potential 'smart' aspects of regulation are usually underdeveloped, including responses to feedback on what works and what does not work. With this issue in mind, Prenzler & Sarre (2008, p. 6) developed six dimensions of smart regulation:

1. Comprehensive licensing would cover all occupations involved in security work and reflect and recognise the high levels of trust and client vulnerability entailed in security ...

2. Regulation would be national, with states and territories endorsing a model Act and Regulations. This would allow interstate portability of licences and removal of 'havens' for licence applicants rejected in other jurisdictions.

3. Development and administration of amended legislation would be consultative, with standing industry and stakeholder committees advising the regulatory agencies ...

4. Regulation would involve exclusion of personnel through a national system of criminal history checks and power over licensees through an enforceable Code of Conduct.

5. Mandated training standards would be based on analysis of security tasks and establishment of basic competencies for all categories ...

6. Regulatory agencies would be proactive, holding a mission both for research and professionalisation. Compliance monitoring and com-

plaints investigation would need to be vigorous, including innovative approaches such as behavioural observation studies and other forms of research into the conduct of security staff ...

Security Industry Contributions to Crime Prevention

The following subsections outline — very briefly — how the industry assists in crime prevention and improved justice.

Legal Powers

Security providers exercise a range of overlapping powers in democracies like Australia. A citizen's powers, and powers associated with the defence of private property, are particularly important (Sarre, 2014a). Licensing systems normally do not confer any particular powers, however. Security providers — whether they are on private property or in public areas such as footpaths — can engage in citizen arrests for a wide range of offences, such as theft or attempted theft, or robbery or attempted robbery. This is a complicated area of law, with numerous ambiguities, so practitioners need to be carefully trained in their powers and responsibilities. Importantly, security providers can also exercise powers of self-defence and defence of others. The principle of proportionality is particularly important here in matching protective force to the level of threat and avoiding excessive force (Sarre, 2014a).

The idea of defensive force extends to a crucial area — trespass. Here the common law empowers property owners to exclude persons from their property. This is a major dimension of the power held by owners of property (including government property) to prevent crime (Sarre, 2014a). This is not an absolute right. For example, property owners must not breach antidiscrimination legislation. But shopping centres and other establishments can set entry requirements, such as a dress code, and also refuse entry to persons suspected of crimes, so long as they do not ban them on grounds of race or sex or any other grounds listed in relevant antidiscrimination legislation. There is a right to use a degree of force in blocking a person attempting to enter premises or removing a person who has been told to leave and who then refuses (Sarre, 2014a). These rights can be delegated to an 'agent', and this gives security staff their authority on private property.

The law is also enabling in terms of the rights of persons to surveille other persons. This gives private investigators and CCTV operators considerable freedom to operate, so long as their actions don't breach a range of laws related to harassment and decency — keeping in mind that there is no general tort of invasion of privacy applicable in Australia (Sarre, 2014a). There is also little to stop private agents attempting to ask questions or obtain information — but, again, there are many laws related to information privacy, as well as property repossession and service of summonses, that need to be observed.

Techniques

Situational crime prevention and CPTED (Chapters 6 and 7) drew in part on established security management techniques (Chapters 8 and 9). The work of Ronald V. Clarke and other pioneers of situational prevention acknowledged the role of security providers in contributing to successful crime reduction. A range of associated professions also contributed, including police, architects, town planners and product designers, facilities managers, and business and resident associations. More recently, information technology (IT) security specialists have become essential to defending against computer-based crime, employing situational measures at the human–cyber interface. Partnerships have been particularly important for maximising yields in crime prevention projects (Chapters 8 and 9).

Security providers make use of a wide range of site-specific 'tailor made' strategies, consistent with the 25 techniques of situational crime prevention. These include mainstays like 'target hardening', including fences, walls, locks, grills and safes. These are often augmented with various forms of surveillance, including alarms and CCTV (Sarre, 2014b); with capacity for rapid response and interventions such as arrests. Additional measures include deterrence and intervention methods similar to traditional police patrols but targeted to the needs of clients. 'Access control', 'facilitating compliance', 'avoiding disputes' 'setting rules' and 'alerting conscience' are all staples of the industry, made possible by the legal framework outlined above. The standard security management process of regular security audits is also consistent with the idea in situational crime prevention of continuous improvement through data-rich evaluation and modification (Chapters 6 and 11).

Security and the Crime Drop

The impact of the security industry is increasingly evident in long-term crime trends. In the 1990s, there were few studies available that included national or international data. Some exceptions included the work of Webb (1994), showing the benefits of steering column locks on motor vehicle theft in a number of countries; and fraud reduction initiatives in Sweden (Chapter 8). Property crime rates began to fall consistently in many countries from the 1990s; followed by smaller falls in violent crimes (van Dijk, 2008, 2012). Australia followed a similar pattern, slightly delayed.

A variety of theories have been put forward to explain these trends, including economic theories and theories related to improved policing and greater imprisonment. In his address as the recipient of the 2012 Stockholm Prize for Criminology, van Dijk (2012) argued that, from a global perspective, the trends appear to operate largely independently of economic cycles, police innovations, and imprisonment rates. While changes in policing and imprisonment may have relevance in specific locations (e.g., the alleged 80% crime drop in New York City; Zimring, 2012), they do not provide an explanation for crime trends at the global level. The most likely explanation for reduced crime relates to the impact of 'self-protection' measures and 'responsive securitization' (van Dijk, 2012, pp. 11, 10; see also Farrell, 2013). In van Dijk's words (2012, p. 11):

> Investments in self-protection have since the 1970s been a mass phenomenon, impacting on almost all aspects of society. A prime example is the huge increases in private security guards and alarm centres ... Measures to prevent crime have become ubiquitous in all corners of modern society. Harnessing new technology, security provisions have been built into homes, cars, stores and parking lots, public transport and public/social housing, schools and hospitals, offices and other work places, entertainment venues and sports stadiums, airports and seaports, and to warehouses and transportation terminals.

Van Dijk (2012) developed this thesis by examining how specific crimes, such as motor vehicle theft and household burglary, have been significantly reduced where security devices were utilised, such as immobilisers and alarms. Government mandating of security devices appears to have been particularly effective. One United States' study of commercial burglary found that the probability of a property without an alarm being burgled was 4.57 times that of an alarmed property (Hakim & Shachmurove, 1996, p. 43). Security devices in combination have also been shown to substantially reduce burglary. For example, a study on burglary in the 2009–2010 British Crime Survey found that:

> Households with 'less than basic' home security measures were six times more likely to have been victims of burglary (5.8%) than households with 'basic' security (0.9%) and ten times more likely than households with 'enhanced' home security measures (0.6%). (Flatley, Kershaw, Smith, Chaplin, & Moon, 2010, pp. 2–3)

'Basic security' included 'window locks and double locks or deadlocks to outside doors'; while 'enhanced' security included these and one other device, such as sensor lights, security grills or an alarm.

Conclusion

The security industry has been growing at a significant pace since the 1960s and is now an established and prominent part of a complex 'policing' apparatus — making use of the legal capacity of citizens and property owners to protect themselves and their assets. This fundamental social change has not been without its problems. However, the industry is thriving because of the many benefits it provides to a very wide range of people in reducing victimisation and helping people feel safe. 'Smart regulation' by government, in cooperation with the industry, is the key to maximising the benefits of this paradigm shift, and minimising harms. Government also has a major role to play in making security work for disadvantaged people. This can be achieved, in part, through improving security in public housing and public institutions, in subsidising security, and in facilitating public–private crime prevention partnerships.

References

Australian Bureau of Statistics. (2013). *2011 census of population and housing, customised data report (security-related occupations)*. Canberra: Author.

Australian Skills Quality Authority. (2016). *Training in security programs in Australia*. Melbourne, Australia: Author.

Born, H., Caparini, M., & Cole, E. (2007). *Regulating private security in Europe*. Geneva, Switzerland: Centre for the Democratic Control of Armed Forces.

Button, M. (2007). Assessing the regulation of private security across Europe. *European Journal of Criminology, 4*(1), 109–128.

Confederation of European Security Services. (2011). *Private security services in Europe: CoESS facts and figures 2011*. Wemmel, Belgium: Author.

Confederation of European Security Services. (2013). *Private security services in Europe: CoESS facts and figures 2013*. Wemmel, Belgium: Author.

Cunningham, W., Strauchs, J., & van Meter, C. (1990). *Private security trends, 1970 to 2000*. Boston, MA: Butterworth-Heinemann.

Davis, R., Ortiz, C., Dadush, S., Irish, J., Alvarado, A., & Davis, D. (2003). The Public accountability of private police. *Policing and Society, 13*(2), 197–210.

Farrell, G. (2013). Five tests for a theory of the crime drop. *Crime Science, 2*(5), 1–8.

Flatley, J., Kershaw, C., Smith, K., Chaplin, R., & Moon, D. (2010). *Crime in England and Wales 2009/10*. London, England: Home Office.

Hakim, S., & Shachmurove, Y. (1996). Spatial and temporal patters of commercial burglaries. *American Journal of Economics and Sociology, 55*(4), 443–456.

Hollinger, R., & Adams, A. (2009). *2008 National Retail Security Survey*. Gainesville, FL: Department of Sociology and Criminology and Law, University of Florida.

Johnston, L. (1992). *The rebirth of private policing*. London, England: Routledge.

Kakalik, S.J., & Wildhorn, S. (1971). *Private police in the United States: Findings and recommendations*. Santa Monica, CA: RAND.

Marx, G. (2002). What's new about the 'new surveillance'? *Surveillance & Society, 1*(1), 9–29.

McCrie, R. (2006). A history of security. In M. Gill (Ed.), *The handbook of security* (pp. 21–44). Houndmills, England: Palgrave.

Prenzler, T. (2004). The privatisation of policing. In R. Sarre & J. Tomaino (Eds.), *Key issues in criminal justice* (pp. 267–296). Adelaide: Australian Humanities Press.

Prenzler, T. (2005). Mapping the Australian security industry. *Security Journal, 18*(4), 51–64.

Prenzler, T., Earle, K., & Sarre, T. (2009). Private security in Australia. *Trends and Issues in Crime and Criminal Justice, 374*, 1–6.

Prenzler, T., & Sarre, R. (1998). Regulating private security in Australia. *Trends and Issues in Crime and Criminal Justice, 98*, 1–6.

Prenzler, T., & Sarre, R. (2008). Developing a risk profile and model regulatory system for the security industry. *Security Journal, 21*(4), 264–277.

Reeve, T. (2013). BSIA attempts to clarify question of how many CCTV cameras there are in the UK. Retrieved from http://www.securitynews-desk.com/2013/07/11/bsia-attempts-to-clarify-question-of-how-many-cctv-cameras-in-the-uk/

Sarre, R. (2014a). Legal powers, obligations and immunities. In T. Prenzler (Ed.), *Professional practice in crime prevention and security management* (pp. 149–162). Brisbane: Australian Academic Press.

Sarre, R. (2014b). The use of surveillance technologies by law enforcement agencies: What are the trends, opportunities and threats? In E. Pływaczewski (Ed.), *Current problems of the penal law and criminology* (pp. 755–767). Białystok, Poland: Temida.

Sarre, R., & Prenzler, T. (2009). *The law of private security in Australia*, 2nd edition. Sydney, Australia: Thomson Reuters.

Sarre, R., & Prenzler, T. (2011). *Private security and public interest.* Sydney: Australian Security Industry Association Limited.

Shearing, C., & Stenning, P. (1983). *Private security and private justice.* Montreal, Canada: Institute for Research on Public Policy.

Small Arms Survey. (2011). *States of security.* Retrieved from http://www.smallarmssurvey.org/publications/by-type/yearbook/small-arms-survey-2011.html

Strom, K., Berzofsky, M., Shook-Sa, B., Barrick, K., Daye, C., Horstmann, N., & Kinsey, S. (2010). *The Private security industry.* Washington, DC: Bureau of Justice Statistics.

van Dijk, J. (2008). *The world of crime.* Thousand Oaks, CA: SAGE.

van Dijk, J. (2012, June). *Closing the doors: Stockholm Prizewinners lecture 2012.* Paper presented at the Stockholm Criminology Symposium, Stockholm.

van Steden, R., & Nalla, M. (2010). Citizen satisfaction with private security guards in the Netherlands. *European Journal of Criminology, 7*(3), 214–234.

van Steden, R., & Sarre, R. (2007). The growth of privatized policing. *International Journal of Comparative and Applied Criminal Justice, 31*, 51–71.

Webb, B. (1994). Steering column locks and motor vehicle theft. *Crime Prevention Studies, 2*, 71–89.

White, A. (2015). The impact of the *Private Security Industry Act 2001. Security Journal, 28*(4), 425–442.

Zimring, F. (2012). *The city that became safe.* New York, NY: Oxford University Press.